HER MAJESTY'S PLEASURE

HER MAJESTY'S PLEASURE

HOW HORSERACING ENTHRALS THE QUEEN

JULIAN MUSCAT

RACING POST

Copyright © Julian Muscat 2012

The right of Julian Muscat to be identified as the author of this work
has been asserted by him in accordance with the Copyright, Designs and Patents Act 1988.

This edition first published in Great Britain in 2012 by Racing Post Books
Axis House, Compton, Newbury, Berkshire, RG20 6NL

1 3 5 7 9 10 8 6 4 2

A catalogue record for this book is available from the British Library.

ISBN 978-1-905156-86-3

Designed by Soapbox
www.soapbox.co.uk

Printed and bound by Butler, Tanner and Dennis Ltd, Frome, Somerset

Every effort has been made to fulfil requirements with regard to copyright material.
The author and publisher will be glad to rectify any omissions at the earliest opportunity.

www.racingpost.com/shop

PHOTO CREDITS: Associated Press: 155; Camera Press: 24; Central Press: 112, 133, 173; Gerry Cranham: 196;
Ronald Frain: 229; David Hastings: 209; Horse and Hound: 51, 54–5, 82, 83, 88–9, 91, 94, 106, 118, 179, 195, 221, 223, 34–5,
236, 243, 247, 249; Hulton Archive: half-title, 48, 61, 64; Irish National Stud: 243; Trevor Jones Thoroughbred Photography:
34; Mirror Syndication: 113; Laurie Morton: 8–9; Odhams: 50, 105, 143, 163; PA Photos: 25, 37, 56, 90, 114, 138, 185, 210,
214; Bernard Parkin: 36–7; Racingfotos: 12, 66, 78; Rex features: 16–17, 204–5; Racing Post: frontispiece, 20, 21, 26, 28, 39,
44, 72–7, 81, 100–2, 108, 128, 145, 188–9, 199, 253; Alec Russell: 207; George Selwyn: 43, 176–7, 198, 201;
Sport and General: 7, 124–5, 146, 171; Edward Wing: 150–1

CONTENTS

PREFACE | 6

1 | MEN AND HORSES SHE HAS KNOWN | 8

2 | AT ROYAL ASCOT AND OTHER RACECOURSES | 36

3 | CARLTON HOUSE: SO NEAR AND YET SO FAR | 72

4 | AUREOLE – AND OTHERS IN VAIN PURSUIT | 100

5 | THE 1950s: A GOLDEN DECADE | 124

6 | THE 1960s: A BARREN DECADE | 150

7 | TWIN PEAKS: HIGHCLERE AND DUNFERMLINE | 176

8 | TWIN TROUGHS: WEST ILSLEY AND HEIGHT OF FASHION | 204

9 | THE CRYSTAL BALL | 232

INDEX | 254

PREFACE

On the face of it, there can be few more daunting projects than to amplify one aspect of a very private life. When that life is the Queen's, however, and when the aspect is her passion for horseracing, the assignment takes on a whole new meaning.

The reservation in accepting Brough Scott's summons for the Queen's portrait within a racing frame was that those who knew the story would hesitate to tell it. That concern proved without foundation. By their reminiscing, the people who bring this book to life reflect the Queen's disposition in all Turf matters. Invariably smiling when on the racecourse, she is also, as Sir Peter O'Sullevan memorably describes, a 'very human being' behind the scenes.

No account of the Queen's involvement would be complete without a brisk gallop through her six decades of patronage. Racing's twin bedfellows of triumph and disaster are regular themes, yet the early running explores the interplay between Her Majesty and some of racing's well-known players. It casts the Queen in a perspective far removed from the solemnity of official duty. If these accounts lack intimacy, the author is entirely to blame.

Those who chronicle horseracing see the Queen in circumstances few others are privy to. Although her commitment to duty is exemplary, she cannot help but project the impression that she is truly at ease at Royal Ascot or Derby day: hence *Her Majesty's Pleasure*.

The Queen's love of racing is well known but her horsewoman's instinct is manifest in subtle ways. Her former trainer, Ian Balding, averred that she never wore scent when visiting his stables, since perfume is prone to 'stir up' excitable colts. Such detail serves to underline why historians maintain that the Queen's expertise eclipses that of all previous monarchs.

An initially daunting project thus became a profoundly enjoyable one. This was due in large part to the generous time given by those within the royal racing circle, among them the Queen's bloodstock and racing advisor John Warren; the Royal Mews' manager and stud groom Terry Pendry; the Royal Studs' manager Joe Grimwade; and the studs' former director Sir Michael Oswald and his wife Lady Angela, who serves a mean lunch.

Half title: The royal party in the Ascot winner's enclosure after Aureole's victory in the 1954 King George VI and Queen Elizabeth Stakes.

Frontispiece: At Epsom, Derby day 1989.

Sincere thanks are also offered to the Queen's trainers past and present, Ian Balding and Richard Hannon; former jockey Willie Snaith; stable lad Peter 'Caz' Williams; BBC racing stalwarts past and present, Sir Peter O'Sullevan and Clare Balding; and Alec Head, a breeder of international repute who has twice hosted the Queen at his stud farm in Normandy.

Less tangible but equally indispensable contributions were made by Catherine Austen in picture research; Sean Magee, whose sensitive handling of the entire project was greatly appreciated; and the aforementioned Brough Scott, whose sharp insight and constant support were invaluable.

The last word is best left to Joe Grimwade, who went beyond the call of duty in providing a comprehensive tour of the Royal Studs at Sandringham on a bitterly cold December day. In common with others inside the royal racing fold, his enthusiasm knows no bounds.

'The Queen is aware of everything that happens to the staff and the horses here,' Grimwade said in closing. 'I know it makes her sound a bit too good to be true, but that's the reality. That is how she is.'

JULIAN MUSCAT
April 2012

1

MEN AND HORSES
SHE HAS KNOWN

Richard Hannon isn't prone to getting flustered. He can raise a storm when he has to, although in the main he is as relaxed an individual as you will find among racehorse trainers in Britain. On this particular morning, however, Hannon is anxious for everything to proceed as planned.

Sitting beside him in the front of his Jeep is the Queen, who is here to see the horses Hannon trains for her. It's a rare treat for the monarch. She has been described as a frustrated trainer who, were she not born of regal roots, would be doing precisely what Hannon is doing. Instead she is a passenger in the vehicle that is edging towards a group of horses in the distance. The horses are detached from the rest of the string, which proceeds over the brow of the hill at Hannon's Herridge Stables, on the edge of Salisbury Plain.

The first departure from the script duly follows. Hannon watches in frustration as a lone horse makes its way towards the group. Its rider is trying to catch up, having been late into work that morning, and inadvertently joins the gathering of the Queen's Thoroughbreds. Muttering apologies, Hannon squeezes the accelerator and is soon alongside the group.

'Get out of there,' he shouts through the car window.

'Yes, boss,' comes the reply, although horse and rider remain impostors in the royal herd.

'Turn right. Go over there,' Hannon commands, his voice betraying mounting irritation.

Only then does Hannon notice the rider is wearing a turban over his obligatory crash helmet. He leans out of the window and starts gesticulating furiously, pointing towards the brow of the hill. 'Over there.'

'Yes, boss,' says the rider, who resolutely refuses to move anywhere.

By now Hannon is aware of an uncomfortable truth. In common with many who work with horses in Britain today, the rider has no comprehension of the English language. He cannot understand a word. The only two he speaks are those he has dispensed to Hannon twice already: 'Yes, boss'.

Exasperated, Hannon turns to the Queen and asks: 'Ma'am, do you speak Indian?'

'No, I'm afraid I don't,' comes the reply.

Which prompts Hannon to exclaim: 'Well you ought to, ma'am. You ruled the place for long enough.'

In different circumstances Hannon's insouciance might have provoked a hint of royal consternation. Not this time. The Queen is smiling broadly, and the mood of jollity is contagious. It extends to the back seat, where John Warren, bloodstock and racing advisor to the Queen, embellishes the moment. His barely suppressed chuckle gives way to unrestrained laughter.

Later on, when the party decamps to Hannon's house for refreshment, the Queen revisits Hannon's rejoinder. 'I imagine you'd have had a bit of a shock if I'd started speaking Hindi,' she says.

'Not half, ma'am,' Hannon affirms. 'Not half.'

The Queen's demeanour on this spring morning, when the promise of the nascent Flat season knows no horizon, will be familiar to all in horse racing. The royal love of racing is well documented. It is not so much a favoured pastime as a full-blooded embrace. Any meaningful profile of the Queen on newsprint is obliged to dwell at length on her passion for the Sport of Kings. It is her calling. From the Royal Studs at Sandringham to the racecourses of Britain, she is at her leisure.

Those who work with horses are of a particular orientation. They wear silken gloves over iron fists. The more extreme among them even prefer the company of horses to people. While it would overstep the mark to suggest as much of the Queen, it is clear she shares the bond that binds

such people together. The fraternity is tightly knit. Taking horses with those of like mind generates more than bonhomie. The sense of kinship is profound: it is almost as if you have discovered a long-lost relative. To know about horses is to understand the multitude of things that can go awry, as it did on that spring morning with Hannon behind the wheel.

'The Queen seemed to find it quite amusing,' Hannon reflected in his soft Wiltshire drawl. 'We've had some good old laughs in that Jeep. After we watch the horses at exercise we always come back to the house so she can chat to the jockeys. She enjoys that part of it almost as much as she enjoys being in my living room. She says it's one of the few places she goes that doesn't smell of fresh paint.'

To succeed with horses requires a keen eye. Hannon's is best amplified by the fact he was champion trainer in two consecutive seasons to 2011, and three times in all. His attention to detail is all the more striking for the nonchalance with which he disguises it. On morning duty in his Jeep, which is akin to riding a fairground carousel, he tackles a series of tasks simultaneously.

As he watches the string he might change the car radio station with one hand and field a phone call in the other while digressing to point out a circling hawk in the distance. All the while he dispenses instructions to riders in staccato bursts. His mind is here, there and everywhere, yet he will always spot a horse wearing the wrong kind of bridle.

It takes one keen eye to know another, of course, and Hannon has seen enough to recognise as much in his patron. That much became clear on the Queen's first visit to his stables in 1999, five months after Hannon received his first intake of royal horses.

'We got a bit confused as to which of her horses were coming up the gallops,' Hannon recalled. 'She found it quite funny, thankfully, but she soon put us right when the horses came past. She recognises every single one of them when she comes here. She knows them like the back of her hand.'

That wasn't all about the Queen's first visit that lingered in Hannon's mind. Having never previously met her, he was understandably nervous at the prospect. He was fortified by the presence alongside her of Warren's father-in-law, Lord Carnarvon, who was racing manager to the Queen

Opposite: The Queen at Newbury races with her bloodstock and racing advisor John Warren (left) and trainer Richard Hannon.

until his death in 2001. Hannon's success with Carnarvon's horses doubtless prompted the latter to recommend him for the royal warrant. Nevertheless, he couldn't help but fret as the royal party swept down his drive for the first time.

He was soon put at ease. 'The Queen hadn't been here ten minutes when we were looking at some horses trotting around the warm-up ring,' he said. 'Then she asked me: "Isn't that Betty Brister on that horse?"'

'Yes it is, ma'am,' Hannon said. 'How do you know her?'

'She used to look after my best racehorse, Highclere.'

Hannon was astonished. 'How she recognised Betty underneath her crash helmet I'll never know,' he said. 'Sometimes I can't do that with people who have been working here for twenty years.'

Hannon was to learn what his predecessors quickly realised for themselves. In addition to recognising her horses, the Queen rarely forgets a face. No less than twenty-five years had passed since Betty Brister bade farewell to Highclere in 1974. It was an emotional parting, since Brister played an important part in allowing Highclere to express the full extent of her ability. Like many others bred by the Royal Studs, Highclere came with her share of temperament. She was what racing parlance would deem a 'proper madam' when she arrived at Major Dick Hern's stables as an unbroken yearling. She would try to bite and kick anyone who entered her box. She was also prone to lash out indiscriminately with her hind legs.

At that time Brister was the only girl working at Hern's stables. She relished the challenge of being around Highclere without unduly imposing herself on the filly. In looking after – or 'doing' – a difficult horse, the groom must dominate the relationship without resorting to force. Patience is the key: hence the iron fist in silk gloves. In this way a difficult horse will see its groom as a comforting presence in a world it has come to regard as a hostile place.

It was Brister who established the parameters of her relationship with Highclere. She set the ground rules to which both parties adhered in their mutual interest. An acknowledged horsewoman herself, the Queen will have appreciated the way Brister handled one of her equine pride and joys. She will have seen Brister perhaps half a dozen times in 1973-74, and then not for a quarter of a century, yet she still recognised what remained of a face not hidden under her crash helmet that morning.

To those who know Hannon, the look of incredulity on his face as he recounts the Betty Brister episode would be no surprise. He is not one for the finer details, especially when it comes to horses' names. He is first and foremost a stockman: the son of a trainer who recognises horses more by their shape and mannerisms than by what owners choose to call them. He connects with them at first glance when they arrive in his yard, often straight from the yearling auctions, towards the end of every season.

At that stage they are equine adolescents about to embark on the formative process of being backed and ridden away. Because they are also unnamed, they tend to be identified by the name of their father, or sire. In this way does the chestnut colt with three white socks becomes known as 'the Galileo colt'. So it is with each new arrival. Owners affix names to their horses in due course, but to Hannon, the chestnut with three white socks always remains 'the Galileo colt,' as it was when he set first eyes on it. There is no room for confusion around the yard, where long-serving staffers know precisely what Hannon means when he asks to be shown 'the Galileo colt'. Beyond Herridge, however, Hannon's creaky memory can be his undoing.

'Oh dear,' he says of the time he lunched at Windsor Castle before the party went on to Royal Ascot in 2000. 'Talk about the hot seat: I was drawn between the Queen and the Queen Mother, whom I hadn't met before. I knew about her love of jumps racing, of course, yet while she was getting on in years her memory for those horses was remarkable. I was into a bit of jumps racing myself, but not like her. She reeled off every one of Ryan Price's Schweppes winners – and he never even trained for her. Speechless, I was. I couldn't remember any of them.'

The Queen Mother's love of jumps racing knew no bounds. She won the Schweppes, a devilishly competitive race over hurdles at Newbury, with Tammuz in 1975. It was just as well for Hannon that she didn't raise the name of Gran Alba. He would have undoubtedly struggled to recall that he trained that horse to win the Christmas Hurdle in 1991.

Gregarious by nature and a generous host, Hannon is one of the most amusing characters in a game not short of them. Many of his owners have

Previous spread: Derby day at Epsom.

been with him since he started out in 1970. Rarely a day passes without one of them – or indeed a small flock – descending on his stables for the morning joyride in his Jeep. The Queen is not alone in enjoying an experience much treasured by those lucky enough to have savoured it.

She anticipates visits to see her horses with particular relish. At her request, they are devoid of ceremony redolent of official duty. There is no red carpet, no speech for her to recite, no statue to unveil. She is in her element in the company of animals that enchanted her from an early age, and with those who handle them. 'She always enjoys a chat with the lads in the yard,' Hannon said. 'Or at least, the ones that can speak English.'

Hannon's propensity for industrial language is offset by a hilarious turn of phrase. It is part of his charm. Before he met the Queen his staff chided that he swore so frequently he would be unable to desist in her company. The story goes that a week before the inaugural royal visit his staff placed a bucket in the corner of the yard into which he would have to drop a coin every time he swore. Hannon denies it vehemently – albeit with a smile on his face.

Just as emphatically, but with an equally broad grin, he rejects an account that has him rushing to the loo in a brief interlude during a royal visit. Incensed at finding the door locked, he loudly exclaimed that 'you can never use your own loo when you bloody well want to!' The door duly opened to reveal Her Majesty as the occupant.

Whatever the authenticity of these stories, Hannon's friends will vouchsafe that they are utterly plausible. He brings a light touch to any proceedings but he felt pride's full force when Carnarvon served him with the royal summons. 'When he asked me whether I would like to have some of the Queen's horses to train, I said: "There is no need to ask me that, m'lord, of course I would." My father would have been very proud if he was here to see it.'

And with that, Hannon wanders over to the desk in his living room, which he only uses when the Queen visits. From a drawer he pulls out a pile of hand-written letters in her own hand. He holds them close to his chest. 'These are among my most treasured possessions,' he declares. 'I don't know how she finds the time to do it, but she does.'

The Queen is a prolific writer of letters to each of her trainers. In this way will they learn each year which young horses they have been allocated. When Hannon receives his letter he stands back and pinches himself before opening it. 'If you'd told me when I started that I'd one day be training some of the Queen's horses, I'd never have believed it,' he says. 'But the best part is the way it has turned out, because she is a delight when she comes here. We always look forward to her visits.'

Admiration is mutual. Now in the twilight of his career, Hannon was given the prestigious Cartier Award of Merit when he was champion trainer at the end of 2010. Through Warren, the Queen paid tribute to a man who was unable to receive the award in person at the glittering London ceremony. Hannon, then 65, had just left hospital after undergoing triple heart bypass surgery. But for that, he would have puffed out his chest at the Queen's message. He is a royalist from head to toe.

The Queen's patronage of Hannon followed on from that of Henry George Reginald Molyneux Herbert, the seventh Earl of Carnarvon. He was the first establishment racehorse owner to acknowledge Hannon's talent by sending him horses to train. The decision paid instant dividends. Between them Niche and Lyric Fantasy, who were contemporaries as two-year-olds, won a hatful of significant races in 1992 – after which Carnarvon sold Lyric Fantasy at auction for 340,000 guineas. The following year Hannon saddled Niche to win the Falmouth Stakes, a benchmark contest for three-year-old fillies, and followed up in the same race for the next two years with Lemon Souffle and Caramba. Each of them triumphed in Carnarvon's scarlet racing silks.

Carnarvon also elected to sell Lemon Souffle, who made another princely sum – this time 400,000 guineas – when she was offered at auction in 1994. The earl, an astute breeder with a taste for a bargain, was not averse to cashing in fillies of high racecourse achievement. They are valuable breeding assets much coveted by those with the means to pursue the dream of having a racehorse to outrun all others.

Both Lyric Fantasy and Lemon Souffle were purchased by John Magnier, whose Coolmore Stud, in Ireland, has dominated the racing and breeding landscape in Europe for the past two decades. The two fillies were in excellent hands, yet as it transpired, none of their offspring would make an impact on the racecourse. They both took excellent credentials to the paddocks, yet both fell woefully short of expectations.

Riding in Windsor Great Park, 1992.

This is all too common within the breeding business. Expertise only counts for so much. As those endeavouring to unearth it have found to their cost, the formula for breeding good racehorses is jealously guarded by Mother Nature. Over the years this elixir has seduced countless individuals of immense wealth. It is what prompted the Aga Khan to describe the quest as akin to 'playing chess with nature.' Money alone cannot buy success.

A footnote to the sale of Lemon Souffle, and in particular how quickly such idyllic aspirations can fall from grace, concerns her second foal. Bois de Citron was sold as a yearling in 1999 – before she was old enough to be ridden, never mind galloped in earnest – for the equivalent of £500,000 at auction in France. She raced for a new owner who was full of hope that such a well-bred filly would excel on the track, yet from twelve starts she won only one insignificant race at Leicester. When her racing days were over Bois de Citron was deemed surplus to requirements and sold on. This time she changed hands for £57,750. Her value had depreciated almost tenfold in three years.

Equally, to sell such valuable breeding assets, as Carnarvon did with Lyric Fantasy and Lemon Souffle, amounts to a calculated risk. Either of these fillies might have established a majestic Thoroughbred dynasty for

The Queen with her mother at Cheltenham races, 1957.

Magnier. Their sons and daughters might have run rampant over the Turf, to be succeeded in turn by sons and daughters of similar hue. That they did not is largely down to happenstance. Although Carnarvon came out on the right side on both occasions he was not so fortunate in 1982, when he sanctioned the sale of the Queen's top-class filly, Height Of Fashion, to Sheikh Hamdan bin Rashid Al-Maktoum. Height Of Fashion did indeed establish an equine dynasty for Dubai's Minister of Finance. Worse still, her sale would trigger a sequence of events that would embroil the Queen in a controversy that raged like a forest fire for more than a decade.

As for Niche, she would meet a cruel fate. Having won the Falmouth Stakes in July 1993, her sights were trained on a big race in France the following month when she fell and unshipped her rider during morning exercise on Hannon's gallops. Running loose, and doubtless traumatised by the fall, she found her way out of the drive at Herridge and onto a minor road – where she ran headlong into an oncoming van.

It was an instant death, an accident of the kind that goes with the territory. In racing, as in other equine disciplines, triumph and disaster are seemingly umbilically linked. Yet even that knowledge cannot immunise against the shock of disaster that invariably comes out of the blue, as it did with Niche. Some people are labelled 'lucky owners' when their successes outweigh their investment. Carnarvon was among them, although the phrase pays scant justice to his intuition and flair for breeding good horses. The Queen, by contrast, has known more than her fair share of ill fortune over more than six decades of involvement.

It has not dimmed her enthusiasm; quite the opposite, in fact. To endure bad times is to appreciate the good in turn. To breed and race Thoroughbreds is to experience extremes of emotion, from harsh disappointment to unbridled elation. These emotions are shared by all connected with the horse, from the Queen as its owner to her trainer, to the horse's groom, to those who nurtured it on the stud, and to the trusty individual on hand to oversee the safe birth of the horse in the first place. This lengthy process of evolution is what brings horsefolk together. They share the same aspirations. Their hearts beat in unison when the stalls snap open at the start of a race. They all hope for a glimmer of encouragement, a sign that here, at last, might be the horse of their dreams.

The Queen has deliberately kept a ceiling on the number of Thoroughbreds she breeds. The consequence is that she knows every one of them intimately. She would not have it any other way. The thrill of watching them run will be familiar to any parent at school sports day. The frisson of willing their children on comes in sharp contrast with the greater concern for their return home free of injury.

It's no wonder the Queen is animated when she visits her horses in training. She will not see them for months on end, yet she always remembers them. So much so that she averted what would have been a major calamity in 1955. On visiting the Freemason Lodge stable of her trainer, Captain Sir Cecil Boyd-Rochfort, in Newmarket, she realised that the identity of two of her horses had been confused. She was shown a yearling colt pertaining to be Agreement and another known in the stable as Doutelle. Although she hadn't seen either horse for eighteen months, she immediately recognised the error.

When, as foals, the two horses had been weaned from their mothers, they were sent to Ireland to graze on that country's fertile pasture. The mix-up arose when they returned from Ireland to Newmarket, where they arrived with no names attached to their headcollars. Nevertheless, their

The Queen and Queen Mother with trainer Captain Cecil Boyd-Rochfort at Royal Ascot after Aureole's victory in the 1954 Hardwicke Stakes.

respective identities were plain to the Queen. When she visits her horses she always takes her camera, as do parents on sports day. So frequently does she pore over the photographs that she could recognise her horses from a distance, as Hannon testified. On that autumnal morning in Newmarket she had no doubt that a horse known to Boyd-Rochfort's staff as Agreement was in fact Doutelle. And that Doutelle was Agreement.

It was a critical distinction, since Doutelle won races of a calibre that placed him in demand as a stallion. On the completion of his racing career he took up stallion duties at the Royal Studs, on the Queen's Norfolk estate at Sandringham, where he was bred to a 'book' of forty mares each year. Had he done so under the guise of Agreement's pedigree – the two horses hailed from quite different parentage – the consequences would have been catastrophic. The Queen herself bred many of her mares to Doutelle. Had Agreement been masquerading as Doutelle, bloodlines at the Royal Studs, which are forensically analysed for optimum matings with stallions of different strains, would have resembled a tangled fishing line. Although the advent of DNA testing and microchips has since negated the possibility of such confusion arising, the danger was very real in the middle of the last century.

The Queen's interest in racing is not confined to her own horses. Each day she takes her breakfast with a copy of the *Racing Post*, the sport's trade newspaper, and is keen to discuss racing-related issues of the day with John Warren by telephone. The former Foreign Secretary, Robin Cook, greatly endeared himself to the monarch when the pair's paths crossed on official business in the Middle East. Cook arranged for a copy of the newspaper he'd read on the flight from London to be delivered to the Queen. First things first, as the saying holds. Indeed, the extent of the Queen's knowledge of racing news beyond her own horses was to surprise Sir Peter O'Sullevan, doyen among commentators and the BBC's 'Voice of Racing' for fifty years until his retirement in 1997.

In November 1974 Sir Peter was commissioned by the Royal Archives, via his employers at the BBC, to talk to the Queen about her Thoroughbreds. Their meeting at Windsor Castle was filmed; much of the material was subsequently released for use in television documentaries. Sir Peter recalled: 'We were walking down to see the yearlings being led through some starting gates when she stopped, turned to me and said: "And what about Be Tuneful? You must be thrilled; he was very impressive."'

Be Tuneful was the first significant winner for the stallion Be Friendly, who was Sir Peter's pride and joy. Be Friendly had won several important races in Sir Peter's silks but it was important he made an impact with his early runners. In this way would the young stallion generate demand for his services. It took Sir Peter aback to learn that the Queen had noted Be Tuneful's promise for herself.

On the Kingsclere gallops with trainer Ian Balding.

'Well, ma'am,' he quipped, 'I hope we are wired for sound as I'd love to be able to use that in a commercial.'

The Queen's memory for horses is matched by her concern for people within the equine fraternity. This detail reinforces the concept of a bond between horsefolk. It is one the Queen has amplified on numerous occasions. In 2002 Sir Peter was invited to lunch at Windsor Castle ahead of a day at Royal Ascot. He went with his wife Patricia, whose death in January 2010 left a gaping hole in Sir Peter's life. With a tear in his eye Sir Peter recalled: 'The next time I saw the Queen she said: "I remember Pat in my prayers." I found it very moving, but then, the Queen is a very human being.'

This 'very human' side to the Queen is well known to people of a racing orientation. Photographs of her on the racecourse invariably show her smiling. When she is not, it is because she is concentrating deeply while assessing horses in the paddock. Her patronage of racing, and of Royal Ascot in particular, is the envy of other sports. Racing is no longer as synonymous with British life as it was in the first half of the last century, when the Royal Family's affiliation enhanced their own popularity by their support of it. Nevertheless, to remove royal patronage would be to strip racing of its bark.

The strength of links between racing and British royalty is most pronounced at Royal Ascot. Numerous races at the five-day fixture are named in commemoration of the Queen's ancestors, among them Queen Mary and Queen Alexandra, George V and Edward VII. Indeed, the opening race on opening day is named after Queen Anne, who established Ascot racecourse in 1711.

Nor does the name-game end there. Races at Ascot's midsummer festival in July commemorate the Queen's sister, Princess Margaret, and her parents, King George VI and Queen Elizabeth. Beyond that, a feature race on British Champions Day, the prestigious fixture inaugurated in 2011, is the Queen Elizabeth II Stakes. This race often determines the champion racehorse over the distance of one mile.

You would expect nothing less of Ascot, with its historic royal links, yet the Queen's affection for the sport is acknowledged in similar vein around the world. Major races embracing Queen Elizabeth II in their titles unfold annually in Australia, Canada, Hong Kong, Japan, Singapore and the United States of America.

The Queen Elizabeth II Cup at Sha Tin racecourse, Hong Kong, October 1986: presenting the cup to Mr E.C. Lowe, owner of the winner Forever Gold.

The advent of Champions Day underlines just how important is the Queen's patronage. Champions Day marked a significant development within British racing. Before its introduction the Flat season tapered away without a grand finale. A fitting stage was required to celebrate Britain's champion racehorses but pinning down a date proved a problem. There were sound arguments for staging it in September and October. An important consideration in choosing October over September was that the Queen was more likely to be free of official duty – and therefore more likely to attend, as she did in 2011. On that day she marvelled at the prowess of Frankel, whose victory in the Queen Elizabeth II Stakes marked his ninth from as many starts.

Clare Balding, who hosted the BBC's television coverage from Ascot on Champions Day, remembers the occasion well. The Queen had already seen Frankel in the flesh twice before. She was at Newbury when the colt made his seasonal debut in April and she saw him again at Royal Ascot, when the magnificent colt won the St James's Palace Stakes in June. 'I knew the Queen would take a lot of interest when Frankel came into the paddock,' Balding said. 'She looked very closely at him. It's as if she was saying: "Let's see what all the fuss is about, let's have a look at this great horse." She could barely take her eyes off him.'

Frankel is due to retire from racing to take up stallion duties at the close of Diamond Jubilee year, and the chances are that the Queen will breed one of her mares to the horse, whose racing excellence identifies him as a stallion with obvious potential to sire superior horses. These are the tenets of the breeding business: it is all in the blood. Although the Queen was not alone in appreciating Frankel's handsome physique, she will have cast a more refined eye over the horse's attributes. She will have noted his overall size, the lines of his forelegs, the shape of his hocks, the size of his chest; these are facets that will help her to choose an appropriate physical mate for him. For example, a broodmare with offset front legs should be bred to a stallion with straight, correct front legs. This lessens the prospect of a foal by their union being similarly flawed.

Alec Head has few peers in that respect. Widely acknowledged as one of the world's most successful breeders, he has twice hosted the Queen at his Haras du Quesnay, in Normandy. The two have conversed about

Opposite: The Queen and Queen Mother, Sandown Park, 1953.

27

Alec Head greets the Queen on her visit to
his stud farm in Kentucky, 1984.

Thoroughbreds at some length and Head readily attests to the Queen's
encyclopaedic knowledge of bloodlines. 'When she came to stay she was
very interested to know how I bred the horses that did well for me,' Head
recalled. 'She wanted to know why a particular mare had bred champions
and why a similar one had not – even though the truth is that nobody
really knows the answers.'

Beyond that, as a Frenchman of English ancestry, Head is perfectly
placed to amplify what the Queen means to British racing – and the thrill
she in turn draws from it. 'Racing in Britain is fabulous for many reasons,
but having the Queen as an owner and breeder makes all the difference,'
he said. 'What the Queen likes, the country takes an interest in. Racing
would get a huge boost if the Queen won a big race like the Derby. It
would be seen on television all around the world. For sure, racing in
Britain would not be the same without her.'

On her private visits to Normandy the Queen wanted to do little else but
talk horses. It was the purpose of her visit, after all, yet it cast her in a fresh
light even though Head had previously met her at the races. 'The first time
she came she could have been any other breeder,' he said. 'It seems clear to
me that what she likes most of all is being around young horses on the farm.
My staff and I were very surprised to find how relaxed she was. She has so
many responsibilities in her life that very few people get to see her as we did.
She cannot relax like that when she is on official business.'

Head and Sir Peter O'Sullevan are old friends. And Sir Peter is plainly
on repartee terms with the Queen. A picture in his book *Horse Racing
Heroes*, published in 2004 and reproduced here, shows Head greeting the
Queen at the stud farm he leased in Kentucky. The pose of each protagonist
is unusual: it appears the Queen is deferring to Head.

Sir Peter knew the Queen had seen his book; he was asked to deliver a
copy to Buckingham Palace on its publication. 'The next time I saw the
Queen I said: "Ma'am, I love the picture of you curtseying to Alec Head."'

To which the Queen replied with a smile: 'So do I. It was one of the first
things I saw when I opened the book.'

The Queen's penchant for the company of racing folk was evident when
she hosted a dinner at Windsor Castle to celebrate Ascot racecourse's
tercentenary year in 2011. Clare Balding was among 300 guests. 'When we

arrived the Queen's lady-in-waiting told us she would be gone by 10.30pm but she was still there after eleven, having a brilliant time in the sort of company she really enjoys.'

On that occasion she spoke at some length to Ruby Walsh, whose neck was in a protective brace after one of those crashing falls from which jump jockey seems to rise in systematic defiance of the odds. As Sir Peter discovered, the Queen remembers her racing comrades-in-arms in times of adversity, often with simple gestures that mean much to those in receipt of them. She was acquainted with Buster Haslam, who was the travelling head lad at Major Dick Hern's stables, where Highclere was trained. Haslam was present when the Queen hosted a party for racing folk at Windsor Castle in the Silver Jubilee year of 1977. 'It was a shock to all when Buster later took his own life,' Sir Peter related. 'I understand the Queen was really upset about it and wrote a private letter to his family.' It was the same Buster Haslam whom the Queen had addressed by his first name at the Silver Jubilee party.

There are happier memories of Willie Snaith, who rode the royal colt Landau to win the Sussex Stakes at Goodwood in 1954 – with Her Majesty in attendance. Attached to the stable of Sir Noel Murless, who trained for the Queen until the late 1960s, Snaith retired in 1972. He lives on the edge of Warren Hill, the famous Newmarket gallop, with his wife Silvia. On stepping down from the saddle he turned his hand to taking visitors on guided tours of a town long known as the 'Headquarters' of British racing. He remains as jovial today as he was in his riding days; all the more so when he was awarded the MBE in 2005 for his services to the Newmarket community. 'So I bowed and said: "Good afternoon, Your Majesty,"' Snaith reflected of receiving his honour. 'And she said: "Good afternoon to you too. It has been a very long time since I last saw you."'

A period of 51 years had passed since Landau galloped to victory at Goodwood, yet Snaith related how the Queen remembered the race, reminisced about Landau and wanted to know all about his work as a guide in Newmarket, a town the Queen knows well. Silvia, meanwhile, was wondering what on earth the two were talking about. She couldn't help but notice the Queen had spent discernibly longer chatting to her husband than anyone else.

'When I got back to Silvia I think she was a bit cross with me,' Snaith ventured of his wife. 'She thought I had spoken to the Queen for too long and was holding her up, but it was the Queen who did most of the talking.' She was in racing company, after all.

Instances of the 'very human being' to which Sir Peter O'Sullevan referred are manifest between the Queen and racing's flock. Back in 1957 'Dodger' Hooper had his hands full with Atlas, a talented royal horse with his share of quirks. Atlas was prone to bite anything that moved – and much that didn't – when he was out of his box. One day, as Hooper was leading him around a racecourse paddock, Atlas clamped his teeth onto the jacket of his suit and ripped it clean off his shoulders. On hearing of this, the Queen sent Hooper funds with which to replace the suit.

First racecourse airing of Princess Elizabeth's racing colours: Astrakhan and jockey Tommy Burn at Ascot, October 1949.

Peter 'Caz' Williams is another from racing's tribe familiar to the Queen. However, much though he'd like all the memories to be fond, it was Williams's misfortune to have been involved in a series of calamities that would have sent a less understanding owner scurrying from the sport.

The Queen's catalogue of misfortune in racing is substantial. Nor do the random fates bow to any kind of symmetry. There is no explanation for a curse that was recognised by Cecil Boyd-Rochfort as early as 1957. After hearing of Almeria's untapped prowess in a post-race debrief with Harry Carr, Boyd-Rochfort warned his stable jockey: 'For goodness sake, don't tell the Queen. Whenever one says that, something always goes wrong.'

Nothing blackens the soul like a promising horse killed in its prime. With half a ton of flesh perched atop fragile limbs, Thoroughbreds are notoriously prone to mishap. They have been refined for optimum speed by selective breeding since the sixteenth century. They can run like the wind until an ill one blows in their faces. The Queen herself recognises that racing cannot exist without the risk of mortal injury. It is part of the covenant.

Anyone working with horses will attest to the overriding concern for their safety. This aspect of stable life is often taken to extremes. Expensive and elaborate measures designed to minimise risk are inbuilt in the daily regime. No equine establishments do more to embrace the principle of safety than racing stables, with their cargo of valuable Thoroughbreds. And no racing establishment houses a better quality of employee than Peter 'Caz' Williams, who has worked at Park House stables for the past 44 years.

Park House, on Newbury's south-east fringe, has a long association with royal racehorses. John Porter trained horses there for King Edward VII, then Prince Of Wales, in the 1860s. The royal link would be renewed in the autumn of 1963, when the Queen sent yearlings to be trained by Peter Hastings-Bass. By the following June, Hastings-Bass, then 44, had succumbed to cancer. He was succeeded by his son-in-law Ian Balding, father of Clare, who took Williams aboard in 1968.

At that time Williams still harboured aspirations as a jump jockey. He was of the old school; he served part of his apprenticeship at Fairlawne with Peter Cazalet, who trained 250 winners for the Queen Mother until his death in 1973. Indeed, it was Cazalet who trained the Queen's first winner in 1949 when, as Princess Elizabeth, she saw Monaveen win in her colours at Fontwell Park. Mother and daughter shared ownership of the steeplechaser who would himself meet a tragic end when he broke a leg in a fall at Hurst Park the following year. It was something of an omen.

At Fairlawne, Williams was assigned to look after the Queen Mother's horse, Three No Trumps, on a daily basis. It would be the first of many royal horses to be placed in his care. In noting Williams's meticulous stablecraft, Balding delegated him to look after the Queen's horses from 1969. So it was that Williams had the misfortune to witness the demise of some of her most promising horses.

The first of them was Musical Drive, whom Balding bought as a yearling on the Queen's behalf in 1967. The following spring, when he was showing abundant promise ahead of his imminent debut, Musical Drive was out at routine exercise when Williams saw a herd of riderless horses making straight for them.

'It was a nightmare of a morning,' he reflected. 'There must have been six or seven running loose and one of them came galloping straight at me. I didn't know which way to turn so I left it to Musical Drive, who suddenly started plunging forward. I sat tight the first time he bucked but the second time he tipped me off. Then he galloped in a circle before heading for an iron gate in the corner of the field. He hit it so hard they had to flatten it out with a tractor. Bent double it was, like a horseshoe.'

Horses are animals of flight. If one starts galloping, those around it are compelled by instinct to follow. A common cause of horses galloping hard in the wild is to flee from perceived danger. Musical Drive's blood was stirred by the sight of his stablemates galloping loose. It cost him his life.

Balding was distraught. The Queen's horses had not been long at Park House and he was obliged to deliver bad news. 'It was one of the earliest telephone conversations I had with Her Majesty,' Balding recalled. 'The accident was so horrific I took a few hours to compose myself before I made the call. I said I was sorry to have to tell her that we'd had the most horrible morning and poor Musical Drive has gone and killed himself.'

The Queen's responded in the way she does when any horse of hers is involved in an accident. 'Instead of asking me how it had happened, her first words were: "Oh dear, Ian, I am sorry. How is the poor lad who was riding him?" Well, Peter [Williams] had been flung a mile but luckily he was fine. And when I relayed that to her, she said: "Good. Now don't worry about it; these things happen." It was a lovely reaction from her. I have never forgotten it.'

Further to the constant drive to minimise risk, Balding took measures to lessen the prospect of a similar accident recurring. There is always danger when a loose horse at the gallop encounters the corner of a railed paddock. It has effectively run into a cul-de-sac. Consequently, the iron gate in the corner of that paddock was resited on the basis that, however small the difference, there is less chance of a horse killing itself by colliding with wooden rails than with an iron gate. The gate itself, in its raw metallic colour on the day Musical Drive clattered into it, was painted white to make it more visible.

Balding was responsible for making those changes, but the Queen herself insisted on amending protocol at Park House when her promising stayer Magna Carta perished early in 1971. Williams inherited Magna Carta at the end of his two-year-old season when John Hallum gave him up take on a new arrival belonging to Paul Mellon. 'In a way John got lucky,' Williams mused, 'because the new horse turned out to be Mill Reef. If John hadn't taken him on, it could have been me.'

Williams instead devoted himself to Magna Carta. The horse was a favourite of the Queen's: his mother Almeria had carried the royal silks with distinction in the 1950s. Early one morning Magna Carta was found prostrate in his stable with his front foot entangled in a haynet. The net, made of strong nylon fibre, was attached to the stable wall and Magna Carta, having become entrapped, flailed wildly with his front legs in a frantic effort to free himself. It transpired he had broken his jaw in two places. He survived the subsequent surgery but he could not process the anaesthetic toxins in his body. He died three days later. As a result of Magna Carta's accident the Queen decreed that hay for her horses should be placed on the floor of their boxes, thus eliminating the risk posed by suspended haynets.

By contrast, no amount of lateral thinking could have spared Special Leave. The colt was bred to be a champion and in Balding's estimation he would not have been far short. Balding trained his sire, the aforementioned

The Queen at Royal Ascot with Lord Porchester, 1981.

Mill Reef, to win just about every race of consequence in 1971. He was the first racehorse to complete the coveted sweep comprising the Derby, the King George VI and Queen Elizabeth Stakes and the Prix de l'Arc de Triomphe. Special Leave's mother Light Duty, no mean runner herself, was a full-sister to no less an equine luminary than Highclere. He was bred, as they say, in the purple – which just happens to be the principal colour of the royal silks.

Special Leave showed his mettle as a two-year-old, which is when Thoroughbreds first take to the races. On his debut in 1982 he landed the Hyperion Stakes, a race historically won by horses of significant potential. Although Special Leave disappointed on soft ground in a Derby trial the following season, his flair was such that Balding persevered with the plan to run him in the Derby itself. With the race imminent, Williams was aboard on a May morning when Special Leave was asked to stretch out at the end of his gallop.

'There we were, going along full tilt on the downs when suddenly, one of his hind legs just snapped,' Williams related. 'It was sickening.'

Most horses are 'put down' on humane grounds when they break a leg. Very few can be saved although, ironically, Mill Reef survived a broken leg and the subsequent, pioneering surgery in 1972 that saved him for what would be an illustrious stallion career. In the majority of instances, however, any compound fracture is terminal. Even if surgery is successful, toxins from the requisite anaesthetic pose a grave threat to horses – as the case of Magna Carta illustrates. And even if a horse can surmount those obstacles, the recuperative process is fraught with danger. No weight can be placed on the broken limb for many months. Humans can lie in bed for the duration but horses cannot be instructed to do likewise. Nor do they spend anything like as much time lying down as humans do. They are able to sleep on their feet, which has helped them to survive in the wild without the defensive armoury available to other animals. They are creatures of flight that can flee from a standing start. Naturally active, they are ill disposed to standing still for very long. Even if one should come through the twin ordeals of surgery and recuperation, the chances of it being able to roam a paddock are extremely remote. It is far better, and far more humane, for one with a broken limb to be euthanised.

Were the prospect of saving a horse not so forlorn, the Queen would certainly embrace it. From an early age there have been countless examples of her forsaking traditional ways with horses for a kinder, less austere approach. Astrakhan, the foal given to her as a wedding present by the Aga Khan in 1947, had troublesome knees. Her trainer, Boyd-Rochfort, was convinced Astrakhan would never stand up to the rigours of training but the Queen, then Princess Elizabeth, moved the filly to Willie Smyth's stables in Sussex for a course of electrotherapy. Astrakhan was treated not by a vet but a physiotherapist, which was a most unusual diversion in the middle of the last century. Her knees responded, and on 15 April 1950 Astrakhan rewarded her owner by winning at Hurst Park racecourse. It was the princess's first winner on the Flat, and the only one to prevail in her own registered silks of scarlet, purple hooped sleeves and black cap. She would inherit the royal silks on the death of her father George VI in 1952.

For all the anguish suffered by Ian Balding and his lad, Peter 'Caz' Williams, the pair would work in tandem to achieve notable success with the Queen's horses. Some of them are represented today in bloodlines at the Royal Studs. Among them is Example, a high-class royal runner in 1971-72 who is survived by her great-great-great-granddaughter Rainbow's Edge – although perversely, Example's own career as a broodmare would meet a tragic end in the act of giving birth to her first foal, the appositely named Pas de Deux.

Ian Balding retired in 2002, to be succeeded by his son, Andrew. They are the only father-and-son alliance to have trained for the Queen, but to Ian alone goes the accolade of the biggest faux pas ever committed by one of her racing men.

Balding was talking to the Queen by telephone on the day Margaret Thatcher was elected Prime Minister in 1979.

'What do you make of that?' he was asked.

'Extraordinary, ma'am,' he replied. 'To think we are going to be governed by a woman … '

It is to Balding's eternal credit that he tells the story against himself.

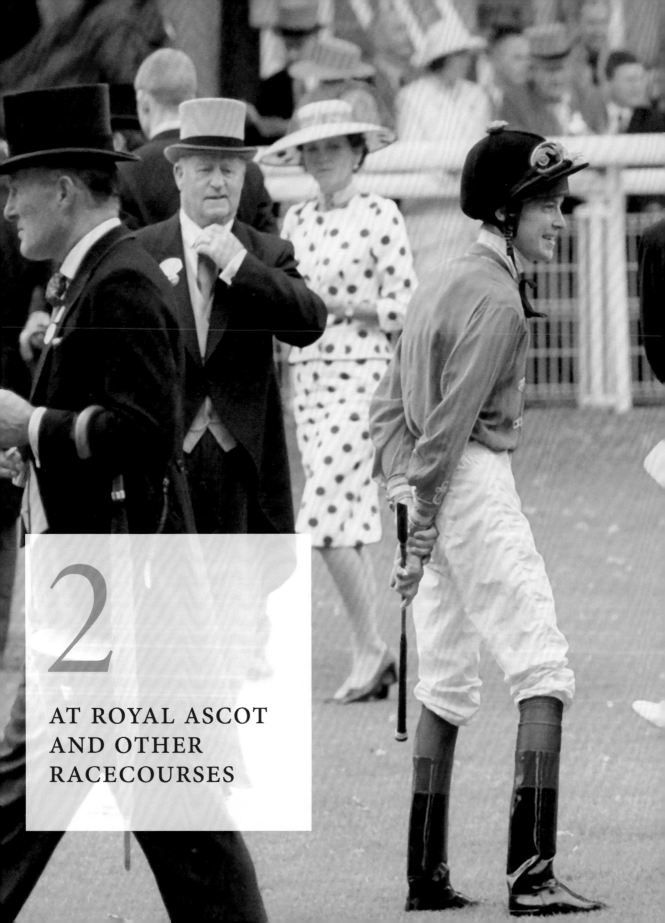

2

AT ROYAL ASCOT
AND OTHER
RACECOURSES

Few couples are more familiar with the rhythms of the Royal Household than Sir Michael Oswald and his wife, Lady Angela. Sir Michael has advised on racing and breeding matters since he was appointed Manager of the Royal Studs in 1970. His present role is as National Hunt advisor to the Queen, who chose to maintain the royal link with jumps racing after her mother, a bastion of the winter code, died in 2002.

In 1949 mother and daughter shared ownership of the steeplechaser, Monaveen. Beyond that, mother expanded her involvement with jumps racing while daughter started preparing herself for the day she would inherit the Royal Studs, with their emphasis on Flat racing. At that point her father George VI was beginning to ail with the lung cancer that would ultimately claim his life.

Lady Angela, for her part, was a lady-in-waiting to the Queen Mother for 21 years from 1981. The couple's standing within the household is such that they were advanced to make public the Queen Mother's affront at criticism of the Queen in the aftermath of the death of Diana, Princess Of Wales, in 1997. The interview they gave to a national newspaper in 2009 could only have come with royal assent.

An avid military historian, Sir Michael is as genial as they come. He became transfixed by racing at prep school and continues very much in that vein. Prior to joining the Royal Studs he managed Lordship and Egerton Studs in their Newmarket heyday. He is universally popular, not least for his boyish charm. Anecdotes tumble from him like ripe apples from a tree, although he is too well versed in royal protocol to give away more than he should. To linger over lunch at the couple's converted rectory in Norfolk is to recognise why they had come to serve at the heart of the Royal Household.

So much so that Lady Angela holds the rare distinction of having a royal racehorse named after her. In January 1996 Shirley Heights – the resident stallion at Sandringham, to where he retired after winning the 1978 Derby – underwent surgery during which veterinarians removed seventeen feet of his intestine. It was a critical operation; one that left his devoted groom fearing the worst. All manner of post-operative medication was tubed into him but Lady Angela insisted on adding some of her arnica-based 'rescue remedy', as Sir Michael called it. Her part in Shirley Heights' revival was recognised by the Queen Mother, who named one of her horses Lady Arnica.

Given the inspiration behind her name, Lady Arnica's career in the royal livery was woefully inappropriate. She was sold on after two undistinguished starts, although Sir Michael is quick to add that she went on to reach a place for her new connections. 'If you asked me to sum her up,' he said, 'I would

The Royal Box at Epsom on Derby day, 1993, as Enharmonic wins the Diomed Stakes.

Opposite: Princess Elizabeth with jockey Tony Grantham at Fontwell Park, 1949. Lord Mildmay (partially hidden) stands between them.

describe her as a well-bred filly with good legs, but who requires strong handling.' And with that he threw a smile at Lady Angela, daughter of the sixth Marquess of Exeter, who looked very much as if she had heard it before. Indeed, Lady Angela knows a little about athletic prowess herself. Her father won gold for Britain in the 400m hurdles at the 1928 Olympic Games. The previous year he had demonstrated his running prowess at Cambridge when he sprinted round the Great Court perimeter at Trinity College in a time quicker that it took the college clock to complete its midday chimes. His achievement inspired the scene's re-enactment in the much-celebrated film *Chariots of Fire*.

It was appropriate that Lady Arnica was a daughter of the royal broodmare, Brand. Having been plagued by a series of physical problems when sent into training in 1991, Brand never made it to the racecourse. Veterinarians' advice was that she wasn't worth breeding from, although Sir Michael thought otherwise. He took Brand under his wing and mated her with the jumping stallion Broadsword, to whom she delivered a robust, attractive foal. Ian Balding then trained Brand's second foal Double Brandy to win in the Queen Mother's colours at Newbury in 1998, which was otherwise a lean year for the royal silks.

Brand duly returned to the pages of the royal stud-book. And to telling effect: she would subsequently produce Banknote, who counted an important race in Germany among eight victories and prize-money earnings in excess of £100,000 for the Queen. She died soon after her last produce, Autumn Fire, was foaled in 2009. It would be apposite were Autumn Fire to reach the winner's enclosure. She is a great granddaughter of Highclere, who has but two surviving representatives at the Royal Studs – and that prospect is down to Sir Michael, who persevered with Brand against overwhelming odds.

In relating one detail, Sir Michael perfectly amplifies the extent of the Queen's devotion to racing. 'The Queen's diary is drawn up in outline eighteen months in advance, and in detail six months ahead,' Sir Michael said. 'Only six days are ring-fenced every year and they are the five days of Royal Ascot and Derby day at Epsom.'

Those entries are made in indelible ink. The Queen has been to Royal Ascot every year since 1945. Logistical complications were brushed aside

in 2005, when York staged the meeting while Ascot racecourse was rebuilt. The monarch still attended all five days. She has barely missed a Derby since 1953, when she watched her first runner, Aureole, finish runner-up soon after her Coronation. These important racing fixtures are annual highlights for the Queen. She must surely have had a pressing engagement for her 2011 visit to Australia to conclude just three days before the Melbourne Cup – although not before the Australian Bart Cummings, who has trained an astonishing twelve Melbourne Cup winners, revealed his sparse knowledge of royal responsibilities by wishing her luck with her bets.

Beyond those ring-fenced dates, the Queen usually manages to go racing a handful of times each year. 'If she happens to be at Windsor one weekend and there is nothing official to do, she will go and watch her runners,' Sir Michael said. Such impromptu visits are glitter on the racing frock. They are also pleasantly informal in an age when others of world status are so assiduously protected as to render them all but invisible. Successive Popes have taken to acknowledging their flocks behind bullet-proof glass walls in their buggies. It is increasingly rare to see President Obama walking freely among his people, yet such suffocating security cordons do not envelop the Queen on the racetracks of Britain. A less obtrusive security blanket is in place, which is as the Queen prefers it.

Nor do visible security measures constrain her annual trip to Epsom on Derby day. The Queen is equally at ease with her subjects when visiting the paddock at Newbury, a destination favoured by its close proximity to Windsor. Nevertheless, she is most synonymous with Royal Ascot, that fusion of racing and high fashion which remains the focal point of 'the Season' in Britain, and much coveted by every other major racing nation.

Truth be told, racing's popularity around the world is on the wane. The sport is in an embattled state in the United States, where as recently as the mid-1970s racegoers flocked in their hundreds of thousands to witness epic jousts between Affirmed and Alydar. Strenuous efforts are now made to cajole 'celebrities' to events like the Kentucky Derby, to little obvious effect. Racecourse attendance is in decline in Ireland of all countries, while most of the best of racing in France plays out before empty grandstands. Only in Australia, Hong Kong and Japan is horse racing vibrant, yet the totems of none of these nations are seen on the racecourse.

It is no exaggeration to say that the Queen is a greater lure to Royal Ascot galleries than the horses themselves. The daily Royal Procession down the racecourse culminates in the paddock, which is far more densely populated for the arrival of the royal party than for any big-race winner. Nor is it possible to move around in the immediate vicinity; the crowds start gathering long before carriages are due. It has been this way since Princess Elizabeth, then twenty years old, was swept down the Straight Mile at Ascot, entering through the Golden Gates first used in 1878 by her great-grandfather, Edward VII. Such gilded history makes the eyes of visitors from abroad turn green with envy.

For all the pageantry, the royal presence is as relaxed as it can be without breaching protocol. You could be standing only yards from the Queen without realising it. As she comes and goes from the paddock she will sometimes stop and chat to the BBC's racing presenters Clare Balding and Willie Carson, whose broadcasting position adjourns her route. The Queen is well acquainted with both. Her first encounter with Balding predates the

Arriving at Royal Ascot in 1983 . . .

43

... and in 2011.

latter's memory: Balding would have been barely out of the cot when the Queen visited the stables of her father, Ian. And Carson was the jockey who rode the royal filly Dunfermline to win two Classic races in the Silver Jubilee year of 1977. 'The Queen often has quite a lot to say to Willie,' Balding said. 'She is always particularly keen to talk to jockey and trainers.'

Such relative lack of formality characterises the Queen's integration within the racecourse community. Mind you, this spontaneous interaction introduces an occupational hazard for presenters in their professional capacity. 'I always try to curtsey when the Queen walks past,' Balding said. 'I don't want to appear rude but sometimes I am live on air, so I can't.'

There is no issue with it. On the contrary, the Queen is there to savour the action, just like any other racegoer. In quiet spells between races she will watch the BBC's output from the Royal Box. 'We occasionally get some feedback on how we are doing,' Balding said. 'After Yeats won his fourth Ascot Gold Cup [in 2009], the Queen apparently thought I did very well in summing up a historic achievement.'

It wasn't the first time Balding was conveyed the royal take on her broadcasting skills. In 2003 the Queen watched on television as Casual Look galloped to victory in the Oaks, one of the five 'Classic' races renewed annually in Britain. She would have followed Casual Look's progress through the race: the filly was owned and bred by Will Farish III, then the serving US Ambassador to the United Kingdom, and whose Thoroughbred stud in Kentucky, Lane's End Farm, was home to the Queen's mares when they visited American stallions.

Farish was not at Epsom to see Casual Look, since American troops had just invaded Iraq. So the post-race interview, which Balding was charged with conducting, could only really involve the winning trainer – in this case none other than her brother Andrew, who had just succeeded her father at Park House Stables. Emotions coursed so strongly through members of a particularly close family that, for once, Clare seemed lost for words. She did well to keep the thread going but was more than grateful when Ian suddenly appeared beside Casual Look's head. What followed was a veritable gem of live broadcasting.

'Dad, can you speak?' Clare inquired.

Just as Ian replied with a resounding shake of the head, Andrew appeared – stage left.

'Andrew? Andrew?' Clare pleaded.

To no avail. Andrew, too, was overcome by emotion while Clare tried vainly to adhere to the broadcasting code of impartiality. It was as touching as it was hilarious; none found it more so than the Queen. Delight at victory for Farish advanced to unrestrained joy as father, son and daughter, all of whom she knew so well, played pass-the-parcel with the microphone.

Some months later Clare fulfilled a request from the Women's Institute, Sandringham Branch, to address the motherhood on her media career. When she took questions from the floor a request came through to relive the sequence of events by a lady in the audience who maintained it was one of the funniest things she had seen on television. The lady in question wasn't wearing her crown.

This sort of interchange between the Queen and her racing subjects is as unremarkable as her presence on the racecourse. Just as she savoured her honeymoon on the Mediterranean island of Malta, where she enjoyed relative freedom from attention, her racecourse visits allow her privately to engage in one of her favourite pastimes. Equally, racecourses open a public window into an otherwise very private life. Before any big race the Queen is always to be found sizing up the field of runners. At the Royal meeting she always presents the winner's trophy after the Gold Cup, the Royal Hunt Cup and the Queen's Vase. You could set your watch by her entering and leaving the paddock. Indeed, her presence at Royal Ascot is so much part of the furniture that racing is almost in danger of taking it for granted.

That thought occurred to Balding at a time when the BBC's coverage of Royal Ascot was produced by a New Zealander, Malcolm Kemp MBE. 'Malcolm was absolutely fascinated by the Royal Family,' Balding avers. 'It would get to the point where he constantly had pictures of the Queen in shot. I used to say to him: "Give it a rest, mate, you're doing a bit too much of it."'

Kemp gained the respect of his peers in an illustrious career. His prowess was such that he was asked to be a route director at Princess Diana's funeral. He won a BAFTA in 2002 for his coverage of the opening and closing ceremonies at the Commonwealth Games in Manchester. Sadness engulfed the BBC two years later when Kemp died of cancer, aged 57. He was succeeded in his Royal Ascot role by a British producer.

'Sometimes I think we have swung too much the other way now,' Balding says. 'We don't show enough of the Queen in the paddock – or the other royals, for that matter. Quite a lot of them tend to go these days.'

Conversely, this lack of ceremony, and the enjoyment the Queen takes from being among like-minded souls, is doubtless much of Her Majesty's pleasure. By contrast, her 2010 visit to Wimbledon, which jousts with Royal Ascot for acclaim as Britain's sporting summer jewel, generated the sort of fuss that is entirely absent on the racecourse. There was a semi-official feel to proceedings. The entire site was cordoned off by ropes to keep the public at arm's length. Security was stepped up; uniformed police were visible around Centre Court.

In contrast to her regular greeting of jockeys in the paddock there was a first encounter for the Queen with Roger Federer, six times Wimbledon champion and one of the greatest players the game has seen. 'I'm just so glad I got a chance to meet her,' Federer said. Wimbledon's desire to make a fanfare of the occasion was understandable: it was the Queen's first visit in 33 years, and only her third in all.

Mind you, it is not all fun and games for the Queen at Royal Ascot. The lunch she hosts at Windsor Castle before racing has official responsibilities. A distinguished daily cast of guests ranges from visiting royalty to ambassadors and diplomats, right through to her racing acquaintances. BBC commentators are obliged to glean at least a working knowledge of them all lest they should appear on television, without warning, during the Royal Procession. The Queen, for her part, must be fully cognisant of them.

A 'working knowledge' of anything has never sufficed for Sir Peter O'Sullevan. Not by accident did the acclaimed BBC broadcaster become as instantly recognisable as the stars he portrayed in his rich, distinct delivery. He achieved it by hard work and an unstinting eye for detail. It is doubtful anyone has spent more time on the racecourse than Sir Peter, who doubled up in his commentary duties as racing correspondent for the *Daily Express*. He has seen it all. He was at Fontwell Park in 1949, when Monaveen opened the Queen's racing account, yet nothing induced in him a fear akin to paralysis like commentating on the Royal Procession.

'For me it was the most nerve-wracking part of Royal Ascot week,' Sir Peter reflects. 'It seems to take an absolute eternity for the carriages to get down the course. In the early days it was always a dark secret what the Queen was wearing, so you had to describe that. And even though you'd swatted up on who was in which carriage, they'd sometimes swap the carriages around. You'd only notice it for the first time when you saw them on your monitor.'

Typically, Sir Peter went further than researching the human contents of each carriage. Each year he would contact Lt Col Sir John Millar, the Crown Equerry who was central to the coach-and-horse aspect of royal pageantry, for chapter and verse on the horses themselves. 'If there were moments of confusion I could always say: "And there's Manitoba, the

Riding her horse Surprise to Ascot
racecourse in 1961 …

twelve-year-old given to the Queen on her visit to Canada, who'd never
pulled a carriage until he came to England ..." It helped me to save myself
many times.'

The boot was on the other foot in 2002. Having lunched at Windsor
Castle, Sir Peter and his wife Pat rode serenely down the racecourse in the
Royal Procession, leaving his successor at the BBC to grapple with who
was who – and in which carriage.

Sir Peter came to appreciate the value of his forensic research many years
earlier. He watched on television as Lord Oaksey, commentating live for
Channel 4 at Epsom, was overcome with panic at his producer's demand
to describe what the Queen was wearing as she emerged from her car on
Derby day. Bracing himself, he paused for a moment before uttering the
immortal words: 'And there's the Queen looking very nice in her … kit!'

Indeed, part of the Queen's 'kit' has become synonymous with what
bookmakers would doubtless choose to describe as their entrepreneurial

flair. Every year at Royal Ascot they offer odds about the colour of the Queen's hat on Thursday, when the running of the meeting's feature, the Gold Cup, sees women in their finery. Feverish exchanges between punters and their sworn enemies have been recorded – not least in 2005, when the fixture decamped to York on Ascot's reconstruction. Sustained betting on a brown hat atop the royal head saw those odds tumble from 33/1 into 3/1 before bookmakers cried enough and closed the book. The money was not misplaced; nor was the significance of the fact that the gamble originated in a Windsor betting shop. The mice were clearly at play.

Sir Peter O'Sullevan's thirst for knowledge has seen him encounter the Queen when she is truly at her leisure. During Ascot week he would arrive with the dawn to watch runners from abroad take morning exercise on the racecourse. And who should be out there among them but the Queen on horseback – often accompanied by Princess Margaret. 'It didn't happen every day,' Sir Peter recalls, 'but it wouldn't be a surprise to see the royal party galloping around the racecourse in their dark glasses and scarves.'

It may be stretching the imagination to think the Queen pretended she was aboard one of her runners later in the day, galloping on to famous victory. Yet most who ride horses indulge the dream that inspired the film *National Velvet*, which struck a powerful chord when it was released in 1944. Such dreams are the essence of horse racing. Every time a foal is born it might just be the one to carry all before it. It could conceivably be the one that skips over the turf while the hooves of others sink into it.

On such random possibilities do individuals of incalculable wealth embrace a dream that also preoccupies the Queen, although she spends a small fraction of that dispersed by Middle Eastern potentates who have transformed the canvas since they rose to the challenge so enthusiastically in the late 1970s. To see their gleaming Thoroughbreds on the racecourse is to see a small fraction of the time and money invested in them. Every one of the hundreds in their livery has been nursed and tutored as though they were themselves of royal descent.

So much about what makes a racehorse happens behind the scenes, and the life of a contemporary groom is a hectic one. Workloads have increased significantly in tandem with the rapidly escalating cost of

keeping racehorses in training. It is not so much a case of cutting corners as cutting the cloth to suit. Anyone who has done the job will attest to its demands. To work for an unappreciative employer is as demeaning as it is rewarding to work for someone who appreciates the toil, the winter hardship, the bumps, bruises and bone breaks that go with the territory.

Equally, anyone versed in the job's demands will know within minutes of walking into any Thoroughbred establishment, however small or large, what kind of employer presides over it. The supressed atmosphere of a tyrant – and there are still many in racing – hangs over his stable like a dark cloud. The converse scenario spawns a joie de vivre; the invigorating sound of laughter, of a united workforce making the best of a hard lot. An unquantifiable satisfaction is drawn from working in such places. It is also true that happy grooms promote happiness in horses, who are acutely resonant to the mood of their handlers.

To visit the Royal Studs at Sandringham is to find a place in harmony. There is banter – respectful, but banter nonetheless – between the manager Joe Grimwade and his staff. Any desire to please is born of respect. The two stallions, Motivator and Royal Applause, are happy as sandboys as they fulfil covering duties that have made downright savages of other stallions. This may be a consequence of natural temperament, an inheritance trait from which the royal horses have not been immune in the past. Again, however, anyone who has worked on studs where most of the stallions are dangerously difficult to handle will verify that ill temper alone does not account for it.

'The Queen will always let us know in advance if she wants to look at a horse,' Grimwade says. 'That doesn't mean she won't go out with the dogs and walk around the studs, but she will always tell us if she wants to see a specific horse.'

That seemingly inconsequential detail is revelatory. It underlines the Queen's respect for her staff, together with the recognition that they take pride in their work. It is an acknowledgement between kindred spirits within the horse community, and of the kind horse people recognise in one another.

The greatest test of an appreciative proprietor is punctuality. Those arriving late for a pre-arranged visit are guilty of taking their staff for

The stallion Royal Applause at Sandringham.

granted. The worst kind of proprietor is one who makes no appointment at all, who simply converges on the place when it suits. Such proprietors are an affront to employees who have no time to make proper preparations, and whose pride demands they should be given it.

Those who lunch at Windsor before journeying to Royal Ascot by carriage attest to the Queen's determination to be punctual for the scheduled start of racing. The logistics alone are formidable, not least for television schedules in a multitude of countries. But there is another reason. Where horses are concerned, punctuality is a byword for courtesy. It is important for the timetable to be adhered to, but those versed in horses acknowledge the strenuous efforts made by others to present them at their best. Grooms take great pride in producing their horses at the appropriate moment so they are literally fit for a queen. It is galling for them when that moment is delayed. Equally, trainers can make elaborate plans to stop a hot-tempered horse from boiling over before the start of a race. The preliminaries can be an ordeal, especially at Royal Ascot. To pull it off, trainers will work in sequence with the timetable. In the quest to stop a nervous horse from boiling over it may be brought into the paddock only seconds before it is due to head down to the start. Any delay in proceedings, even one lasting a few minutes, can leave the plan in ruins. In that short time months of intense preparations can be undone.

The Queen is cognisant of this. She has seen similar preparations made in advance of royal carriages entering the public domain – as they do at Royal Ascot. Brass is re-polished right up to departure time. The horses' manes and tails are re-brushed, their plaits re-checked, their girths re-tightened, their hooves re-blackened with oil, the sides of their mouths re-wiped clean of spittle. The attention to detail never stops. It would not do to spoil such elaborate preparations for the sake of a diplomat refastening his tie for the umpteenth time. To that end guests are briefed in advance not to delay the departure from Windsor to Ascot, where racehorses cannot enter the paddock until the procession has run its course.

Although royal protocol is a fundamental requirement it can sometimes suffocate moments of joy. It is not widely known that television cameras and photographers cannot aim their lenses into the Royal Enclosure at Ascot. The code is largely adhered to, although the one occasion when it was deliberately breached conveyed more about what racing means to the Queen than the capacity of a thousand words. This spontaneous decision by the BBC to override protocol came in 2008, when the Queen's colt Free Agent landed the Chesham Stakes.

It was something of a seminal moment: a first royal victory at the royal racecourse in nine years, and a first royal winner for Free Agent's trainer, Richard Hannon. Spirits in the royal box were soaring as the colt reached the winning line, and BBC cameras had filmed the Queen's reaction. Moments later, with Free Agent making his way back to the winner's enclosure, pictures showing the Queen's delight were dispatched around the world. Her beaming smile said it all. She practically punched the air in celebration. The winning feeling had been a long time coming. In its enactment the pleasure it brought the Queen, then 82, was witnessed by millions of television viewers in her colonies and beyond. But for the fact she is instantly recognisable, she could have been any other owner caught in the moment when decorum is overwhelmed by effervescent joy.

Tellingly, there was no formal complaint from the Palace. Nor was one forthcoming from her entourage of managers and advisors. It was, after all, a delightful image. 'When the race was over the Queen raced to the paddock like she was twenty years old,' John Warren recalled. 'We were struggling to keep up with her. There was a wonderful picture of her on television, smiling and throwing her arms up in the air. And for the next two months on her public duties, wherever she went, it was the one thing that people wanted to talk to her about. When it comes to racing, people can really glimpse her personal side through her love for the sport.'

Conversely, over in her studio by the edge of the paddock, and thus unable to gauge the royal party's mood, Clare Balding was beset by apprehension. 'I was nervous when I first saw the images on my monitor,' Balding related. 'I wasn't sure we should have shown it; the protocol on that sort of thing is pretty strict. But as a snapshot of her passion for racing, you just couldn't beat it.'

That a breach of protocol was required to amplify the Queen in spontaneous celebration, and so obviously in her element, is more than a little ironic. Protocol helps to keep subjects at a respectful distance from the monarch. The case for adhering to it is unarguable, even it can be

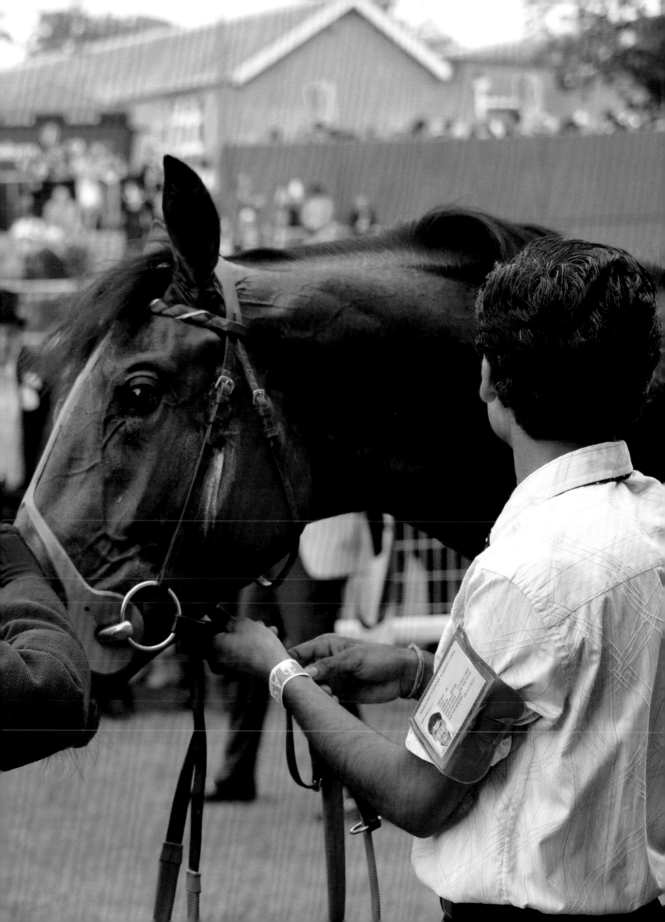

Previous spread: With Free Agent after the colt's victory in the Chesham Stakes at Royal Ascot, 2008.

Opposite: Sharing a joke with Willie Carson, 1978.

a double-edged sword. On the one hand, exclusivity serves to maintain intrigue and awe. On the other it can make a monarch appear remote and aloof. Clive Smith would have forever inclined to the latter but for the Queen's involvement in racing. He was presented to her ahead of the 2008 Gold Cup at Cheltenham, for which his horse, Kauto Star, was a strong favourite. 'I was not much of a royalist until I met her,' Smith related afterwards, 'but I am now. In the past the Queen appeared too distant, and the pomp was a put-off.'

The concept of a distant monarch also runs contrary to the grain of twenty-first century life. Social media is rampant in its twin projections of inclusiveness and the instant reaction everyone craves. It has claimed another layer of protective skin, even from those unwilling to shed it. The British monarchy has gone with the flow on this: it has a Facebook page and also interacts via Twitter, although its orientation towards social media is largely cosmetic. In terms of public relations, more might be made of the Queen's patronage of racing. Perhaps her advisors counsel against it: her involvement attracts critical comment on internet forums redolent of the age, even though not a penny of the public purse is spent in its pursuit. An immediate disbanding of the Royal Studs would spare the taxpayer nothing at all, since funding is derived entirely from the Queen's private income. So much so that in the 1970s the Royal Studs' offices were transferred to Sandringham because of the cost of maintaining vast perimeter walls around Hampton Court Palace, near London. With responsibility for their maintenance resting with the Ministry of Works, as it was then, the office was relocated to prevent it becoming an easy target for anti-royal sentiment. Quite what Henry VIII would have made of it does not bear thinking about. It was he who founded the 'Royal Paddocks' at Hampton Court in the sixteenth century.

It might further provoke those who baulk at the Queen's 'indulgence' to see a greater prevalence of images of her at ease on the racecourse. Yet what racing regulars see is a monarch mixing happily among her people. The setting is devoid of pomp, uncluttered by claustrophobic security. It would add a more 'human' dimension to a figure most often seen in ceremonial duty in distant outposts of the world. It is easier to relate to the Queen standing in a paddock at home than to see her inspecting

Maori warriors at the conclusion of a tribal war dance. It would also be in harmony with contemporary times for social barriers, perceived or otherwise, to be vaulted. In its absence, those who go racing when the Queen happens to be present are among the few afforded a glimpse of what Sir Peter O'Sullevan described as 'a very human being'.

Anecdotal evidence of the value of a racing-driven slant to public relations already exists. The Queen's assured presence at Royal Ascot and the Derby, where she acts in an official capacity at both events, allows the BBC to tailor its coverage accordingly. Balding averred that the corporation's agenda is highly influenced by it. And this, in turn, is how untold millions of television viewers around the world will come to see the monarch. 'Much of the opening part of our daily programme from Royal Ascot is governed by the fact that the Queen is there,' Balding said. 'It basically accounts for the first forty minutes, which is why the programme does so well in the ratings.'

In this way is the relationship between the Queen and racing symbiotic. There is a clamour among visitors to Britain in June for tickets to Royal Ascot. Much of the meeting's glamour would disappear without royal patronage. The Queen, for her part, greatly anticipates a week when official duties are light at an event she would only miss for the gravest intrusion. She is captured at her best by television cameras which portray images for the world to see. Television's all-embracing eye has certainly played a significant part in advancing Royal Ascot's allure beyond Britain's shores.

Further to the theme of changing with the times, the Queen has broken with long tradition on the appointment of some of her key racing aides. Her Majesty's Representative at Ascot, Johnny Weatherby, is the first not to have originated from the commissioned ranks of the Armed Forces or been titled at birth. Weatherby follows in the footsteps of the Marquess of Hartington (now Duke of Devonshire), Sir Piers Bengough, the Marquess of Abergavenny and the Duke of Norfolk. The same is true of her bloodstock and racing advisor, John Warren. He followed on in the role from Lord Carnarvon, Major Sir Richard Shelley, Brigadier A.D.R. Wingfield, and, before him, Captain Charles Moore, who held the position when the Queen acceded to the throne. Indeed, the Queen's early racing years were punctuated by pictures of her flanked by the twin towers of Moore and her trainer, Cecil Boyd-Rochfort. Both men stood well over six feet tall.

Another regular presence by her side is also significant in height, although in the Duke Of Edinburgh's case, he is no aficionado of horse racing. That does not preclude his having a strong affinity with horses. He was president of the International Equestrian Federation for 22 years, during which he attended four Olympic Games, until he retired from the post in 1986. A keen polo player in his youth, Prince Philip subsequently took up carriage driving, at which he helped to win team gold for Britain at the World Championships. Thoroughbreds, however, are not his favourite equine messengers.

By all accounts, the demands of Ascot week can render the royal consort of more than sixty years liable to the sort of chance remark seized upon with perpetual glee by the media. Richard Hannon's stable jockey, Richard Hughes, once elected to ride wearing what became known, during their brief fad, as 'Technicolor' goggles. Their makers were adamant they afforded jockeys better vision even though to look at them from the outside was akin to peering into a kaleidoscope. Feigning alarm when Hughes wore a pair in the Ascot paddock, Prince Philip told the jockey he sincerely hoped he could see out of them. 'So do I,' Hughes responded in kind, 'for your sake as well as mine.'

Nor is Prince Philip much inclined to watch racing. Once he reaches the sanctuary of the royal box at Ascot he is more disposed to watch England play Test cricket on television. Ian Balding tells the story of how the prince was rebuked by his wife on his sole visit to Balding's stables, having declared that all her horses looked too thin. 'If you did but know it,' the Queen retorted, 'that is how a fit racehorse should look.'

When it comes to pleasing her, however, Prince Philip knows the way to the Queen's heart. It would tax the most imaginative of minds to choose an appropriate Silver Jubilee present for the woman who has everything. The prince's solution was to commission Barry Linklater, the acclaimed equine artist, to paint the Queen's favourite broodmares, together with their foals of 1977. The canvas depicting Highclere, Escorial and Albany will have rekindled many fond memories of their racing exploits. Each of them took high rank – in particular Highclere, whose victory in one of France's classic races, the 1974 Prix de Diane at Chantilly, is indelibly etched in her owner's mind.

Of all the royal racehorses Highclere represents the pivot within the Queen's lengthy involvement. Highclere's legacy, through her daughter Height Of Fashion, would bring the Queen much angst, but Highclere's grandmother Hypericum was instrumental in conveying the thrill of racing to Princess Elizabeth – as she was when she first saw Hypericum as a foal at Hampton Court Stud in 1943.

The previous year George VI had taken the princess, then sixteen and accompanied by Princess Margaret, to visit the Beckhampton stables of Fred Darling. It would prove a seminal experience for her to see her father's best racehorses in the flesh as they progressed towards their next racing engagements. As the Queen recalled during her filmed discussion with Sir Peter O'Sullevan in 1974: 'I suppose I first became interested in racing during the war ... when my father took me down to see Big Game and Sun Chariot working, which I had never seen before. I was able to pat them in the stable afterwards. I had never felt the satiny softness of a Thoroughbred before. It's a wonderful feeling.' So much so that she would not wash her hands for several hours afterwards.

Big Game had already won the Two Thousand Guineas and Sun Chariot the One Thousand Guineas; each of them triumphed by the decisive margin of four lengths. In a royal annus mirabilis they would go on to win four of the five Classic races in Britain. Their deeds plainly inspired Princess Elizabeth. The convert immediately became a regular visitor to Hampton Court Stud, camera in hand, to run her evolving expert's eye over the royal homebreds. On one of her inaugural visits in 1942 an unnamed foal by Hyperion, the potent stallion of the day, caught her attention. She thus followed Rising Light's career with particular interest, especially when he contested the 1945 Derby (run at Newmarket's July Course), which she attended in person for the first time – and wearing her khaki ATS uniform. During her visits to Hampton Court in 1953 another foal by Hyperion, this one a filly, engaged the princess's imagination. She would be named Hypericum, and she more than repaid the faith of her royal admirer.

In 1945, Hypericum approached one of the season's defining races for two-year-olds, the Dewhurst Stakes in October, with a favourite's chance. With her parents otherwise engaged, Princess Elizabeth made arrangements to travel to Newmarket to watch Hypericum run. The war was now over, and with it, the need to keep the movements of the royal children secret. Hypericum's movement was equally unimpaired as she strode to a comfortable victory – much to the princess's evident delight. Dwarfed, as ever, by Boyd-Rochfort and Moore, yet standing out as one of the few women in a crowded winner's enclosure, the princess felt a sensation the like of which very few racehorse owners get to enjoy.

Duly smitten by Hypericum, Princess Elizabeth joined her father at Hurst Park racecourse the following spring to see the royal filly make her three-year-old debut. Defeat did little to dampen the belief that Hypericum, who was short of peak fitness, was entitled to line up for One Thousand Guineas won four years earlier by Sun Chariot. Come the day, however, and Hypericum displayed the worst of her wilful behaviour.

With her father's 1946 One Thousand Guineas winner Hypericum in the Newmarket winner's enclosure. Flanking her are Captain Charles Moore (left) and Captain Cecil Boyd-Rochfort.

She charged through the tapes at the start, in the process decanting her jockey, Doug Smith, and galloped riderless down the course before finding her way to the edge of the Newmarket car park, where she was finally retrieved. She delayed the start for upwards of fifteen minutes and was lucky to escape unharmed – although there was nothing fortunate about the late run that swept her up towards the winning post in splendid isolation. The princess was in raptures. As she subsequently related to Sir Peter O'Sullevan: 'I was there as a very young girl. It was a source of terrible excitement when Hypericum disappeared into the car park and was brought back [to the start]. The extraordinary thing was, she then won.'

The natural progression for any filly winning the One Thousand Guineas is to make for the Oaks at Epsom. Just as the One Thousand Guineas is the fillies' equivalent of the Two Thousand Guineas, the Oaks is the fillies' equivalent of the Derby. All four are designated Classic races and Hypericum duly advanced to Epsom, although her task was rendered more arduous by the distance of the Oaks. At one and a half miles, it is fully half a mile further than the One Thousand Guineas.

Pre-race concerns that Hypericum might be racing over a distance beyond her best seemed to find expression in the Oaks. In the early stages she fought against her jockey's wish to restrain her, in the process expending valuable energy, and could not stay with the leaders in the closing stages. While respectable enough, fourth place came as a disappointment to a royal party in which Princess Elizabeth accompanied her parents.

No matter. Hypericum's One Thousand Guineas victory had animated George VI. He had known previous Classic triumphs with the aforementioned Big Game and Sun Chariot, although his enjoyment was somewhat tempered by the pair's origins. Both horses were leased to him by the National Stud, which bred them, and to whose ownership they returned at the end of their racing days. Thus Sun Chariot and her foals never grazed the pastures at Sandringham. Such horses became known as 'the hirelings' – and on Fred Darling's retirement in 1947 they were trained by Sir Noel Murless.

Hypericum, by contrast, was a product of the Royal Studs, which were in the doldrums in the 1940s. The fact she was 'family' made George VI proud.

VI proud. The king came to savour racing late in his life. He was to the sport made, rather than born – although it is down to him that the Royal Studs are still located at Sandringham, where they were established by his grandfather Edward VII in 1887. Having succeeded George V in 1936, Edward VIII put Sandringham up for sale on his abdication. He had found a purchaser before George VI, who succeeded him, intervened to buy the estate from his brother. To this day the estates at Sandringham and Balmoral remain the private properties of the monarch, as distinct from properties owned by the Crown Estate. As for George VI, he freely admitted he knew little about racing but vowed to take an interest while learning about the mechanics of a sport many of his forebears had pursued with zest.

With George VI in the vanguard, Princess Elizabeth was able to go racing almost as much as she liked. However, with the king's health deteriorating from 1950, his eldest daughter's racecourse visits became rarer as she readied herself for hereditary duty. By that stage she was fully immersed in a sport that would continue to fascinate her, albeit from a greater distance.

Hypericum was the first royal homebred winner of a British Classic since Scuttle, who raced for George V, eighteen years earlier. Because his Turf exploits were plagued by bad luck, George V was immensely proud of Scuttle. Princess Elizabeth had just celebrated her second birthday when Scuttle won the One Thousand Guineas in 1928; George V would regale her with tales of a victory gained despite Scuttle losing ground at the start, which she retrieved with a late flourish. He would also name a racehorse Lilibet, after his favourite granddaughter. Two years later he would buy the young princess her first pony, Peggy.

From these seeds flourished the princess's preoccupation with horses. She had, of course, learned the rudiments of horse care long before her inaugural visit to Fred Darling's stable in 1942. She was taught to ride at Windsor, where her instructors attested to her acute understanding and appreciation of horses, both from the saddle and in matters of horse husbandry. She became proficient at many of the equine disciplines, among them carriage driving and riding side-saddle, the latter a prowess she displayed at Trooping the Colour ceremonies.

The question of whether Thoroughbreds preoccupy the Queen more than other breeds of horse is moot. Nor does it much matter, since the overriding impression she conveys is that she simply loves horses – and dogs, for that matter. In any case, the feeling engendered by one of her racehorses in full flow will differ markedly from the one she gets when riding a favoured horse through the grounds of Windsor Castle, or up at Balmoral, in Scotland.

Just as the Queen is patron of both the Jockey Club and the Thoroughbred Breeders' Association, she holds the same positions in the Fell Pony and Highland Pony Societies. Just as she breeds Thoroughbreds at Sandringham, she breeds Highlands at Balmoral. Among her choice of morning rides at Windsor is a Fell named Emma and a Highland named Melody.

'Duty and service to her country is first and foremost for the Queen,' said Terry Pendry, manager and stud groom at the Royal Mews, who rides with the monarch at Windsor Castle. 'But here at Windsor, the horses are all about recreation, exercise and fresh air. She rides in all four seasons and adores the wild birds, flowers and animals.'

Nevertheless, to embrace racing was to discover a world unique within the varied equine disciplines. In its purest form it requires the detailed study of form and pedigrees. As Princess Elizabeth her appetite for both was voracious. She was already well versed in her mid-teens, although even then she was more preoccupied by bloodlines from which the best horses descended than by events on the racecourse. One thing was clear: the Royal Studs would one day pass into safe hands.

In addition to its intellectual fascination, the process of assimilating knowledge of bloodlines is fundamental to the process of breeding good racehorses. Many traits are passed down from one generation to the next. Just as a mare with incorrect front legs should not be mated to a stallion with the same flaw, hot-tempered mares should not be bred to stallions of a similar propensity. To do so would be to flirt with the prospect that the offspring of such unions are difficult to handle, or in some cases downright dangerous. The best progeny of Hypericum's sire Hyperion, winner of the 1933 Derby and champion sire six times, came laced with streaks of temperament. As the Queen herself noted of Hyperion: 'He

Opposite: Princess Elizabeth with her pony Greylights on her thirteenth birthday, April 1939.

At Newbury races, 2011.

was a dear little horse but some of his daughters were absolute devils. Temperament one has to watch very carefully when one is planning the breeding [of Thoroughbreds].'

This, more than racing itself, is what the Queen finds fascinating. Much though she enjoys hearing tales of derring-do from jockeys, whose skills she can relate to, she is most engaged when discussing bloodlines and breeding theories with others of like mind. Hence her two visits to Alec Head's Haras du Quesnay, his stud in the heart of Normandy. While there, the Queen immersed herself in the company of fellow experts Head invited for dinner on most evenings. At other times the gathering dined locally, on one occasion at a two-star restaurant in a delightful river setting at Canapville.

No dietary requirements were sent in advance. Chef Paul Chêne, a close friend of Head brought in from Paris for the week, was given a free hand.

'At first I was unable to tell Paul why I wanted him to come,' Head related. 'All I could say was that my guest was very important. He said he was very busy, but I told him that if he came he would look back and be glad of it.' The proof is in the pudding: to this day a framed photograph of the Queen hangs proudly on the wall of Chêne's restaurant in the Trocadero area of Paris, which is now run by his nephew. The restaurant is small and intimate, as were gatherings when the Queen sat round Head's dinner table discussing pedigrees with such breeding luminaries as the Aga Khan. 'Everyone followed bloodlines closely,' Head said. 'There was a lot to talk about.'

Some breeders are devoted to the cause of blending together proven strains of blood. It dominates their thinking. They are happy to breed from a mare of poor racecourse performance but who hails from regal roots. Others are not sold on this approach; their primary focus is soundness. They will overlook the lack of lustre in the blood for the blessing of breeding a sound, hardy individual that will stand up to the rigours of training. Ultimately, however, as Head avers, it is impossible to be certain of the source of a racehorse's talent. That is why so many breeding theories abound. Affluent breeders have spent untold millions in their efforts to demystify the process, yet Mother Nature is unyielding. Despite the restless promptings of kings, queens, sheikhs and the wealthiest entrepreneurs, she will not give up her secrets.

Daniel Wildenstein stands out as one who ignored a previously rigid principle he applied in the running of his stud. No filly could retire to his paddocks unless she had achieved the minimum criterion of winning a race. It was the golden rule and it served Wildenstein well: he became one of Europe's most successful owner/breeders. But the fates played tricks on the mercurial art dealer. In the mid-1970s Wildenstein's great racemare Allez France swept to a series of majestic victories in the highest class. Her racing merit made her as exciting a broodmare prospect as anyone could wish for. Yet Allez France had an aversion to motherhood. Year after year she would not conceive, and on the few occasions she did, she gave birth to foals so flawed it was clear they had no racing future. Time was running out for Allez France to leave a single daughter for Wildenstein to perpetuate her line. So when, late in her life, a filly, Ave France, was born healthy, she was admitted to the Wildenstein stud even though she was unable to win a race. When Wildenstein was challenged about it, he flew into an uncontrollable rage. 'So what do you want me to do?' he demanded of his inquisitor. 'If I sold Ave France, then somebody else would have the blood – the pure blood – of Allez France. And I? I would have nothing!'

Time would show that Wildenstein should not have made the exception. Ave France proved fertile but she produced nothing of any consequence. It may be that one of her granddaughters will one day produce a superior runner, yet should that come to pass it will only serve to trigger speculation on the true source of that talent. And so the debate goes on ...

In discussions on the subject the Queen is firm in her conviction that good bloodlines are fundamental to the production of good racehorses. Nevertheless, she recognises this is only part of the overall equation. A horse's physical traits are equally important to the mix. When she ascended the throne, the Queen felt she wasn't seeing enough of her young homebreds growing up. A foal's physical characteristics can change significantly from one month to the next, yet when she inherited the Royal Studs she would not see her foals for upwards of eighteen months. They would go their separate ways in late summer: the Queen to Balmoral and her foals to Ireland, where they would graze until they were dispersed among royal trainers towards the end of the following year.

This enforced separation was far from ideal. After years of thought over the production of every foal, the entire crop would suddenly be herded out of the country. In their absence they would advance from fragile children to strapping adolescents. With the Queen anxious to observe at first hand this critical phase of development, the foals stayed at home from the late 1960s – by which time the Queen had leased Polhampton Lodge, a stud on the outskirts of Newbury which replaced Hampton Court as the rearing ground for weaned foals. It was a period when Lord Carnarvon – who, as Lord Porchester, had accompanied Princess Elizabeth to Newmarket when Hypericum won the Dewhurst Stakes in 1945 – became increasingly influential in advising on racing and breeding matters. It was he who advanced the merits of Polhampton Lodge so that the Queen was no longer deprived of seeing her developing foals. She would glean much that would serve her well when in choosing appropriate mates for them when it was their turn to embrace motherhood.

The same sense of frustration was highlighted by another passionate horseman, HH Sheikh Mohammed bin Rashid al-Maktoum of the royal family of Dubai, who took an unprecedented step to redress the imbalance. The sheikh was prevented from seeing his horses in Britain as much as he wanted. The demands of his position ensured that months would pass between his visits to Newmarket. He missed his horses too much, so in 1993 he announced to a disbelieving racing community that he would take the best of them home to be trained in the desert. From there they would fly back to Britain in April to compete in the best races. They would return to Dubai in October for rest.

Sheikh Mohammed's project, which he baptised Godolphin after one of the Thoroughbred's founding fathers, certainly raised eyebrows. It was typically adventurous of him, although it seemed scarcely credible that a Thoroughbred, for whom the greensward seemed so imperative, could flourish on dry sands. So when Balanchine, Godolphin's inaugural runner in the 1994 Oaks, ran away from her opponents, there was much rejoicing in the sheikh's camp. The concept was vindicated at a single stroke.

Godolphin would enjoy outstanding success over the next decade, although by those standards the stable's subsequent fortunes would go into decline. The reasons for this are much debated by racing folk around the world, since Godolphin would soon have international roots. Yet whatever the conclusions on an immensely complex subject, Godolphin was born from one man's desire to see more of his Thoroughbreds. They meant too much for him to abandon them for six months every October.

The Queen understands better than most how Sheikh Mohammed feels. The two are united by their love of an animal that played an important role in their respective and diverse upbringings. Over the past two decades the sheikh's stallions have been omnipresent in the list of matings drawn up for the Royal Studs' broodmares. This crossing of Thoroughbred blood means that success can be savoured by both parties, each of which has contributed one-half of the genetic mix. The racing relationship forged between these two heads of state also led to a recent exchange of horses that came agonisingly close to the Queen realising her ultimate racing ambition in 2011.

In Highland Glen, the Queen owned a horse with sufficient ability to compete at Sheikh Mohammed's winter racing carnival in Dubai. The sheikh's agents duly offered to buy the horse but the Queen's agents, in return, highlighted Highland Glen's occasional aversion to enter the starting stalls. The horse might well arrive in Dubai and stubbornly refuse to race, in which case he would be an embarrassment to his royal heritage. In consequence it was agreed to transfer Highland Glen into the sheikh's ownership, but that no money would change hands.

Sheikh Mohammed reciprocated by sending the Queen four young horses he had bred himself. Three of them proved painfully slow, yet the fourth was anything but. Carlton House would bear down on the 2011 Derby with a favourite's chance. His preparation was compromised by a late injury scare, he encountered traffic problems in the race itself, and he shed a racing plate from one of his front legs as he strained hard for the lead in the closing stages. For a few tantalising strides it looked as though Carlton House might win it. He could not, although in finishing a gallant third he carried the royal silks to their best Derby placing for 58 years. Of the Queen's ten Derby runners, only Aureole had fared better. He had finished runner-up to Pinza just four days after Her Majesty's coronation in Westminster Abbey on 2 June 1953.

Meanwhile over in Dubai, Highland Glen consented to enter the stalls on his debut for Sheikh Mohammed at the glittering Meydan racecourse in February 2010, when he ran out a comfortable winner under Frankie Dettori.

3

CARLTON HOUSE:
SO NEAR AND
YET SO FAR

There is no disputing what the Derby means to the Queen. In a filmed conversation with Sir Peter O'Sullevan for the Royal Archives, she put it thus: 'My philosophy about racing is simple. I enjoy breeding a horse that is faster than other people's. I enjoy going racing but basically I love horses. A Thoroughbred epitomises a really good horse to me, and my particular hope for the future, like all breeders of horses, is to breed the winner of the Derby.'

Although the Queen's expression of that hope is unequivocal, her words require context. She spoke them in November 1974, soon after Highclere had won Classic races in Britain and France. It was a time when the Royal Studs were on a high after rebounding from a fallow decade in the 1960s. There was no reason to believe they could not produce a colt as naturally talented as Highclere.

Charles Moore did much to bring the Royal Studs out of another spell in the doldrums on his appointment as racing manager to George VI in 1937. His policy with the broodmare band was to focus on stamina. It proved highly successful throughout the 1950s but it would fail in the following decade.

Having shown reluctance to do so, Moore eventually retired from the position in 1962. Then 82, he was a fine tutor to a highly inquisitive Princess Elizabeth but had become rather long in the tooth. In 1958 he gave contrary riding instructions to Joe Mercer, a late replacement for injured regular jockey Doug Smith, aboard Doutelle in the King George VI and Queen Elizabeth Stakes. Mercer had scant knowledge of one of the monarch's favourite horses. That made Moore's briefing doubly important, especially with illness detaining the Queen from Ascot. However, a horse who thrived on racing aggressively was this time ridden from behind as Ballymoss collared the Queen's second runner, Almeria, to land the prize. Doutelle rallied from the rear to finish third but he could never land a blow on a horse he had beaten on a recent encounter at Chester – where Doutelle dictated a strong gallop from the start. It was impossible to reconcile Mercer's tactics, as dictated by Moore on the day, with the approach agreed ahead of the race by the Queen and Doutelle's trainer, Cecil Boyd-Rochfort. Doutelle would probably not have beaten Ballymoss however he was ridden, but that was beside the point.

For seven years after Moore's retirement in 1962 the Queen did not employ a racing manager. Richard Shelley took over management of the Royal Studs in 1963, but by then the Queen increasingly turned for racing advice to her friend Lord Porchester, who was formally appointed as the Queen's racing manager in 1969. Lord Porchester's credentials were impeccable. His father, the sixth Earl of Carnarvon, bred the 1930 Derby winner, Blenheim, at his Highclere Stud near Newbury. It was Lord Porchester who helped to inspire the revival of the Royal Studs, which produced not just Highclere but another talented filly, Escorial, in the year the Queen expressed her 'particular hope' to win the Derby.

Her wish did not seem unreasonable. Several close relatives of Highclere and Escorial were alive and well in the Royal Studs, which would soon welcome those two fine racemares into the brood. Meanwhile, two more fillies, Firework Party and Joking Apart, had won their only starts in well-contested races for two-year-olds at York and Newmarket respectively. Joking Apart in particular had the potential to take high rank as a three-year-old, when the ability of a racehorse is properly gauged. One thing was irrefutable: the Queen's decision to heed Lord Porchester's advice to use stallions with faster bloodlines than Moore had for so long advocated was paying dividends. Highclere herself was by Queen's Hussar, an inexpensive stallion who excelled over a mile and who stood at Lord Porchester's Highclere Stud. There was good reason for royal optimism in the years ahead.

Almost simultaneously, however, the Sport of Kings was increasingly tickling the fancy of Middle Eastern potentates with vast oil revenues to spend. Their petrodollars would flush through the racing and breeding communities like a giant tide, sweeping away much in its path. Their investments in racehorses, breeding stock, training centres and stud farms were on an unprecedented scale. In the space of one decade their ambition evolved from the drawing board to an opulence that threatened to swamp the entire business, which was at a collective loss to know how to compete.

Many of them came and went, but the few who persisted were to change the face of a game that had ground the fortunes of countless wealthy individuals before them into the dust. The difference this time was that there seemed no limit to the new players' resources. Arab royalty descended on the Turf from Middle Eastern domains many Britons had never heard of. Like the Queen, they wanted success above all else in iconic middle-distance races like the Derby.

The implications were profound. From competing with operations of a similar size, the Royal Studs became one of a number of historic breeding outfits to feel a tsunami force which had Dubai's Maktoum family at its crest. Every broodmare purchased on behalf of Maktoum studs was of immaculate lineage. Every filly granted entry to those studs was of a calibre other breeders could only expect to behold in a leap year. There were literally hundreds of them, every one with apposite credentials to deliver a Derby winner to the blue-blooded stallions they would visit. And the Maktoums were far from alone.

The consequences for the Derby were inevitable. The first new player to win the sport's Blue Riband was Dubai's Minister of Finance, Sheikh Hamdan al-Maktoum, whose Nashwan prevailed, to the gnashing of royal teeth, in 1989. Nashwan's dam was Highclere's daughter Height Of Fashion, who had been sold by the Queen to Sheikh Hamdan for $2 million in 1982. But the fact that Nashwan was an outstanding racehorse was merely the tip of the iceberg. He was one of a number of supremely talented runners produced by Height Of Fashion, whose daughters also excelled when they were retired to stud. So much so that Height Of Fashion was demonstrably the outstanding broodmare of her generation, a once-in-a-lifetime asset who had slipped through royal fingers. Where the Royal Studs were concerned there was far more significance to Nashwan than his status as the first Derby winner owned and bred by Middle Eastern interests.

Nashwan's victory served to open the Derby floodgates. He was immediately succeeded by Quest For Fame, whose 1990 triumph for his owner Khalid Abdullah was the first of three Derbys won to date by the Saudi Arabian prince. A year after that, in 1991, it was Prince Fahd Salman, a relative of Abdullah's by marriage, who claimed the coveted prize with his colt Generous. And so it went on: Nashwan's triumph started a sequence that saw Middle Eastern owners win the Derby thirteen times in twenty-three renewals up to 2011.

However, the traffic is no longer one way. In an extraordinary recent development, Arab hegemony has been strongly challenged by another gargantuan concern much closer to home. The Coolmore Stud partnership, with John Magnier at its helm, has risen with rare assurance in Ireland to joust for the game's highest honours. It has done so through a combination of factors, not least the expertise of its personnel. The initial driver was the vast income streams generated by Coolmore's tribe of stallions, which is the most potent in the world. Incalculable millions have accrued from that tribe's prowess, and by adopting a meticulous approach to every aspect of the business, Coolmore has parlayed those millions into millions more. To those thirteen Middle Eastern Derby winners since 1989 can be added three more won by the Coolmore partnership, which first struck with Galileo in 2001. The combined Arab and Irish entities have become very hard to beat. At their current rate of success the chances of either entity winning the Derby stands at 70 per cent. Anyone versed in racing will tell you that those are formidable odds. For the Queen and like-minded owner/breeders with smaller broodmare bands, the prospect of winning the Derby has never been so elusive.

Recognition of that fact doubtless propelled the wave of expectation that engulfed Britain in 2011, when Carlton House emerged as a front-line candidate. So dominant was the Coolmore/Arab axis that the royal silks had not been worn in the Derby since Church Parade sported them in 1981, the year the Queen's granddaughter Zara Phillips was born. She would marry Mike Tindall, the England rugby captain, soon after Carlton House ran with such gusto at Epsom.

On the Newmarket gallops in spring 2011 with John Warren (left), Coral Pritchard-Gordon and trainer Sir Michael Stoute.

Media coverage of Carlton House's preparation was intense in a country where the Queen's Derby designs are matched by her subjects' desire to see her attain the goal. As a two-year-old, Sheikh Mohammed's gift horse was given plenty of time to find his strength. He had shown his trainer Sir Michael Stoute clear signs of ability in his formative homework, but because he was relatively late in arriving at Sir Michael's Newmarket stables, he was not on the fast track. The trainer was actually on his annual holiday in Barbados, from where he hails, when Carlton House first arrived in his yard in January 2010.

When Sir Michael joined the ranks of royal trainers in 1998 he renewed the monarchy's links with a stable that ceased on Cecil Boyd-Rochfort's retirement thirty years earlier. Sir Michael operates out of the same Freemason Lodge stables where Boyd-Rochfort trained for forty-five years. He also runs a second stable, Beech Hurst, which sits opposite Freemason Lodge on the other side of Newmarket's Bury Road. The champion trainer ten times, Sir Michael is not one to make excuses in defeat, although he is not alone in advancing the Queen's Flight Of Fancy as an unfortunate loser in the 2001 Oaks at Epsom. Despite a troubled passage through the race, Flight Of Fancy rallied to make her challenge approaching the final furlong when she started hanging sharply to her left.

This is not unusual at Epsom, where the cambered home straight tends to carry tired horses with it. Soon after the race, however, it became clear Flight Of Fancy was physically uncomfortable. X-rays revealed a hairline fracture to her pelvis, which was doubtless the cause of her wayward passage in the closing stages. 'I think she would have won if she hadn't hurt herself,' Sir Michael reflected. 'She hung very badly after she injured her pelvis and could never race again.' In the circumstances her effort in finishing runner-up was all the more commendable. It was rough luck on all concerned, although in Sir Michael's case, Carlton House's early promise encouraged him to believe he had another royal Classic prospect on his hands.

His case advanced significantly when Carlton House went to Newbury for his second racecourse start in October 2011. Although he'd performed well enough when runner-up at Salisbury four weeks earlier, he greatly surpassed that effort in running away from some lightly raced but well-heeled opponents at the Berkshire track. Travelling strongly throughout the one-mile race, Carlton House seized the initiative two furlongs out and galloped clear to win by nine lengths. Everything about his victory augured well: the runner-up beat the third horse home by two lengths, with the fourth horse a further seven lengths adrift. Such exaggerated margins speak of a significant difference in ability – and there were fourteen others even further behind.

Sir Michael is loath to see an inexperienced racehorse burdened by great expectation. Too many show promise in their homework only to flunk the racecourse test. For all that, Newmarket in spring is always abuzz with stories of extraordinary deeds on the gallops from horses that have transformed physically over the winter recess. In human terms, a two-year-old Thoroughbred resembles a young teenager. At that age it may outstrip all others but when racing on turf ceases in October, its resumption in March often heralds a change in the order of merit. Horses of greater physical maturity as two-year-olds are often supplanted by later-developing types that have gained in strength over the winter.

Carlton House was very much in the latter category. He had been spared tough competition in his two-year-old season, yet come March, when he would normally be asked to step up his homework, he contracted a minor foot infection. It was of no great concern, and it had the added benefit of detaining Carlton House from those early gallops so beloved of Newmarket work-watchers in their anxiety to identify the new season's nascent stars. Sir Michael thus elected to start Carlton House's three-year-old campaign in the Dante Stakes at York. The Dante is the last recognised Derby trial – and usually the most significant.

There was no prospect of the Queen travelling to York. She was committed to attending the Royal Windsor Horse Show, which opened on 11 May with the release of a photograph showing her riding happily in Windsor Great Park alongside her two grandchildren born to Prince Edward and Sophie, Countess of Wessex. On the same day the Queen surpassed the reign of George III, who died in 1820, to become the second-longest reigning monarch in 1,000 years of British history. Only her great-great-grandmother Queen Victoria has ruled for longer. One day on, and Carlton House would take aim at the Dante.

The word was out by then. Carlton House's early dormancy had given way to a series of encouraging homework reports. On the day of the Dante Stakes he was usurped in betting exchanges by Seville, a colt from the Coolmore collection, yet Carlton House took the race by the scruff of the neck when he charged through a narrow gap between horses approaching the final furlong. From that moment he was in complete control. Jockey Ryan Moore barely resorted to his whip to bring him home a decisive winner of the Derby's premier trial. The dream was alive and well; so much so that some bookmakers quoted odds as short as 6/4 about Carlton House winning at Epsom.

Down at the Royal Windsor Show, the Queen excused herself just before the Dante was run. A deft reorganisation of the royal schedule left her free for a brief return to the castle to watch the race on television. Unaware of the revised arrangements, John Warren rang in from York by prior arrangement to relay the running of the race. The Queen was plainly taken by the manner in which Carlton House had 'spilt horses' en route to victory. 'She was very excited by it,' Warren related afterwards.

Up at York, Warren was flushed by what he had seen. The race may have been an untidy affair, but Carlton House exceeded the expectations of everyone except a confident Moore. 'I would have been disappointed if the horse had been beaten today,' the jockey ventured.

Every conceivable Derby omen was favourable. In addition to showing raw ability, Carlton House had quickened through a narrow gap without hesitation, which was encouraging for one of his inexperience. The Derby

The 2011 Dante Stakes: Ryan Moore and Carlton House burst clear – and straight to Derby favouritism.

is always a gruelling test in which horses have to handle the rough and tumble of a big field clattering round Epsom's severe gradients. The bay horse had shown at York that he boasted sharp acceleration, without which any horse will struggle to win at Epsom. And the Queen will have noted that Carlton House hailed from a female bloodline that had made a previous impact at Epsom. Two close relatives in Three Tails and Maysoon – the latter trained by Sir Michael – had finished third in successive renewals of the Oaks in 1986 and 1987.

There was one more encouraging pointer. Sheikh Mohammed had made previous gifts of two horses to run in the Derby. In 1995 he had bequeathed Lammtarra to his nephew; thirteen years later New Approach had donned the silks of his wife, Princess Haya of Jordan. Both horses won at Epsom. And to cap a memorable week, Carlton House's triumph was augmented the following day when the Queen's horse St James won a class for veteran hunters in Windsor Park.

These were happy days for the Queen as the countdown to Epsom gathered momentum. Her state visit to Ireland had been an unqualified success: the first by a British Monarch since the 1911 tour by her grandfather George V to what is now the Republic of Ireland but was then part of the United Kingdom of Great Britain and Ireland. And the country still bathed in the afterglow of Prince William's marriage to Kate Middleton. After years of upheaval, the House of Windsor had returned to public favour. It almost seemed preordained that the Queen would surf this wave of happiness all the way to the winner's enclosure at Epsom, and profound media interest in the build-up illustrated just how much her patronage boosts racing's profile. A sport rarely in the spotlight for reasons other than a corrupt underbelly at its lowest levels was having a rare run of it. Newspapers traced the long history of royal involvement with unabated enthusiasm. Even Sir Michael Stoute, with his well-known media reticence, welcomed writers from far and wide onto Newmarket Heath as Carlton House continued preparations for the biggest day of his racing life.

The purest statement of all about the Queen's relationship with racing came on Derby day itself. Accompanying her were her husband the Duke of Edinburgh, the Prince of Wales and Duchess of Cornwall, the Duke and

Opposite: The Queen and the Duke of Edinburgh arrive at Epsom Downs racecourse, while (above) her granddaughters Princesses Eugenie and Beatrice get into the Derby day mood.

Duchess of Cambridge, Prince Harry, Prince Andrew and his children Princesses Eugenie and Beatrice, together with Prince Edward and the Duchess of Wessex. That so many of her children and grandchildren were present was testament to their acknowledgement of the Derby's place in the Queen's affections. The gathering was suffused with joy, the family at ease with itself in the relaxed public environment of Epsom Downs.

John Warren himself played a part in gathering the family together. 'Because many of them don't follow racing closely they probably didn't understand how hard it is to actually get a horse to line up in the Derby,' he recalled. 'I sent out some messages to the effect that it would be great if they could make it because Carlton House stands a chance of getting in the shake-up, and they responded brilliantly. The excitement in the build-up to the race was immense, quite fantastic. It was a special day – apart from the result.'

Clare Balding, who fronted the BBC's coverage of Derby day, was aware of Warren's efforts. 'It was the first time Prince William and Prince Harry had been to watch Flat racing and I understand they both really enjoyed the day. It might have been a key moment if royal interest [in racing] is to be perpetuated.'

Balding's last remark is something that preoccupies all those professionally engaged in the sport. Although horses continue to be a central tenet of royal life, none of the Queen's children or grandchildren has her natural affinity for the Sport of Kings. As much was evident on Derby day. In the spate of photographs taken of the royal party in the paddock, where they mingled with connections of other Derby runners, the younger royals smiled broadly as they chatted to one another. They had little time for Thoroughbred aesthetics. Conversely, the Queen's face was a mask of concentration as she assessed some prime horseflesh. Her keen eye evaluated the French-trained runner Pour Moi as a likely threat to Carlton House. And so it proved.

Mind you, it is too much to expect any among the Queen's brood to match her love of the sport. Only two of her forebears were true pillars of the Turf. Charles II maintained a royal palace in Newmarket, to which his court would relocate twice a year so that he could indulge his passion for racing – and also for his mistress, whose infamy is remembered by the annual running of the Nell Gwyn Stakes at Newmarket. Edward VII, the Queen's great-grandfather, was the other significant royal patron. By a quirk of wonderful symmetry, his mistress is remembered by the annual running of the Lillie Langtry Stakes at Goodwood. Edward VII won the Derby three times around the turn of the twentieth century, twice as Prince of Wales. Appropriately, his winner in 1900 was named Diamond Jubilee in commemoration of his mother's long reign. The colt was foaled in 1897, when Queen Victoria celebrated her own Diamond Jubilee. It was Edward VII who described racing as 'the glorious uncertainty', a phrase that retains all of its resonance today.

For all that, the extent of the Queen's calling is said by historians to exceed that of both kings, and she will be a hard act to follow. Much speculation concerns the future of the Royal Studs: who will take them forward; will they even continue? These questions preoccupy all who appreciate the near-umbilical connection between racing and the monarchy. Who, if any among the younger royals, would get so excited at winning the royal box's annual Derby sweepstake as the Queen did when Generous prevailed in 1991? The moment was captured by BBC television cameras. It was almost as if the Queen had won the race herself. Almost ...

Television dictates how millions of people around the world see the royal family. And for the BBC, Carlton House's Derby bid made a perfect excuse for a trawl through the archives. Three decades had passed since the last royal runner; three whole generations had grown up without seeing televised footage of the royal bond with the world's most famous race. That lull has coincided with – perhaps even helped to influence – horse racing's receding popularity with the public. That was certainly not the case when the royal silks were regularly represented throughout the 1950s. From Aureole in 1953, the Queen had runners in five of the next six renewals.

Earlier that century, the symbolic importance of the royal connection with the Derby was amplified by the militant suffragette Emily Davison. Her motives for throwing herself among flailing hooves during the 1913 renewal are disputed, yet one aspect of the grisly incident is beyond doubt. Of all the runners in the race Davison took aim at the king's horse Anmer, who fell and trampled her to death at Tattenham Corner. With George V's presence at Epsom assured, there could not have been a more public platform for her to make her stand.

No such protest unfolded in 2011, even if Carlton House did not enjoy the run of the race. The colt's participation was the subject of a late scare when he banged the fetlock joint in his near (left) foreleg during routine exercise five days beforehand. As Sir Michael and his staff worked hard to contain the inflammation without recourse to medication that would have resulted in Carlton House failing a post-race drugs test, racing's rumour-mill sparked into life. The would-he-wouldn't-he saga over his participation reached fever pitch. During the Derby Club Dinner at London's Savoy Hotel, John Warren was asked to make a statement on Carlton House's well-being. He was called to the podium ahead of the traditional Derby auction, when a cast of distinguished guests bids for each Derby runner. The bids are then aggregated, a sum set aside for charity and the rest paid out to the winning bidder. As the favourite, Carlton House was the last horse to be auctioned. On Warren's positive bulletin he fetched £20,000 more than the next most popular horse; far more, in fact, than he was worth within the context of a thirteen-runner race around Epsom's extreme undulations. There was clearly a premium to be paid for the royal runner. It was a measure of the expectation.

The Queen could certainly have done without the setback to Carlton House. The timetable for bringing a colt to the Derby in mint condition permits few stumbles along the way. All trainers ask is that they are afforded a trouble-free preparation. Carlton House should have been out on Newmarket Heath in the warmth of early summer, feeling happy in himself. Instead he was largely confined to his stable. It was far from ideal so close to the preordained day, although the Queen was philosophical.

She was more preoccupied by the mechanics of Carlton House's preparation. 'The Queen was fascinated by how the horse was being trained for the Derby,' Warren said. 'She wanted to know how he galloped at home, how he recovered from those gallops, how far he was galloping, who was riding him – everything. For the first time in my experience, she went into every detail. She wanted to understand the entire build-up.'

Having been prepared for his day of destiny for the previous eight months, Carlton House was deemed sufficiently recovered from the injured fetlock for him to his to take his chance. Ryan Moore was legged aboard in the paddock, and the combination of man and horse ambled down to the Derby start. Carlton House got agitated when the stalls handlers ushered him forward, and for a while he was reluctant to load. Much the same had happened at York, with no obvious detriment to his performance, yet the Dante had drawn a small cast of six runners. More than twice as many were lining up here. It was important for him to break cleanly from the stalls – especially from his wide draw.

The Derby start is a crucial aspect of the race. Horses may have a mile and a half ahead of them but to be more than halfway down the field in the early stages is something of a burden. The early pace is often strong, dictated as it is by a horse prescribed that role in the interests of a better-fancied stablemate, or alternatively, by one who is there to give his deluded owner the opportunity to brag that his horse had led the Derby field. Such horses are the bane of all jockeys riding against them, since they have no realistic chance of winning. When they drop back through the field they can interfere with fancied runners which are simultaneously moving forward into challenging positions.

Before the race Warren was sufficiently concerned by Carlton House's wide draw to seek advice from Lester Piggott, who won the Derby a record nine times. 'Lester said it was not ideal,' Warren related. 'He said it made it more important for Carlton House to break quickly and get into a good early position.'

As fate would have it, Carlton House blew the start. He was one of the last to find his stride, leaving Moore with little option but to thread his way through the field from the rear. Moore improved into midfield at halfway but was soon obliged to angle Carlton House wide, away from the running rail, as Castlemorris King, an exhausted 150/1 shot, back-pedalled furiously around Tattenham Corner. This is the most treacherous part of the racecourse. Any horse swinging wide must contend with a contrary camber that rolls away from the running rail, yet Carlton House maintained his rhythm and balance. Having evaded Castlemorris King, Moore was still in a fair position, albeit a little further back than he might have chosen. However, just ahead of him a more serious melee was in the making.

Previous spread: Treasure Beach (striped sleeves) goes for home in the 2011 Derby. Carlton House (scarlet sleeves) tries his hardest despite losing a shoe, but Pour Moi (extreme left) is about to come from the clouds.

As the field approached the exit from Tattenham Corner, Marhaba Malyoon, this one a 100/1 shot, veered sharply away from the rail. He carried Masked Marvel and Ocean War with him, in the process obliging Moore, who was tracking that pair, to bring Carlton House wider still. The concertina effect was typical of Epsom on Derby day but it cost Carlton House valuable ground. The prospect of a royal victory was disappearing fast.

Unbowed, Carlton House rallied from the setback. Moore rebalanced the horse and drove him forward on reaching the long home straight. Stride by stride, inch by gruelling inch, Carlton House made inroads into the lead. So much so that Clare Balding, in her makeshift studio high above the hallowed winner's circle, anticipated a historic denouement. 'I'd prepared myself thoroughly to tell the story without really believing it was going to happen,' she related. 'And then, two furlongs out, I thought: "Oh my God, it is going to happen." At that point I thought Carlton House would win.'

Well inside the final furlong and Pour Moi (9) is now poised to swoop.

The field's progress down the home straight seemed to take an eternity. It was an optical illusion created by Carlton House's slow progress; all eyes were on him as he continued to erode the deficit. Up in the grandstand younger occupants of the royal box, Prince Harry to the fore, were punching the air in excitement. And then, almost out of nowhere, Pour Moi emerged at a rate of knots. No sooner did he catch the eye than it was clear he had built up inexorable momentum. As Carlton House faltered, his bravery no longer able to resist the clamour from aching muscles, Pour Moi lunged late to collar Treasure Beach half a stride from the winning post. Carlton House finished right on their tails. He was beaten by less than the length of one horse, but it was only good enough for third place.

Moore was inconsolable in the heat of the moment. Returning with a face like thunder, he raged against the no-hopers he believed had cost him victory. 'The horse was slowly into his stride but I had to go wider than I wanted because of the rubbish in the race,' the jockey said, in reference to the retreating outsiders. 'He started to get there after that, but [the outcome] was disappointing.'

Might Carlton House have won without trouble in running? To Moore's sense of injustice must be added another in-running setback: it later transpired Carlton House lost a horseshoe attached to one of his front legs 100 yards from the finish. This can affect a horse's balance; Moore was unaware of it when he said in the post-race debrief: 'The horse was not quite comfortable during the last furlong.'

Although Moore was adamant, John Warren was more circumspect. 'Ryan felt that if circumstances had been different, so would the result. I would say the run of the race did us no favours. If Carlton House takes on the same horses again, the result might be different.'

Sir Michael Stoute, for his part, lamented the collective influence of a series of unwanted obstacles. 'Carlton House has run very well but things just haven't gone right,' Sir Michael said. 'He had a hold-up [with his injured front leg] close to the race, he got too far back during it and then he had to run wide into the straight.'

Subsequent analysis of Carlton House's effort brought little variation to the original themes. Together with Warren, and in contrast to the rest of her family out on the balcony, the Queen watched the race on television inside the royal box. 'The crucial moment came at the top of Tattenham Hill, when horses started coming back to Ryan,' Warren recalled. 'When she saw what was happening the Queen gently shook her head and said: "He is too far back." She has watched the Derby all her life, she knows better than anyone what it takes to win. I don't think there was ever a moment when she genuinely thought the horse was going to win. From the way it all unfolded I think she knew in her own mind that it just wasn't meant to be. And I think Sir Michael [Stoute] touched upon a crucial thing when he said that in the build-up to races at this level, every little margin counts for something.'

It isn't unusual for the Derby to provoke a diverse range of opinions. It is part of the sport's appeal that different minds read different things into the same race. Carlton House's defeat, though lamented by connections, was hardly the biggest shock in Derby history. It cannot measure up to Dancing Brave's seismic reverse at Epsom twenty-five years earlier, when the Two Thousand Guineas winner came from far back to fail by less than a length. Did jockey Greville Starkey ask too much of the wonder horse? Did the horse fail to handle the camber, as Starkey suggested? The answers will never be known. Dancing Brave would comprehensively avenge that defeat by Shahrastani later in the season, when he would sweep all before him. But on Derby day, when it mattered most, the record books state that Dancing Brave came up short. And while Carlton House is unlikely to match Dancing Brave's deeds, Sir Michael was far from despondent about his future. 'Carlton House is still a high-class horse who will have a big day,' he said.

Not the one that mattered, though. The Derby dream lingered for all but the closing seconds after two-and-a-half minutes of frenetic galloping in which Carlton House's fortunes ebbed and flowed. For all that, the narrow distance by which he failed might as well have been a country mile. To the winner goes the glory; to the vanquished go commiserations that are quickly forgotten. The difference between Pour Moi and Carlton House, though small in terms of merit, was now vast on the balance sheet. Victory in the Derby bestows more than glory. At £10 million, there would have been takers for Pour Moi immediately after the Derby. Carlton House, by contrast, was worth around one-fifth of that.

By such slender margins does the breeding industry propel itself. The owner of a Derby winner will collect vast sums as breeders queue up to use the horse on his commencement of stallion duties. Other races make instant millionaires of their winners, but the Derby has no peer. It is a unique, gruelling test of a horse at an age when Thoroughbreds are deemed just about physically strong enough to undertake it. Warren's post-race musings about a potentially different outcome were Carlton House to tackle the same horses again alluded to races further down the line. A horse has but one opportunity to win the Derby, since the race is confined to three-year-olds. Blow the start, as Carlton House did, and there is no chance of redemption in the race that matters most.

In no other sport is the Blue Riband so exclusive. The Derby is a one-off, ambivalent to chance and intolerant of failure, however unjust the circumstances. Every year the best three-year-olds line up at Epsom for one to be hailed. It is then beholden to this totem of equine adolescence to take the fight to his elders. He must defend three-year-old honour, in the process affording judgements on the merit of his generation against the one preceding it. Each Derby winner is one link in the perpetual chain by which horses racing in different decades can be compared.

Acclaimed breeders have always set great store by the Derby. One of the best, the Italian Federico Tesio, had no doubt about its status. In the first half of the twentieth century Tesio bred the winners of twenty-two Italian Derbys, twenty-one of which he trained himself. He also bred a pair of international champions in Nearco and Ribot, both of them undefeated through lengthy careers. Although he never won the Derby at Epsom, he observed of it: 'The Thoroughbred exists because its selection has depended not on experts or zoologists but on a piece of wood: the winning post of the Epsom Derby. If you base your criteria on anything else you will get something else, not the Thoroughbred.'

It is hardly surprising that the Queen, whose approach to breeding horses is equally purist, holds the Derby dream so dear. The unconverted who cheered for Carlton House cannot have comprehended the essence of the quest, yet the Queen proved the conduit between the complexity of her hobby and the simplicity of the public's desire to see her prevail. As Clare Balding put it: 'The Queen is deeply interested in the science of it but the public just wants a story. They latched on to her attempt to win it without understanding how difficult it is to achieve.'

Ironically, the first Derby-winning owner of royal descent kept as his London residence Carlton House, in Pall Mall. The house no longer exists; it was demolished in 1825 after George IV acceded to the throne. Some years earlier, as Prince of Wales, George IV won the 1788 Derby with the odds-on favourite, Sir Thomas. Victory came nine years after the race was inaugurated when Lord Derby won the toss of a coin to determine whose name the race would carry. Sir Charles Bunbury, vanquished in the toss, extracted a measure of revenge by winning the first-ever renewal with his colt Diomed.

Sir Thomas's victory thus cemented the royal affiliation with racing, and with the Derby in particular. Interestingly, although the Derby has been won six times by members of the royal family, it has only fallen once to a reigning monarch. And even then, Minoru, who scrambled home in 1909, was no product of the Royal Studs. He was leased by Edward VII for his racing career at a time when the Royal Studs were not producing horses of the calibre the king demanded.

Sir Thomas was George IV's sole Derby winner but his brother Frederick, Duke of York, savoured a brace in six years. First up in 1816

King Edward VII with his Derby winner Minoru (Herbert Jones up), 1909.

was Prince Leopold, who holds the extraordinary distinction of winning the Derby on his racecourse debut. Unlike Sir Thomas, Prince Leopold's victory was unexpected: he started at odds of 20/1. It was a popular one: the previous year the Duke of York presided as commander-in-chief of the Army when troops led by the Duke of Wellington prevailed over Napoleon's forces at the Battle of Waterloo. It was Frederick who inspired the nursery rhyme about the grand old Duke of York, who had 10,000 men. The duke triumphed a second time when Moses had the better of a tense duel with Figaro in 1822.

More than seventy years would lapse before the Derby baton passed to Edward VII, whose mother, Queen Victoria, came to thoroughly disapprove of horse racing after the death of her husband Prince Albert. Having dissolved the Royal Stud at Hampton Court in 1838, she re-established it fifteen years later with the proviso that all foals born to royal broodmares were sold as yearlings, rather than put into training. One of them, Sainfoin, went on to win the 1890 Derby for Sir James Miller.

Edward VII, then Prince of Wales, would have taken a dim view of Sainfoin's sale – and several others, for that matter. For the fact is that Hampton Court Stud during Victoria's reign was a remarkably successful nursery. In the year Sainfoin won the Derby another of its graduates, Memoir, won the 1890 Oaks and St Leger after her sale to the Duke of Portland. Later that year, demand was intense when Memoir's full-sister was offered at the Hampton Court auction. She realised the fantasy sum of 5,500 guineas to the bid of Baron de Hirsch. Many thought the price absurd but the German banker would have the last laugh when La Fleche, as she was named, landed the One Thousand Guineas, Oaks and St Leger in 1892. La Fleche would almost certainly have won that year's Derby had her jockey, George Barrett, not ridden what was by common consent a shockingly inept race.

It is a constant source of source of amazement to all but the finest judges of horseflesh that one yearling can draw a king's ransom at auction when another of equally illustrious origins barely raises a bid. Their physical differences are invisible to the untrained eye but the acute one, as La Fleche showed, is rarely deceived. So it was with Richard Marsh, who started training horses for Edward VII, then Prince of Wales, in 1892. Frustrated by his mother's antipathy towards racing, a sport which he pursued with relish, Edward VII established his own stud at Sandringham in 1887 to provide him with horses to race. Within a year of the royal summons Marsh took one look at a foal grazing the Sandringham paddocks and was moved to declare: 'I must say I have never set eyes on a more beautiful foal.' Marsh's judgement was impeccable, since Persimmon would carry all before him. After winning Edward VII the first of three Derbys in1896, he would develop into an iconic racehorse and sire.

Persimmon's superior merit was plain from the start. After winning at Ascot and Goodwood his sights were set on the Middle Park Stakes, probably the most important test for two-year-olds of its time. Yet Marsh was a reluctant participant come the day. Persimmon had developed a respiratory problem and Marsh's fears proved well founded when the royal colt could not match strides with the winner St Frusquin.

Defeat did little to dampen Persimmon's prospects for the following season's Classics. He grew such a shaggy coat over the winter recess that he resembled a sheep. His natural defence against inclement weather suggested he might take time to flourish in spring, so there was no cause for concern when he was slow to thrive on returning to work early in 1896. Yet concern there most certainly was when, according to reports, the lad who looked after Persimmon was ambushed outside a pub in Newmarket by a gang of rogues. A knife was put to his throat, a small package thrust into his hand. At a time when doping racehorses was rife, the message was unambiguous. Persimmon's lad must empty the sinister contents of the package into the horse's feed. By rendering him a physical wreck, Persimmon's participation in the imminent Two Thousand Guineas would be out of the question.

Gambling was rife around the turn of the nineteenth century; indeed, Edward VII enjoyed a flutter himself. But the sums bet on races were so huge that the unscrupulous fringe, from bookmakers and stable staff right through to racehorse owners, would stop at nothing to gain an edge. It wasn't uncommon for a majestic Thoroughbred to be reduced overnight to the state of a crippled carthorse. Thanks to fate's intervention, the threat to Persimmon never came to pass. He performed so abjectly in his home trial for the Newmarket Classic that he was withdrawn from the race itself. His lad was thus able to empty the sinister sachet anywhere but into Persimmon's feed bucket.

Even if the threat of doping was real, it is open to question whether Persimmon's lad would have been able to execute it. Trainers were acutely aware of the threat and took elaborate measures to counter it. Something of a tyrant, Marsh was fastidious in the way he ran Egerton House Stables. In common with many trainers he locked up his riders at night to stop them from frequenting Newmarket pubs, which were hotbeds of gossip. But Marsh went even further to keep the lid on the well-being or otherwise of his horses.

On leaving the Army in 1962, Sir Michael Oswald spent his formative years in the breeding business at Egerton Stud – Marsh's former stables that were subsequently bought by Lady Macdonald-Buchanan in 1942 and amalgamated with her neighbouring stud, Lordship. During interminably long night hours, when he oversaw broodmares giving safe birth to their foals, Sir Michael was regaled by colourful accounts of life at Egerton House Stables by 'Simmy' Simmonds, who'd worked for Marsh in his youth. It was Simmonds who exercised Minoru, Edward VII's third Derby winner, around the contours of Epsom on the morning of the race in 1909.

'They were the most lurid stories imaginable,' Sir Michael recalled. 'Marsh was particularly secretive about which of his horses went out to gallop each morning. He would conduct his trials at first light because he didn't want anyone to see them. The horses went out with bits of sacking around their feet so that none of the other lads in the yard would know [from the grass stains] they had been out at all. Some of Simmy's stories sounded extremely fanciful but I checked out everything he told me, all the data, and it was absolutely accurate.' Sir Michael was plainly forearmed about royal horses of yesteryear when he was appointed manager to the Royal Studs in 1970.

As for Persimmon, he recovered so robustly that he was soon ready for his pre-Derby trial. A delicate problem arose when the prince and his wife, Princess Alexandra, expressed a desire to watch it. Marsh had just fired his cook, which required the swift deployment to Newmarket of replacement chefs, together with butlers and waiters, from London's Savoy Hotel. The royal luncheon was duly prepared after Persimmon outlined his state of Derby readiness with a blistering gallop.

Come the day and Persimmon locked horns with St Frusquin two furlongs out. The two colts had a compelling tussle that saw Persimmon wrest the lead from his battling foe just 100 yards from the finish. Thousands of hats soared in a spontaneous outpouring of support for the prince. An epic encounter had whipped the 300,000-strong crowd into a state of high excitement, which found expression when the prince emerged from the stands to lead Persimmon into the winner's circle. Witnesses maintained they had never known anything like it. Cheers rang out for fully fifteen minutes as police struggled to clear a path for the horse and his popular owner.

Persimmon's triumph was celebrated by all, with one notable exception. As the *West Coast Times* in New Zealand reported: 'Queen Victoria, it is said, was not at all pleased with her son's success, as she detests horse racing, but she was gratified, in spite of herself, to read of the tremendous enthusiasm with which the nation as a whole hailed that success.'

The prince revisited the winner's enclosure with Diamond Jubilee in 1900, when he also won the Grand National with Ambush II. He remains the only owner to have completed that unlikely double in the same year, and will almost certainly be the last. Diamond Jubilee was a full-brother to Persimmon and equally fractious in temperament; he even contrived to bite a finger off the hand of his stable lad. Nine years later, and now King Edward VII, Diamond Jubilee's owner returned victorious to Epsom one more time with the aforementioned Minoru.

Although Diamond Jubilee went on to complete the Triple Crown, there is no doubting Persimmon's superiority to him – both as a runner and at as a stallion at Sandringham, where he retired after a four-year-old season that saw him land the Gold Cup at Ascot by the extravagant margin of eight lengths. He was in his prime when, aged fifteen and in much demand with breeders, he slipped in his stable and fatally fractured his pelvis. Persimmon's legacy was already secure: he was champion sire four times and produced a remarkable daughter in Sceptre, whose achievement in winning four of the five Classics in 1902 has no parallel to this day. It will never be matched, let alone surpassed.

By these deeds did Edward VII assimilate a formidable record on the Turf. He was so devoted to his racehorses that he sent them all Christmas cards, which he signed 'Edward R'. In many ways he set the standard to which subsequent horse-owning monarchs should aspire. In 1875 he registered the royal silks that are still in use today. They were inspired by coachman's livery from the Royal Mews, with gold braid adorning the front of a purple jacket with scarlet sleeves and a gold fringe to the black velvet cap. The silks were seen in public for the first time at the Newmarket July meeting of 1877.

As for Carlton House, he is the second horse of that name to have raced for the Queen. Names remain unique to racehorses for a period of twenty-five years, after which they can be recycled. There were high hopes for Carlton House's forerunner, who won a competitive race for two-year-olds at Ascot in 1974, but the horse never realised them. Conversely, aspirations never rose above the ordinary for Abergeldie. Together with Carlton House, she was given to the Queen by Sheikh Mohammed towards the end of 2009. Nor was much hope ever entertained for Abergeldie's namesake, who raced for the Queen in 1953. Yet by her infamy, this particular Abergeldie earned herself a permanent place in racing's history books.

On 3 July 1954, Abergeldie reared over backwards at Sandown Park, in the process crushing her jockey, the twenty-six-times champion Sir Gordon Richards. Sir Gordon fractured his pelvis so badly that he would never ride again. A year earlier he had finally ended his Derby drought when riding Pinza to victory at the twenty-eighth attempt. He did so at the direct expense of Aureole – who was owned by the Queen.

4

AUREOLE – AND OTHERS IN VAIN PURSUIT

The Queen and Prince Philip greet the freshly knighted Sir Gordon Richards at Epsom before the 1953 Derby.

On the morning of her Coronation in 1953, the queen-in-waiting was asked by a lady-in-waiting how she was feeling. She replied that she was very well: Cecil Boyd-Rochfort had just called to relate that Aureole had completed his Derby preparation with a pleasing gallop in Newmarket earlier that morning.

The exchange is revelatory. On this of all mornings, very few messages would have been deemed sufficiently important to relay to a woman who already had more than enough to think about. Conversely, of course, Aureole would have been very close to the Queen's heart: he was bred by her late father, whose myriad responsibilities were about to be formally invested in her. There was a pleasing symmetry to the parallel that Aureole had shown himself to be as devoted to his own cause as his owner was to hers.

Her response also endorsed what those in her racing employ have long maintained. The welfare of her horses is paramount. For six years from 1963 her former trainer, Ian Balding, spoke frequently to her by telephone. The Queen had no racing manager, so Balding was encouraged to dispatch his news as it arose. Her racing manager today, John Warren, attests to the same thing. 'The well-being of Her Majesty's horses comes first,' he said. 'I can ring at any time, day or night, to update her on the welfare of her horses.'

There was no welfare issue with Aureole on this day. Quite the opposite: he was in rude health as the Queen contemplated what lay ahead. In a few hours she would take the Coronation Oath before 8,000 invited guests, among them numerous prime ministers and heads of state. She would be bound to serve her people, and to maintain the laws of God. Outside Westminster Abbey, an estimated three million people lined the streets of London for a first glimpse of the new queen. Beyond the capital, more than 20 million people watched on television in Britain and countless more around the world, courtesy of a BBC broadcast in forty-four different languages.

She had ascended the thrones of the United Kingdom, Australia, Canada, Ceylon, New Zealand, Pakistan and South Africa in addition to her role as Head of the Commonwealth. It is also fair to say that sixteen months of coronation preparations were about as long as she had entertained the Derby dream on Aureole's behalf. Aureole had a peak of his own to scale on the day *The Times* exclusively proclaimed that Everest had finally been conquered.

Coronation Day also carried a broader significance. George VI had been ill for some time before he would die of lung cancer in February 1952. In the post-war chapter of his reign, his absences from public life meant that he was unable to rally the public in the same way that he and his wife had done during the war, when they became symbols of the fight against fascism.

The fact that they refused to leave London – and kept their children with them – saw them confront the same wartime dangers as their subjects. However, optimism was in short supply in the post-war years. With victory gained at incalculable cost, Coronation Day was seen as the emblem of a new beginning. A vibrant, attractive, twenty-six-year-old princess would be crowned on 2 June 1953, when street parties broke out the length and breadth of the country.

Over in Newmarket, Aureole did his bit to maintain the celebratory mood. Boyd-Rochfort, who attended the Coronation, felt sure the horse was ready excel in the royal silks at Epsom. He was certainly bred for the part. His dam, the Oaks runner-up Angelola, was half-sister to no less a runner than Hypericum, whom the Queen had seen winning the 1946 One Thousand Guineas in her father's silks. Given that Hypericum was by Hyperion, it made perfect sense to breed Angelola to the same sire. The consequence was Aureole, who was among the first wave of royal foals dispatched to Ireland for a change of scene in 1950.

Aureole thus spent a formative year at the Mondellihy Stud of Peter FitzGerald, in County Limerick, where he relished nothing more than evading capture in the paddocks by stud staff obliged to return him to his stable every evening. It was an early sign that Aureole had, in racing parlance, 'his own way of going'. In that respect he mirrored the traits of Hypericum. Provided Aureole was amenable, it was a source of encouragement. The best progeny of Hyperion, among them Hypericum, all tended to be high-mettled.

As it turned out, Aureole was quite a handful. There was no malice in him, as there had been in Diamond Jubilee, but he would do little unless he consented to what was being asked of him. He was both impetuous and inclined to decant his rider while exercising on Newmarket Heath. Some horses shed their riders through taking fright, in which case they represent a danger to themselves and everything in their path. Their state of agitation inclines them towards panic, which triggers them to run indiscriminately at full pelt. Along the way they might spook violently at anything unfamiliar, which often serves to frighten them further. They enter into a spiral of fear that feeds on itself until they calm themselves – often when they are too exhausted to run any further.

Aureole was never like that. It was more of a game to him; a statement of his independence. Despite his propensity to shed his rider for the joys of running loose, he never came to harm. What's more, Boyd-Rochfort had him tagged from the start as a colt of great potential. He would handle him accordingly, racing him sparingly in his two-year-old season until Aureole strengthened into his then-unfurnished frame.

Boyd-Rochfort was slightly unsure what to expect when Aureole made his racecourse debut. So much so that he was sent not to Ascot or Goodwood but further afield to York, where any misbehaviour on Aureole's part would resonate less. He needn't have worried: Aureole recovered from a slow start to run down the leader and win a competitive race at the first time of asking. He ran once more in 1952 when he trailed throughout the Middle Park Stakes at Newmarket, but the fact Boyd-Rochfort chose to start this inexperienced colt in the season's most important two-year-old race was a harbinger of things to come.

Aureole exercises at Newmarket, spring 1953.

Following the winter recess, Aureole's passage to the Derby went as planned. The Queen watched him run with promise in the Two Thousand Guineas to finish close up in fifth place behind Nearula, who had beaten Aureole pointless in the Middle Park Stakes. Aureole was subsequently sent to Lingfield, where he cut a dash in winning the Derby trial, and his preparation for Epsom was now complete. He had improved with every outing and was ready to run with the best.

If Coronation Day unfolded around pomp and ceremony, Derby day allowed the nation to let down its collective hair. A rainy preamble gave way to glorious sunshine as the hordes descended on Epsom. An estimated

500,000 racegoers flocked to the famous Downs, where Aureole was the overriding story but my no means the only one. Sir Gordon Richards, knighted in the Coronation Honours List just days earlier, had yet to win the great race. His twenty-seven previous rides had all come up short; the unwelcome prospect loomed that a jockey many still maintain was the best of all time might never savour the thrill of Derby victory.

'There were mixed emotions on the day,' remembered Sir Peter O'Sullevan. 'Although it would have been brilliant for the Queen to win at her first attempt, it was always a concern to the public and those of us involved in the game that Gordon was running out of time. In those days there was always a tremendous crowd on Derby day. It would be stretching things to say the atmosphere was particularly electric that year, because it was electric every year, but the Queen obviously enjoyed walking down to the old paddock. It was quite a way from the grandstand and she was smiling constantly at the people waving flags on both sides of the rails.'

Aureole was not quite so relaxed. In the paddock his pre-race nerves were manifest as he broke out into a sweat, and he took a strong hold of his bit when jockey Harry Carr guided him down to the post. Carr later related that he was still hopeful of winning until he saw the imposing figure of Pinza, with Richards aboard, at the Derby start. And so it transpired. Pinza ran out a clear winner from Aureole, who came forward from midfield to claim second place, four lengths adrift.

The vast crowd displayed no sense of anticlimax. Any regret that Aureole had been outrun was more than mitigated by victory for Richards. Back then, with racing in its heyday, Sir Gordon was one of Britain's iconic sportsmen. His unstinting honesty in the saddle, combined with a record-breaking number of winners, made him the supreme ally of punters. He was feted then as the footballer David Beckham would be fifty years later. No-one could take exception to him breaking his Derby duck in the twilight of his career. Certainly not the Queen: she'd wished Richards luck in the paddock before the race and he had reciprocated. Now she summoned him for a private audience. 'She knew time was running out for me and she showed herself a marvellous sport,' Richards said afterwards.

Aureole performed with aplomb, though Pinza proved a class apart. Unlike Carlton House in 2011, the prospect of victory for Aureole was never real. Pinza was always a good bit ahead of him in the home straight. And while Aureole battled manfully when his thick white blaze emerged from the pack two furlongs out, his finishing kick lacked the vigour of Pinza's. Still, there was no disgrace in finishing second.

In the aftermath of defeat the Queen might have consoled herself with the thought that she wouldn't run into as formidable a galloper as Pinza in years to come. She might have thought many things in the flush of the moment. She might even have felt the Royal Studs were in such rude health that they were bound to deliver a Derby winner further down the line. She certainly had a vivid recollection of the day twenty-one years on. In her filmed conversation with Sir Peter O'Sullevan in 1974, she said: 'I think it was very exciting to have a horse so soon as an owner to run in the Derby. Aureole ruined his chance in the parade before the beginning and one shouldn't really be sad not to win because Sir Gordon, at last, had won the Derby.'

Perhaps the one thing that never crossed the Queen's mind on that day was that Aureole was as good as it would get for the next 59 years. For that is how it stands in the year of her Diamond Jubilee. Aureole's bold effort marked the start of a golden chapter for the royal silks. He posted some sterling victories the following season. Foremost among them was an emotional triumph in the race named after the Queen's parents, the King George VI and Queen Elizabeth Stakes at Ascot – before which Aureole shed his jockey once more, this time down at the start. It did him no harm. As the Queen succinctly observed in conversation with Sir Peter many years later: 'Aureole was always an independent and frankly naughty character. He was often loose at Newmarket when he was in training, which is why I think it didn't disturb him when he got loose at Ascot before he won the King George VI.'

The 1954 King George VI and Queen Elizabeth Stakes: Aureole (Eph Smith) just holds off Vamos, whose jockey Roger Poincelet has lost his cap.

The Queen's purple patch would extend to the close of the decade, which was then six years distant. It was a time when the Royal Studs were at their most fertile, the barometer set fair. As is racing's way, however, relative drought would follow. The Royal Studs would suddenly turn on their axis. The likely reasons for fallow periods are only evident with hindsight, but in the early 1960s the Queen's broodmare band was awash with stamina-laden blood. It was a policy strongly advocated by Charles Moore, who was responsible for reviving the Royal Studs in the latter part of George VI's reign. In the breeding of Thoroughbreds, however, time is restless. Studs that fail to change with the times are soon left behind. Breeders across the Atlantic were experimenting by blending faster strains of American blood with British racehorses imported to North America as stallion prospects. Over time this created a more nimble Thoroughbred with sufficient stamina for middle-distance races, but with greater all-round speed. Those breeders would reap rewards.

Equally, horses bred in North America and imported to Britain were becoming increasingly successful. Even the Derby was not immune: it was won in three successive years from 1970 by such imports. Each of them endorsed Federico Tesio's declaration on the Derby's primacy, since Nijinsky, Mill Reef and Roberto all went on to illustrious careers at stud. It marked a sea change in the type of horse required to win Britain's coveted middle-distance races.

For the Queen on Derby day 1953, however, such developments were distant. Up in the royal box Prince Philip asked Richards if he planned to retire with the Derby under his belt. Richards had no time to respond before the Queen insisted that he would not, since he would be riding her colt, Landau, in the following year's Derby. Only part of the Queen's crystal ball-gazing would come to pass. Richards missed the 1954 Derby through injury and never rode again after his paddock accident the following month on Abergeldie, whose name derives from the castle near Balmoral that was leased to the Royal Family until 1970. He would otherwise have been aboard Landau.

As it was, Landau was given a positive ride by Richards's replacement, Willie Snaith. The colt advanced from a prominent position to lead the 1954 field into the home straight, but if Snaith harboured any thoughts of victory they were quickly dashed. Landau's stamina for the one-and-a-half mile distance was suspect; it wasn't long before he beat a dignified retreat into eighth place. Up ahead of them, eighteen-year-old Lester Piggott was on his way to the first of his nine Derby triumphs aboard Never Say Die.

Landau's Derby bid was of no consequence. Yet by dismissing the horse in a handful of sentences it is easy to overlook the impact it made on the man who rode him. Although Snaith rode in seven more Derbys, none gave him a frisson to match donning the royal silks. Snaith is as proud a royalist as they come. He finds it hard to amplify what it meant to be part of the royal story on the most vibrant day in the racing calendar. 'The Derby's the Derby,' he said. 'It was a great day, and a great honour to be riding for the Queen.'

For Snaith, it didn't end there. Just as Aureole rebounded successfully from his Derby exploits, Landau galloped on to victory in the Sussex Stakes at Goodwood's prestigious July Meeting, after which Snaith was presented to the Queen. There could be no better occasion to meet your monarch than in the warm afterglow of victory. Some 57 years later, as Snaith relayed the memory, he shed a soft tear. It was a priceless moment. Here was simple and sincere testament to the meaning of the Queen's patronage.

Later that year Snaith accompanied Landau to Maryland for the Washington International, a prestigious race in the USA. It was the first time the royal silks would be worn outside Britain, and one more experience for Snaith to cherish, even if Landau failed to contest the finish. Sir Noel Murless, who trained Landau, arrived with Charles Moore two days before the race. Anxious at the quality of fare in the on-track canteen, Snaith warned Murless that Moore should be taken somewhere else for his breakfast. Murless replied there was little option; they were miles from anywhere. There was nothing else for it even though the Queen's jockey and trainer could barely imagine the upstanding former Guardsman relishing his eggs, over-easy, with fritters and hash browns. 'We had a bit of a laugh about it,' Snaith said, 'but when the time came Captain Moore tucked in. He really seemed to enjoy it.'

Snaith's aching body compelled him to quit the saddle in 1972 but his mind continued to race until his exasperated wife Sylvia threw him out of the marital bed. 'For many years after I retired I kept dreaming that I was riding in races,' Snaith said with an impish smile. 'I was throwing myself around the bed in my sleep.'

At 50/1, Atlas is the longest-priced Derby runner for the Queen to date. She has never believed in running an outclassed horse for the sake of it, and while Atlas started at long odds he earned his place in the 1956 renewal by winning an established trial: the Dee Stakes at Chester. He vindicated the decision to run him, too, when he closed from the rear to finish a respectable fifth behind the French colt Lavandin.

Ironically, Atlas probably wasn't the Queen's best Derby prospect that year. His stablemate at Boyd-Rochfort's, High Veldt, showed dramatic improvement in his early three-year-old starts but had been scratched from the Two Thousand Guineas and Derby on account of his poor two-year-old form. High Veldt's cantankerous nature had blighted his formative racing days. Towards the end of his two-year-old season he was visited regularly by Dr Charles Brook, a London neurologist who pioneered a soothing treatment of the highly-strung – both humans and animals – by running his hands over nerve-sensitive parts of their bodies. Having successfully becalmed many of the ceremonial horses used at her Coronation, Dr Brook had been asked by the Queen to run his hands over Aureole when the colt became difficult in the build-up to the St Leger. Just as Aureole was becalmed, the improvement in High Veldt was discernible – although jockey Harry Carr later opined that High Veldt could not have matched strides with Lavandin at Epsom. Against that, High Veldt might have made an impact in an average Two Thousand Guineas renewal that went the way of a 50/1 outsider, Gilles de Retz.

Atlas was a proper handful when he was out of his box. He would bite anyone and anything. His half-brother was another equine Jekyll. Miner's Lamp spent much of his two-year-old days rearing up in his box and striking out with his front legs. It seemed only a matter of time before he injured himself, although like Aureole, he probably knew exactly what he was doing.

Some fractious horses will settle down in the company of another non-threatening animal. The aforementioned Allez France, a fabulous racemare who ran for Daniel Wildenstein in the mid-1970s, always had a sheep for company in her box. The sheep travelled everywhere with her, even when she ran in Britain – although for reasons known only to her, Allez France never gave of her best outside France, where she was an undisputed champions. A sheep was worth trying with Miner's Lamp but the experiment was short-lived. On hearing of a scuffle in Miner's Lamp's box Boyd-Rochfort's blacksmith looked in to find the horse setting about his unfortunate companion, which was swiftly removed. Dr Brook was also summoned to attend to Miner's Lamp, but the horse cut little ice in the 1958 Derby. He never threatened in finishing sixth.

Doutelle represented the royal silks at Epsom in 1957, between the years of Atlas and Miner's Lamp. He was a particular favourite of the Queen who, on seeing him for the first time in eighteen months at Boyd Rochfort's

Allez France with her soulmate and constant companion.

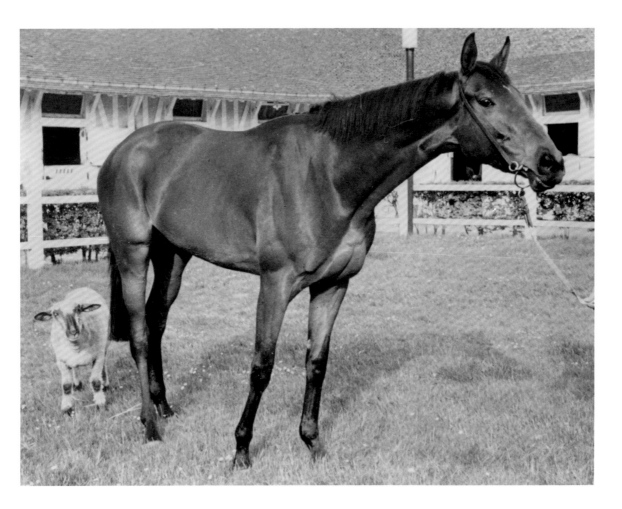

Doutelle (white face in the centre of picture) in the rough and tumble of the 1957 Derby.

stable, instantly recognised – as previously noted – that Doutelle and Agreement had mistakenly assumed each other's identity. Doutelle was a late-maturing horse who thrived in the Derby build-up. In his last gallop before Epsom he strode away from stablemate Tempest, himself bound for the Derby, with consummate ease. The feeling was that Doutelle might just surprise some better-fancied opponents – among them Crepello, facile winner of the Two Thousand Guineas five weeks earlier.

However, Doutelle was never able to show what he was capable of. In one of the roughest Derbys on record he was buffeted about like a seagull in a storm. Jockey Carr said Doutelle's hooves barely touched the ground around Tattenham Corner, where he was sandwiched between horses. It was a chastening experience for the young colt, who laboured home in tenth place. Doutelle's only defeat in five starts that year left Carr feeling disconsolate. He pointed to Tempest, who finished in fourth place, as evidence of what might have been. In reality, however, Crepello was an emphatic winner. Game and talented though Doutelle was, nothing he subsequently achieved suggested he might have outrun Crepello on Derby day.

Doutelle was Carr's favourite royal horse, and among the dearest to the Queen. His dam was Above Board, the last significant winner for the Queen's father when she won the Cesarewitch in 1950 – a victory that prompted George VI to ask Boyd-Rochfort questions of probity after Above Board had landed a sizeable gamble. Like Aureole, Doutelle would prove his mettle as a four-year-old, although his tilt at the King George VI and Queen Elizabeth Stakes, in which he finished third, was compromised by Charles Moore's contrary riding instructions. As we have seen, Moore's pre-race brief to Joe Mercer aboard Doutelle caused controversy at the time. The general feeling was that his advancing years – he was then 77 – had caught up with him. If it occurred to anyone that he might not, in consequence, be best placed to continue dictating the policies of the Royal Studs, it went unsaid. Although they were old friends, Moore and Boyd-Rochfort were always uncomfortable bedfellows in their respective royal roles. As for poor Doutelle, he would meet a sorry end.

It is virtually impossible to groom or put tack on a horse if it is not standing still in its stable. To achieve this, one end of a strong chain is attached to a secure metal ring on the box wall, the other to a piece of baling twine that is looped around a ring in the horse's headcollar. The baling twine is sufficiently strong to resist placid movement in a horse's head. Should a horse take fright, however, the sudden jerk of its head will snap the twine and free the horse, in the process disengaging its natural urge to free itself at any cost. It is one more simple but effective safety measure deployed in the daily care of horses. If there is no twine between the chain and the headcollar, a horse induced by panic will pull violently against the chain until something gives. It is not always the headcollar. In the ensuing struggle the horse might pull the ring clean away from the wall. Alternatively, he might slip over and momentarily suspend himself by his head from the box wall. In these circumstances the potential for injury is obvious.

Some horses quickly realise that by pulling backwards they can snap the baling twine any time they choose. Such horses are playing games. They are having fun at the expense of a groom who has no option but to keep re-looping the twine for the horse to break once more. But Doutelle had another way of amusing himself. He liked to play with the chain, running his teeth along its length. It was his way of passing the time while his groom attended to him.

Above Board wins the 1950 Cesarewitch at Newmarket for King George VI.

There was a hidden danger in this. Once sprung, the clip on the end of the chain is as sharp as a nail. For this reason a piece of rope replaced the chain when Doutelle was with Boyd-Rochfort, yet when he moved to Sandringham to take up stallion duties the chain was reintroduced. One night Doutelle was playing with the chain when he unintentionally sprang the clip. Its sharp, exposed tip dug into his mouth. Doutelle was like a hooked marlin in the struggle to break free, and met with a similar fate. One of the most promising young stallions to enter the Royal Studs would perish in a million-to-one freak accident.

Above Suspicion, the Queen's Derby runner in 1959, went into the race with little sense of expectation. Like Miner's Lamp, he'd finished runner-up in the Newmarket Stakes, and like Miner's Lamp, he ran respectably at Epsom to finish fifth without ever threatening to win. It was an unremarkable run. Good horse though he turned out to be, the only significant detail about Above Suspicion's participation was that the Queen would not have another Derby runner for nineteen years.

In those two decades the royal racing and breeding landscape would change significantly. Two generations of broodmares came and went from the Royal Studs. The two royal trainers, Boyd-Rochfort and Murless, followed Moore into retirement. Lord Porchester was now in his ninth year as Racing Manager to the Queen, and much to Ian Balding's consternation, Margaret Thatcher was not far off becoming Prime Minister when English Harbour, whom Balding trained, ventured to Epsom in 1978.

English Harbour did not exactly set Epsom alight. He finished much nearer last than first, a long way behind Shirley Heights, who was bound for Sandringham on his retirement. As with Landau, however, the human element within English Harbour's bid deserves amplification. English Harbour's daily needs were the preserve of Peter 'Caz' Williams, a long-standing stalwart of the Balding stable. The horse was Williams's pride and joy for the simple reason that he took his loyal handler all the way to Epsom on the biggest day of them all.

Williams's relationship with the royal horses had known dark days. He'd seen the first of them, Magna Carta, fatally strung up in his own hay net. The promising Musical Drive had dropped him in fright and clattered headlong into a gate. And Special Leave would shatter a hind leg when galloping, with Williams aboard, on the downs above Kingsclere. English Harbour, by contrast, was fit and healthy, and had every opportunity to express his inherent talent.

There was a fair bit of it, too. 'He was the best horse I "did" for the Queen,' Williams related. 'Mind you, he was a bit of a tithouse. He had to have his head in front all the time, even on the gallops at home. Otherwise he would just back off.'

English Harbour earned his place in the Derby by defeating Ile de Bourbon, subsequently winner of the King George VI and Queen Elizabeth Stakes, in a trial under Willie Carson at Goodwood. Come the Derby and with Carson otherwise engaged, Joe Mercer received the royal summons.

Before any race the jockey, trainer and owner will discuss the best tactical approach to winning it. A plan is thus hatched but any jockey riding a horse for the first time will always have a quiet word with the horse's lad after he is legged aboard in the paddock. What passes between them is often completely at odds with what had just been decided. Against that, jockeys recognise that stable lads know their horses best of all, especially when they are of Williams's calibre. In attending them every day they become aware of any idiosyncrasies, which is why Williams now impressed upon Mercer the absolute need for English Harbour to lead throughout.

'Joe was a brilliant jockey,' Williams related, 'but he said to me: "Don't be an idiot, you can't make all the running and win the Derby." I told him it had been done before, but he wasn't having it. So I told him there and then the horse might just as well stay in his box. It was annoying that Willie [Carson] went and rode something else. He would always listen to what you told him.'

Williams's eyes dropped to the floor of his local pub in Kingsclere once he had finished reminiscing. It was as if the son he had raised with unstinting devotion had preferred the advice of a stranger. He wasn't for a minute suggesting victory had been snatched from his grasp, even though a form line embracing Ile de Bourbon and the eventual winner Shirley Heights spoke encouragingly of English Harbour's prospects. Nor was he expressing dissent. It was simply that English Harbour hadn't had the chance to do himself justice. As much as the Queen's, English Harbour was his horse, his protégé, his pride and joy. It was also his once-in-a-lifetime chance to engage the dream that in making the journey to Epsom he might return to Kingsclere with the Derby winner in tow. From tens of thousands of foals born each year, it always comes down to one. English Harbour: his English Harbour, the horse whose every waking whim he had catered for without protest for the past eighteen months.

Williams had dreamt of nothing else for several days before the Derby. 'At times it was a nightmare,' he said. 'I was so excited I couldn't get to sleep at night. It would have been a great honour to do a Classic winner for the Queen – and the Derby, of all races. It must have been a great feeling for the lads who did Highclere and Dunfermline.'

There was a happier outcome when Williams took Insular, a horse owned in turn by the Queen and the Queen Mother, to York for a charity race in the summer of 1988. Insular's target was the Queen Mother's Cup for lady amateur riders, in which he was ridden by the Queen's daughter. 'As Princess Anne got into the saddle she asked me to tell her about the horse,' Williams related. 'And I said: "I'm not insulting him, but he is a bit of a boat. If you ask him to do too much too quickly, he will fall in a heap."'

The Princess wanted to know more. 'I told her that Insular would get himself into contention two furlongs from the finish, but that she should sit still and kid the horse he was running away with her.'

This time Williams's promptings were heeded. Sitting as still as a mouse, Princess Anne eased Insular into the lead approaching the final furlong, from where the combination drew further and further clear to win by twelve lengths. 'I could hardly believe it,' Williams said. 'I don't think I've ever cheered so loudly in my life, and Princess Anne showed exactly why she is a proper horsewoman. When she came in she thanked me for that bit of guidance. It was a special moment for me.'

As with Willie Snaith, Williams's life has been enriched by his relationship with the royal horses. It even won him a prize from a local radio station which asked listeners to phone in and tell of the most famous person they had ever met. Unbeknown to Williams, his wife Rachel made the call and he won by a landslide after photographic evidence of Williams's encounters with the Queen was supplied on demand. 'Rachel only told me that she'd called after she sent in the picture,' a sheepish Williams related. 'I suppose I was a little proud.'

The 1979 Lingfield Derby Trial: Milford first, the rest nowhere.

After the nineteen-year hiatus, English Harbour amounted to the first half of the London-bus syndrome, since Milford contested the Derby the following year. Milford: the colt vividly described by Carson as a playboy, a colt extravagant in talent yet brittle of mind. Mind you, Carson's frank appraisal of Milford came some years after he had spurned the Derby ride for the promise of Troy, a stablemate of Milford's at Dick Hern's stables in West Ilsley, Berkshire. It wasn't an easy call. Both horses approached the race with flawless credentials after impressing in their respective trials.

Carson rode Milford to a wide-margin victory at Ascot before injury deprived him of another reconnaissance mission in the Derby Trial at Lingfield, which Milford won with ease under Joe Mercer. Carson returned to action in time to ride Troy in the Goodwood trial which the jockey had won twelve months earlier aboard English Harbour. Troy's commanding victory, by seven lengths, left Carson with a dilemma. Would he ride the

Queen's horse or the one owned by the alliance of Sir Michael Sobell and his son-in-law, Arnold Weinstock?

It is sometimes suggested that royal horses down the years were extended latitude by owners in competition with them. There may even be cause to believe as much in Edward VII's time. In the build-up to the 1896 Derby, when Persimmon would collide with the outstanding St Frusquin, rumour held that no sane man should bet on the outcome. A story doing the rounds was that St Frusquin's owner, Leopold de Rothschild, was prepared to run his horse short of peak condition to aid the royal colt's prospects. Turf patrons at the time railed against the insinuation, although there might have been foundation to the belief that Edward VII's Minoru may not have won the 1909 Derby in his scrambling finish with Louviers. Many felt that the judge, without the benefit of today's photo-finish cameras, had conveniently erred in awarding Minoru the verdict by a short head.

In the case of Milford and Troy, however, no such frivolity governed Carson's choice. He was allowed to make it unfettered and free from any sense of loyalty to the royal cause. Indeed, any pressure felt by Carson emanated from the opposing camp. In a rare interview Weinstock (by then Lord Weinstock) gave to this writer in 2001, he recalled the alternative arrangement in place should Carson plump for Milford. 'I told Carson that if he went for Milford I had Lester Piggott lined up for Troy,' he said with a thin smile.

As tenacious in life as he was in business, Lord Weinstock was not one to trifle with – especially when the going rate for Derby winners at the time approached eight figures. His casual mention of Piggott, the doyen of Epsom and eight times a previous winner of the Derby, was designed to concentrate Carson's mind. At that stage Carson wasn't to know that Piggott would simply switch to Milford if he chose Troy.

As it transpired Carson had made up his mind some weeks earlier, when he rode Troy in a piece of homework with Milford. He never really warmed to the royal colt, whose immaculate lineage came with strings attached. By the outstanding racehorse and sire Mill Reef, Milford was Highclere's first foal. He was contrived by the union of two Classic-winning parents, each with a strain of temperament. And while Milford raced close to the lead from the early stages of the 1979 Derby, Carson was happy to bide his time on Troy.

In the event Milford's challenge didn't last much beyond the exit from Tattenham Corner, and he offered little when Piggott asked him to run down the leader. In beating a retreat he was passed two furlongs out by Troy, who galloped from there to an overwhelming victory. To Carson, it was never in doubt.

In the wake of Troy's triumph Weinstock ventured that winning the Derby was a sensation so euphoric that to win it again – in the process depriving someone else of the feeling – would be 'vulgar.' His sentiment perfectly illustrates why those who have tried and failed for so long are loath to abandon the quest. Weinstock himself strived hard for a second victory. His Golan finished second behind Galileo in 2001 but he did not live to see North Light carry the family silks back into the winner's circle in 2004.

Highclere's racing prowess governed the mating that delivered the Queen's last Derby runner before Carlton House. In view of Highclere's merit her parents were brought together again in the breeding barn. The result was Church Parade – a bay like Highclere, but one with a fraction of her ability. His speculative attempt on the 1981 Derby saw him toil home, like the rest of the outclassed field, behind Shergar.

Mention of Shergar, and his sad fate at the hands of his kidnappers, makes another powerful statement about the Derby. He achieved instant fame by his record-breaking victory at Epsom. That fame is what tempted political mercenaries in Ireland to believe they could blackmail a king's ransom from his owners before returning him in a healthy state. Shergar's legend was such that the mission successfully accomplished would even represent a propaganda coup, a stroke of daring in which the horse was returned safely for the price of a ransom from the rich.

Their botched job in 1983 would backfire badly. It caused great sorrow in a horse-loving country when it became clear, after months of silence from the kidnappers, that Shergar was no longer alive. It also underlined that any royal broodmare sent to Ireland would have been subjected to the same risk. At that point royal horses had been absent from Ireland for some years, and would remain so until such time as the political upheaval subsided. It would prove an immense but necessary constraint on the Royal Studs at a time when Ireland was beginning to attract most of Europe's best stallion prospects. With their blood unavailable, the Royal Studs would endure another period of decline from which they have yet to recover.

As for the Derby, the Queen's overall record bears scrutiny against other private breeding ventures of comparable size. It may be the most coveted race of all but there is life beyond it. Most of the Queen's Derby runners went on to make an impact after Epsom. Aureole, Landau and Above Suspicion won races that carry championship status today, while Atlas, Doutelle, Miner's Lamp and Milford triumphed in the next tier down. They were all thoroughly admirable racehorses capable of holding their own with the best of their generation. The fact that none could win at Epsom emphasises just how difficult it is to win the Derby.

The thirty-year hiatus in royal Derby runners between Church Parade and Carlton House demonstrates that the Queen does not care to be represented for the sake of it. Her horses must earn the right; they do not run for her amusement. Any royal trainer suggesting a Derby run from a horse patently out of its depth is likely to receive the royal nod of disapproval. Interestingly, the Queen made a rare foray into the yearling sales market for a colt that might have developed into a Derby contender in 2007. Harvest Song certainly had the pedigree: he was by multiple-champion sire Sadler's Wells out of La Mouline, whose grandmother Detroit had won France's most prestigious race, the Prix de l'Arc de Triomphe. But Harvest Song proved the rule rather than the exception. In common with most Thoroughbreds that are born to race, he proved disappointing.

The chances of buying a Derby winner at a yearling auction are extremely remote. Even if the keenest eye can identify the best prospect among thousands of horses auctioned annually, the horse in question may only be tenth-best when matched against the might of the Arab/Coolmore axis, whose best homebred yearlings are never sent to auction. Yet the dream endures. It is appositely described by Sheikh Mohammed, whose exchange of horses with the Queen came so close to realising a lifetime's ambition with Carlton House. 'If at first you don't succeed,' he maintains, 'try, try and try again.'

Sir Michael Stoute addressed the question of the royal Derby quest in the days before he saddled Carlton House at Epsom. 'The Queen is first and foremost a horsewoman,' he said. 'She adores her horses and the subject engages her; it is a great source of relaxation. But she is also a great realist. It would be nice if she could win the Derby, but a lot of people don't. If that happened she would be very philosophical about it.'

For the Queen, winning races like the Derby is a by-product of breeding horses, but not necessarily its apogee. She does not see her broodmare band as a competitive tool to measure against those of other breeders. Comparisons are inevitable, of course, but they are only part of it – just as a child should not be judged entirely on his examination results in comparison with those of his classmates. There are other, equally important aspects to school life. Just as some children are born brighter than others, some Thoroughbreds are born to run faster than others. They all have a natural ceiling they simply cannot exceed, no matter what is invested in them. It is all a breeder can do to work with what nature bestows at birth.

Breeding and rearing Thoroughbreds is about doing your utmost to ensure each individual is given the chance to realise its potential, whatever the level of performance that may amount to. It can be just as invigorating for breeders to win a race with a horse plagued by problems all its life as it is to win the Derby. No two horses are alike; each is its own case study. For breeders, fulfilment arrives when a horse they have reared expresses the full range of its talent on the racecourse. Many do not. Their method, their entire philosophy, is vindicated when any one horse, no matter its limitations at birth, achieves as much as it possibly can.

'I have learnt that the Queen's fundamental interest revolves totally and utterly around the horse itself,' John Warren explained. 'Her fundamentals are based on the thorough enjoyment of looking at what she has bred, watching each horse develop and seeing how it performs. She regards breeding as a sophisticated intellectual challenge. I don't see in her the total ambition to beat a neighbour. Her ambition is to develop a horse to be as good an athlete as it can be, according to the way it is bred, reared, managed and trained. That's why she wants to know about everything in great detail. I think she is absorbed by what she has. She is incredibly satisfied with her lot, which is something to admire. She never says she would like this type of horse, or that type. I think she is wise enough to realise how little control you have.' Like the Aga Khan, she plainly enjoys playing chess with nature.

There is also a lot of fun to be had in trying to breed a superior racehorse. Hope is renewed with every crop of foals, when it is customary for stud staff to pick out the one they think will be the best. On one of her first visits to Hampton Court Stud in 1942, Princess Elizabeth was struck by one particular foal in the royal herd. Three years later she would see that horse, Rising Light, carry her father's silks into fifth place in the wartime Derby at Newmarket. For a few strides Rising Light even threatened to win until he was obliged to give best. It was a seminal moment for a young princess attending the Derby for the first time.

Inevitably, however, these early 'stud picks' rarely scale the heights. Most are consigned to ignominy, as was Sir Michael Oswald's pick from the 2009 foal crop. The former manager to the Royal Studs plumped for Sign Manual, whose mother New Assembly traces back to Highclere's dam Highlight. Early reports of Sign Manual's progress in 2011 were encouraging, but when the colt returned to Sandringham for his winter break he was bereft of a critical part of his anatomy. Unbeknown to Sir Michael, the vet had been summoned to discharge Sign Manual of his testicles. This is sometimes the only way to help a horse realise his full racing potential, but it comes at a price. No 'gelding', as such horses are described, is allowed to run in the Derby, since a prerequisite is that the winner must be able to perpetuate his bloodline at stud. In this painful way did Sir Michael's 2012 Derby dream die.

Spend any time with the staff at Sandringham and they are bound to speculate on which young Thoroughbred they believe has what it takes. To wander down the barn housing the royal yearlings is to hear of their strengths and weaknesses, their likes and dislikes, and of course, opinions on their untapped potential. Such barns are incubators of dreams. And there was no mistaking enthusiasm for a bay colt by Elusive Quality out of Medley, a fast runner in her day. The colt is expected to run as a two-year-old in 2012. Named Sea Shanty, he comes by royal endorsement from on high. You heard it here first …

5

THE 1950s:
A GOLDEN
DECADE

In tandem with the mood of a nation rejoicing at the Queen's Coronation, the Royal Studs were on a high in 1953. They emerged from a lean spell towards the end of George VI's reign to produce horses capable of making an impact in racing's premier division. Over the next seven years they would take high rank among Thoroughbred nurseries in Britain.

The absence of a Derby winner was offset by successes gained in other important spheres. Victories at Royal Ascot were celebrated in each year until the turn of the decade. Two Classic winners, Carrozza and Pall Mall, were backed up by a tribe of superior runners that brought regular garlands to Sandringham. This wave of triumph came in contrast to preceding decades when success, though not elusive, was far less pronounced.

The architect of that revival was Charles Moore. Initially appointed racing manager to George VI, he continued in that capacity for the first ten years of the Queen's reign. Before his appointment Moore developed a small but successful stud at Mooresfort, in County Tipperary. He was respected by peers who recognised in him the instincts of a natural horseman. In racing parlance, he knew a good one when he saw one.

Princess Elizabeth learnt much from this well-connected Irishman, to whom she paid tribute in her filmed conversation with Sir Peter O'Sullevan. 'In my father's time he left the breeding policy to the manager, Charles Moore, and when I succeeded I came in for all the successes of that policy – rather unfairly,' she said.

On Moore's appointment in 1937, the poor state of the Royal Studs spoke for itself. In that year George VI had just six inconsequential winners from twenty-one horses in training. It could hardly get much worse – but it did the following season, when the royal haul dwindled further to two. When 1939 yielded five winners and still no horse of note, Moore made an arrangement that had served Edward VII so well in lean times four decades earlier. Edward VII's 1909 Derby winner Minoru was leased to him by Colonel William Hall Walker, whose Tully Stud in Ireland was a source of talented runners at the turn of the twentieth century. On his death, Hall Walker made his entire bloodstock holdings over to the British government, which led to the creation of a National Stud. It was to this institution that Moore turned as he sought to revive the royal racing fortunes. He secured a lease on some of the stud's young stock, and as chance would have it, among the first intake into the royal fold were Big Game and Sun Chariot.

The pair won four Classics for George VI in 1942. Just as importantly, Princess Elizabeth's first encounter with them in the spring of that year converted her to racing's cause. On that morning at Beckhamptom the future monarch, who was just sixteen, left onlookers in no doubt that the royal racehorses would be in good hands. She stood alongside her father on the training grounds and identified each horse as it galloped past. She had only made their acquaintance in the flesh a few minutes earlier, although she was probably familiar with their markings from studying photographs of them.

Big Game and Sun Chariot came at an opportune time, since the reinvigoration of the Royal Studs would take time. A prerequisite of the success of any breeding venture is patience. The worth of any young mare taken to the paddocks cannot be accurately gauged for years after her introduction. Her first three-year-old runner will arrive four years after she was bred to her first stallion, and no real inference of her ability can be drawn until she is represented by three or four runners. In this respect a stud is like a seafaring tanker: it takes a mighty effort to turn it round.

Moore knew precisely the course he wanted to chart. Until the Royal Studs started bearing fruit he filled the void by leasing racehorses from the National Stud. He arranged for them to be sent to Fred Darling, who

The Queen and Princess Margaret with
trainer Noel Murless at Royal Ascot, 1955.

by then had already trained five Derby winners. There was symmetry to Moore's choice, since Darling had previously trained horses from this source. He was familiar with the inherited traits of the stud's bloodlines and would achieve much success until his retirement in 1947, when he was replaced by Noel Murless.

Moore made one more important decision in the reorganisation of the royal racing affairs. Towards the end of 1942, after Darling had trained Big Game and Sun Chariot to carry all before them, he advised the king to replace Willie Jarvis, who retired from the royal training ranks, with his friend and occasional sparring partner, Cecil Boyd-Rochfort. Until then Jarvis handled the royal horses that were bred at Sandringham. Moore's blueprint for short-term racing success was now in place. Now he would confront the challenge of culling broodmares superfluous to the king's requirements at the Royal Studs. There was much to do. Despite the stellar exploits of Big Game and Sun Chariot in 1942, the Royal Studs themselves were only able to chip in with one, solitary, inconsequential winner. They had hit rock bottom.

The process of culling mares is complex, and one undertaken with a heavy heart. It may seem obvious from their poor breeding records which mares are ripe for culling. Many will be daughters or granddaughters of mares with a combination of solid racecourse achievement and illustrious blood. Sometimes Mother Nature bestows those qualities to her offspring; sometimes not. In the majority of instances she does not, but to sell such a well-related mare without affording her an opportunity to prove herself is either very brave or very foolish.

When any stud hits upon a mare who throws superior racing stock, it will hoard any subsequent fillies the mare produces even if they themselves were short of racing merit. As sisters to a superior runner, they are more likely to throw a good one than a mare lacking that status. This is how a stud develops its female families. It concentrates on lines that have delivered recent success and discards the rest. As breeders like to say: it is all in the blood. In this way will a stud farm accumulate a cluster of closely-related mares, any one of which might throw a high-class runner. The question is: which one? To that there is no answer. A stud may opt to sell a young mare of little racecourse account on the grounds she has

two or three of her sisters, yet that one – and that one alone – will turn out to be the golden hen. The remainder of her relatives may collectively produce a herd of rubbish; hence the sense of foreboding when mares are culled. It is not a task to undertake lightly.

It is also far from uncommon for so-called 'superior genes' to skip a generation, sometimes two, before they manifest themselves once again. When this happens it may be down to factors unrelated to the merit of a grandmother, although in the absence of any scientific proof, it is usually she who takes the credit. So it is that when the granddaughter of a Thoroughbred scion is sold on for her apparent inability to transmit superior racing genes, her new owner may reap significant benefits.

There are even occasions when a mare's value will rise and fall several times in the short course of her life. A recent example is Ventura, who was bred and raced by that master trainer of Ireland, Vincent O'Brien. This well-related filly was offered for sale at the close of her racing career in 2001. O'Brien's links with Coolmore were such that the partners, O'Brien among them, could have retained Ventura if they so wished – although they were doubtless happy to part with her when she fetched the princely sum of 500,000 guineas at auction. Ventura's new owner was George Strawbridge, who bred her to the best stallions until, after a series of disappointing runners, he decided to cut his losses and sell her on at auction for 58,000 guineas in 2009. Twelve months later Ventura was back in the auction ring after her two-year-old filly Moonlight Cloud had made an exciting start to her racing career in Strawbridge's silks. With Ventura's stock back on the rise, she changed hands for 260,000 guineas. A handsome profit had been turned, but the oscillating values attached to Ventura still had a way to go.

One year on and Moonlight Cloud added further to Ventura's lustre by winning a championship race. Ventura's new owners again chose to cash in their profit, so she returned to auction in 2011 and changed hands again, this time for 900,000 guineas. Ironically, the winning bid came from the Coolmore partnership, which had sold her ten years earlier for half that sum and had returned to buy her back even though they knew Ventura, who was now thirteen, could not produce many more foals on account of her advancing age.

These are the snakes and ladders of the breeding business. A broodmare's value at any given time is no different from the shares of a company with a Stock Exchange listing, which rise and fall with the company's fortunes. Buyers trade in and out of shares; breeders trade in and out of mares. The only difference is that the value of mares fluctuates more wildly that the most volatile of shares. In the sixty seconds it takes to run a race the winner can suddenly raise the value of his mother by 500 per cent, sometimes more. One minute a mare can be grazing anonymously on pastures in Brazil, to where her lack of success has seen her exported. In the next, her perplexed owner is fielding dozens of phone calls from hawk-eyed bloodstock agents in Europe who have just seen one of her offspring win an important race in France. Few sports are as genuinely international as the racing and breeding business.

Her first Royal Ascot as monarch – with Prince Philip in 1952.

As for Ventura, she traded profitably for any number of people. Even Strawbridge, who bought and sold her for a thumping loss, ended up in the black through Ventura's aforementioned daughter Moonlight Cloud, whose value soared well into seven figures on her racing exploits in 2011. Indeed, the sole party yet to profit from the cycle of buying and selling Ventura is the Coolmore partnership. And with the mare now back in their hands, who's to say that they, too, won't have cause to celebrate further down the line?

It was against this backdrop of risk that Moore set about culling the royal mares. His efforts were somewhat abetted by the outbreak of war. It would be impolitic for the Royal Studs to be turning out large crops of foals – and in reality, the quality of mare didn't warrant it. By 1943 George VI's broodmare band had shrunk by half to ten. Moore then replenished the numbers with new purchases, in the process introducing fresh strains of blood from which to build the foundations for future success.

Moore culled vigorously. The branches of existing families he retained would go on to flourish, although inevitably, not everything he cast away fell on fallow ground. A grave exception was Knight's Daughter, whom Moore sold out of the Royal Studs in 1951 when she was ten years old. For her new owner, the Hancock family's Claiborne Farm, Knight's Daughter would produce a racing icon in North America. Her son Round Table is still fêted today as the finest turf runner ever seen on that continent.

He was voted Champion Turf Horse for three consecutive years from 1957. Round Table won forty-three races, setting or equalling record times on fourteen occasions, before he became Champion Sire in 1972. His influence was such that when the Queen visited Kentucky in 1984 she specifically requested to see Round Table at Claiborne Farm. She would almost certainly have remembered his mother from the days when Knight's Daughter grazed the royal paddocks.

The reputation of Moore's lengthy spell as caretaker of the Royal Studs would have been governed by that disastrous sale, had he not posted notable achievement to counter it. Fortunately for him, Knight's Daughter was one of a number of daughters of Feola who were breeding talented racehorses. Indeed, Feola would go on to carve out her own equine dynasty. She was a veritable gem of a broodmare who had few peers in her generation. Her influence would disperse to all parts of the world, although the sale of her great-great-granddaughter Height Of Fashion in 1982 proved a blow from which the Royal Studs are still reeling. It was the misfortune of Lord Carnarvon, who engineered her sale on the Queen's behalf, that while Height Of Fashion would establish her own dynasty, none of her many relatives on the Royal Studs could match her vigour.

Moore, by contrast, was fortunate that Feola's prolific daughters rendered the sale of Knight's Daughter nothing more than an irritating footnote. It is typical of the culling process that Knight's Daughter should yield little in her six years at the Royal Studs before she bequeathed Round Table. The beneficiary, Claiborne Farm, is probably the most celebrated stud in North America's history. Its founder, Arthur 'Bull' Hancock, was among the first to realise the benefits of importing mares from Europe to cross with faster American stallions. Yet Hancock went further. In 1936 he made headlines in Europe when he headed a syndicate that bought the 1930 Derby winner Blenheim for £45,000. Blenheim had been bred by Lord Carnarvon's father, the sixth Earl.

Feola, who cost 3,000 guineas as a yearling in 1934, raced with such purpose for George V that she was ranked the second-best three-year-old filly of her year. Her impact as a broodmare was immediate, and she quickly became the mainstay of the royal breeding cause. Among her early produce were Hypericum, the One Thousand Guineas heroine, and

Aureole and Eph Smith winning the Victor Wild Stakes at Kempton Park, May 1954.

Angelola, who was rated the best staying three-year-old filly in 1948. The Royal Studs had struck a rich vein: when Angelola retired to the paddocks her first foal would trigger a run of success that would give the Queen the best of her racing times. Aureole could not win the Derby but his exploits the following season swept Her Majesty to the top of the leading owners' table.

For all his sterling deeds as a three-year-old, Aureole was a different proposition with another winter behind him. He won the Coronation Cup ahead of a date at Royal Ascot, when he scrambled home by a short-head

A stirring finish to the 1954 Hardwicke Stakes: Aureole (Eph Smith, near side) has to dig deep to beat Janitor (Manny Mercer) by a short head.

– photo-finish cameras had been introduced by then – in a desperately tight finish under Eph Smith, who had replaced Harry Carr in the saddle. Charles Moore felt that Aureole, a headstrong sort, was more relaxed under Smith – as he had been on his final start in 1953, when Carr was too heavy to make the weight Aureole was allocated for the Cumberland Lodge Stakes. Boyd-Rochfort disagreed but Moore overruled him, not for the only time.

Smith certainly helped Aureole better to express himself, although the jockey with 'soft' hands was decidedly hard of hearing. He wasn't aware Aureole had damaged one of his eyes in the build-up to Royal Ascot. When told of it just before the race he said to the Queen: 'Then we are both handicapped, Ma'am. Aureole is half-blind and I am half-deaf. We are a dilapidated pair.'

Victory at the royal meeting suggested Aureole had few peers among horses of his own age. It was now time for him to confront the younger generation in the King George VI and Queen Elizabeth Stakes. In their number was Two Thousand Guineas winner Darius, although Never

Say Die, that year's Derby winner, was not involved. It was nonetheless a strong cast Aureole repelled to gain his finest hour. Having moved into the lead two furlongs out Aureole repelled Darius – only for Vamos to attack him late on. But Aureole, as courageous as they come, dug in to keep the French challenger at bay by three-quarters of a length.

It was a struggle every bit as draining as it was exciting to watch. Doubtless invigorated by the intensity of the finish, the Queen did something that has never since been documented. She hurried down from her box, and on reaching ground level she made her way with great taste towards the winner's enclosure. Moore, all six foot and three inches of him, was well and truly outpaced. Some who saw her maintain the Queen was actually running, propelled by the joy of the moment towards her chestnut colt with the big white blaze who now returned to unsaddle in a blaze of glory.

The royal archives may contain filmed footage of a young princess at school sports day, but this was different. It was a spontaneous emotion, and one more affirmation, if any was needed, of what racing means to the Queen. Any owner will verify that in the heat of the moment, as your horse duels for the lead in the shadow of the winning post, any attempt at restraint is futile. British reserve wilts. Decorum loses its own duel with the urge to celebrate. Here was the Queen, visibly moved by Aureole's heroics, showing her very human side.

This improbable scene unfolded before a crowd of ecstatic racegoers at Ascot in July 1954. No ropes segregated the crowd from the monarch. No human security mountains obscured their view. There was no punctuating pomp, no ceremony, none of the trappings of official functions when the Queen often appears sombre. During her father's long illness her visits to the racecourse brought relief from the heavy responsibility of representing him at such a young age. Now she had won the race named after her parents with a horse bred by her late father.

It is hard to understate Aureole's place in his owner's affections. His retirement to Wolferton Stud, an annexe of the Royal Studs at Sandringham, would generate even more excitement in the breeding realm from which her love of the sport emanates. Aureole would claim honours as the leading sire in 1960 and 1961. The Queen followed his unfolding stallion career with forensic interest. It was a source of immense pride to her. As much was evident twenty years later, when the Queen's Highclere chased home Dahlia in the same Ascot race. Five months later, in her filmed conversation with Sir Peter O'Sullevan, she said: 'Aureole's influence on the first four home in the King George VI was quite remarkable, really. He was grandsire of Dahlia's sire, Vaguely Noble. Buoy, who was fourth, was Aureole's son. There was no influence as such with Highclere except that they [Highclere and Aureole] are both descended from Feola. One [Aureole] is her grandson and the other [Highclere] is her great-granddaughter.' Of the many owner/ breeders with bigger outfits than the Queen, few could amplify inter-relationships within their bloodlines in such precise detail.

Aureole was not alone in hoisting the royal pennant in 1954. After his fruitless tilt at the Derby, Landau, a lessee from the National Stud, rebounded to win the Sussex Stakes, the feature race at Goodwood's July Meeting. Another royal dart had found its target. It also saw the Queen caught up in a three-way joust for the accolade of leading owner. Victory for her two-year-old Alexander at Ascot in October saw her inch ahead of Sterling Clark, who owned Derby and St Leger winner Never Say Die, and that's the way it stayed when the curtain fell in November. It was a memorable season all round. Boyd-Rochfort, who handled Aureole with a sure hand, was champion trainer for the third time, while the Royal Studs finished third on the list of breeders. Those once-dark days were consigned to the memory. Indeed, none connected with the Royal Studs could have known it, but as this vintage year unfolded the royal broodmares were nursing a crop of foals that would become an even more formidable racing force when their turn came in 1957.

Jardiniere's triumph at Royal Ascot marked the highlight of 1955, an achievement emulated by Alexander at the same venue the following year. Atlas also made his mark in winning the Doncaster Cup, but 1956 was notable for the purchase of Stroma. It came at the Queen's behest when she travelled to Doncaster for High Veldt's attempt on the St Leger. Hopes were entertained for High Veldt, who'd made Federico Tesio's unbeaten champion, Ribot, work hard to win the King George VI and Queen Elizabeth Stakes in July. But that sterling effort on testing ground took its toll: a physically drained High Veldt was soundly beaten at Doncaster. The

Queen, meanwhile, was smitten by a yearling she'd seen at the Doncaster sales in company with Moore and her future racing manager Lord Porchester. A bid of 1,150 guineas was all it took to secure Stroma, whose superior racing merit was matched by her subsequent deeds at stud. In the mid-1970s she would play a pivotal role in helping the Royal Studs to emerge from their next spell in the wilderness.

At the start of 1957 there was no hint of what lay ahead. The Queen has some lightly raced three-year-olds of potential in training, although horses so described are usually quick to join the cast of also-rans. It is said that trainers never retire when they have a top two-year-old in their care for fear of missing out on success the following season. If horses of untapped potential were sufficient to keep them going they would never retire at all. Optimism is at its height when trainers cast off the winter rugs at the onset of spring. The promising colt that was too immature to train hard last season now looks a million dollars. The filly who needed time for her knees to strengthen is now an equine powerhouse. And so it goes on until, one by one, they take to the track and retain their anonymity.

Yet 1957 was different. Boyd-Rochfort was convinced that a pair of fillies, Almeria and Mulberry Harbour, had the requisite talent. Meanwhile, up on Warren Hill at Newmarket, not far from Boyd-Rochfort's Freemason Lodge stables, Murless was struck by Carrozza's development over the winter recess. Murless had moved from Beckhampton to Warren Place stables five years earlier to engage in a keen rivalry with Boyd-Rochfort. The two were polar opposites: Boyd-Rochfort a voluble character not averse to landing a gamble, as he had with George VI's Above Board in the 1950 Cesarewitch; Murless a Yorkshireman solely preoccupied by winning the major races. They were masters of their profession who advocated different ways. Needless to say, each was anxious to outdo the other by their achievements with the Queen's horses. As it turned out, both men were right on the money in their assessment of royal fillies in their care.

All three were bred to appreciate racing over middle-distances, which rendered the Oaks, run over one and a half miles, a more suitable target than the One Thousand Guineas. This gave rise to a potential problem. It is inopportune for the owner of three talented fillies to see them running into one another in trial races ahead of the Classics, although the issue

The Oaks, 1957: the Queen leads in Carrozza and Lester Piggott after their pulsating victory.

resolved itself when Almeria finished a tame third on her comeback run. In contemplating Almeria's effort the Queen resolved to give her more time. At her prompting Almeria would miss the Oaks and wait instead for Royal Ascot.

By then, however, Carrozza had already shown her mettle – initially in winning at Epsom and subsequently with her fine fourth place in the One Thousand Guineas. Mulberry Harbour, meanwhile, won easily on her Kempton comeback and followed up by coasting to victory in an Oaks trial at Chester. After that, Boyd-Rochfort felt sure Mulberry Harbour, who was improving fast, would run with distinction at Epsom.

She did not. After chasing the leader for much of the Oaks Mulberry Harbour started backpedalling just when she was expected to go forward. It was baffling only for as long as it took Mulberry Harbour to return to the racecourse stables. Boyd-Rochfort's assistant Bruce Hobbs took a look at her distressed state and felt there was but one explanation. Mulberry Harbour had been 'got at'. The filly had been doped to prevent her showing her true worth, which saw her start a well-backed second favourite to give the young Queen her first Classic winner.

Patriotism was no deterrent to those motivated by money to remove Mulberry Harbour from the equation. The portents looked promising when Mulberry Harbour rounded Tattenham Corner in second place, running strongly, seemingly poised to make an early strike for the winning post. Then she was gone in a stride, her rhythm suddenly overcome by an intense fatigue as she listed like a sinking ship. Halfway down the straight, those heartfelt Classic aspirations seemed to be sinking with Mulberry Harbour until the eye re-focussed on Lester Piggott poking through a narrow gap along the inside rail.

Piggott was aboard Carrozza, his distinguishing white cap denoting the Queen's second colours in deference to Mulberry Harbour. He'd seen the leader crack just ahead of him and seized the initiative, driving Carrozza to the front with two furlongs remaining. Royal allegiance now switched to the little bay filly whose relentless stride soon had the Aga Khan's favourite, Rose Royale, in trouble. Elation rose from the depths of despair as Carrozza galloped ahead – until Silken Glider emerged from the pack in hot pursuit. The two fillies locked horns in a desperate struggle to the line, with Carrozza on the verge of wilting until Piggott implored from her one final thrust. Back Carrozza came as the line approached; on reaching it the pair flashed past as one blurred entity.

It was much too close to call with the naked eye. Even Piggott, normally a dead-eyed marksman in these circumstances, was unsure of the outcome. Many racegoers felt that Silken Glider had it, which added lustre to the cheers when the judge declared Carrozza the winner by a short head.

Carrozza was fazed by the resultant commotion. She would not enter the winner's circle until the Queen turned her on her heels and walked the royal horse into a berth last occupied after an Epsom Classic by Minoru in 1909. The Queen's delight was obvious as photographers recorded an inaugural Oaks winner in the royal silks at Epsom; Sun Chariot's had been gained in a wartime substitute at Newmarket. As for the race itself, rarely can the fortunes of one owner have fluctuated so wildly in so short a time.

Poor Mulberry Harbour was out of sight and out of mind. The euphoria of Carrozza's victory doubtless blinded the Epsom stewards, who failed to order a post-race dope test on the stricken filly. As for Piggott, his winning ride was so complete that doubters who questioned Murless's sanity in appointing the nineteen-year-old as Sir Gordon Richards's replacement two years earlier would not do so again. Piggott's ride spoke of an uncommon talent. It would hold the sport in thrall for the next three decades, when the jockey imposed himself as the master of Epsom. Two days earlier Piggott had won the Derby by finessing Crepello, a heavy horse racing on unsuitably fast ground, to humiliate his opponents. A set of very different skills was required aboard Carrozza.

Mulberry Harbour returned to action at Royal Ascot, when another poor run persuaded Boyd-Rochfort to give her a long rest while he plotted a course for Almeria. The Queen was on hand to see Almeria gallop on the course before her facile Royal Ascot triumph in the Ribblesdale Stakes. From there it was onwards and upwards. Another victory, this time at Goodwood, preceded two more in the Yorkshire Oaks and Doncaster's Park Hill Stakes – with Silken Glider among the vanquished both times. Her progress coincided with an injury to Carrozza that foreshadowed her retirement. And while Almeria rested on her laurels from mid-September, Mulberry Harbour reappeared to win two races of a quality commensurate with her ability.

This trio of royal fillies dominated the season. They had no peer in the year-end classifications when Almeria, Carrozza and Mulberry Harbour filled the first three places, in that order, in the three-year-old filly category. They were not alone in their successes. His rough passage in the Derby aside, Doutelle won four times from as many starts for Boyd-Rochfort, each of them in superior company. He'd opened his campaign by winning the Two Thousand Guineas Trial at Kempton, in the process completing a hat-trick of royal triumphs in that race. All in all, it was a year when one success followed another with a pleasing frequency.

The Queen ended the season as leading owner for the second time in four years, and almost certainly for the last time in her reign. It is inconceivable she will ever be able to match contemporary Middle Eastern behemoths that now roam the British turf, since sheer weight of numbers renders it an unequal contest. Doutelle's last victory of the season, at Ascot in October, secured her the accolade, yet try as he might Boyd-Rochfort could not top a trainers' listing headed by Murless at his direct expense.

Taken as a whole, 1957 has to supplant the achievements of Aureole three years earlier as the Queen's best season on record. It certainly put a spring into Her Majesty's step. On a visit to Newmarket she astonished Boyd-Rochfort with her agenda for the day. Having arrived in time for the trainer's 'first lot' at the crack of dawn, she raced away to see her mares and foals at nearby studs before returning in time for 'second lot'. She then changed for the races and went back to Freemason Lodge for evening stables, where she saw every horse ahead of the drive back to Sandringham. Boyd-Rochfort was left reeling in her wake. Against that, he was giving the Queen, then thirty, exactly four decades.

Another welcome legacy of the 1957 campaign was that Almeria and Mulberry Harbour would become prized additions to the Royal Studs. Carrozza, leased for her racing days, would return to her birthplace at the National Stud. Throughout his rivalry with Murless, Boyd-Rochfort fortified himself in the belief that his horses were the Queen's true pennants. Murless was training horses that passed in and out of royal ownership; 'the Hirelings', as Moore had dubbed them. In this Boyd-Rochfort had allies in just about everyone involved in a royal racing capacity. George V certainly drew the distinction. Following Scuttle's victory in the One Thousand Guineas of 1928, he wrote in his diary: 'I am very proud to win my first Classic, and that I bred her at Sandringham.'

Such sentiments are inevitable. Years of intense preparation goes into the production of each and every foal. Success from this source, rather than one of 'the Hirelings', was bound to be more cherished. To the public, however, there was no distinction. The royal silks are just that, and each victory promoted the same sense of joy in those who savoured their racing. 'In the public and journalists' mind it didn't matter whether the horses came from Sandringham or the National Stud,' Sir Peter O'Sullevan observed. 'It made no difference at all.'

If Boyd-Rochfort was piqued to be beaten to the Classic punch by one of the Murless 'Hirelings', he would be assuaged a year later. The colt in question came from a most unexpected source, and only after Moore had chosen to cleanse the Royal Studs of any trace of his origins. In 1949 Moore embarked on an experiment in breeding theory when he bought Malapert, a slow but well-bred filly, for a pittance at public auction. For the next five years he bred her to stallions of his choice, to no tangible benefit. Duly frustrated, Moore recommended Malapert for culling and thought no more of her after she recouped 910 guineas in 1955. The following year Moore recommended the same course of action for Malapert's two-year-old daughter Cheetah, who was sold for 460 guineas. There was but one son of Malapert left in production: a yearling colt whose front legs were so ill-conformed that he was thought unlikely to stand the rigours of training. Inevitably, he would be the one to flourish.

In 1958 Pall Mall lived in the shadow of his much-vaunted stablemate Bald Eagle at Freemason Lodge. The royal colt was left trailing when matched with Bald Eagle in one of those spring gallops beloved of Newmarket work-watchers. Both colts won their prep races ahead of the Two Thousand Guineas, although Bald Eagle's victory was the more visually arresting. Accordingly, Harry Carr, with Boyd-Rochfort's blessing, elected to ride him over Pall Mall – for whom Doug Smith, victorious aboard George VI's Hypericum in the One Thousand Guineas twelve years earlier, was engaged.

Bald Eagle was dispatched a warm favourite at Newmarket. Pall Mall's prospects were assessed at 20/1, but Smith had a very different take on the race two furlongs out. With Bald Eagle foundering, Smith brought Pall Mall through to challenge his brother Eph, aboard Major Portion, before grinding down that combination to win by half a length. Pall Mall's resolution won the day. He never once flinched under a hard drive from Doug Smith.

For his reward Pall Mall earned distinction as the Queen's first homebred Classic winner, although the Queen herself was not at Newmarket to witness the welcome surprise. She was laid low by a cold; that she

didn't travel in hope probably reflected the consensus surrounding Pall Mall's slim prospects of winning. Hindsight decrees her absence from Newmarket more regrettable for the fact that Pall Mall remains the only colt owned by the Queen to win a Classic.

Such improbable victories often come with strings attached. On the one hand it would have plainly thrilled both the Queen and Boyd-Rochfort, who can never have been so delighted to be proved so wrong. Yet while the Classic garlands were theirs, Harry Carr felt only acute despair. The Two Thousand Guineas outcome was beyond comprehension to a jockey who had seen Bald Eagle repeatedly saunter past Pall Mall on the home gallops. And it wasn't the first time a significant royal victory had been dashed from Carr's lips. He was replaced aboard Aureole for a four-year-old campaign that saw Aureole brush all-comers aside. And he'd looked on from the rear aboard Mulberry Harbour when Lester Piggott won the Oaks on Carrozza. The very same nightmare resurfaced twelve months later, this time with Pall Mall. Carr would not have believed Pall Mall had beaten Bald Eagle but for seeing it with his own eyes.

As for Moore, Pall Mall's victory was bitter-sweet. Although his breeding experiment with Malapert had paid off, the Royal Studs were in no position to capitalise. Every bloodline to do with Malapert had been expunged. To make matters worse, Malapert's daughter, the aforementioned Cheetah, would soon sow a rich seam for her new owner – none other than Murless, trainer of the 'Hirelings'. Murless would subsequently train Cheetah's granddaughter Caergwrle to win the One Thousand Guineas in 1968.

The vagaries of chance were in play once again. Moore gave Malapert six years to prove herself but it was not quite long enough. One more year and the Royal Studs would certainly have retained both Malapert and Cheetah. And Moore would have been hailed as something of a magician on account of his exploits with a mare for which he paid just 100 guineas in 1949.

Still, Pall Mall ensured that the Queen's 1959 season opened as the previous one had closed. The colt went on to further success in the Lockinge Stakes, a race now accorded championship status. He was one of just three royal three-year-old colts in Boyd-Rochfort's care; each would demonstrate superior racing class. Restoration vindicated his trainer's daring approach when he won Royal Ascot's Edward VII Stakes on his racecourse debut. And Miner's Lamp came forward from his Derby run to win the feature race at Newmarket's prestigious July meeting.

This run of success was enhanced by Doutelle, who had opened his four-year-old campaign in 1958 with important victories at Newbury and Chester. As the days unfurled ahead of Britain's midsummer showpiece, the King George VI and Queen Elizabeth Stakes, it was not lost on the Queen's advisors that she had sound prospects of becoming leading owner for the third time in five years. She would be represented in the imminent Ascot race by Almeria in addition to Doutelle. Victory for either would make her hard to overthrow.

This was the race in which Moore overruled prearranged instructions, agreed between the Queen and Boyd-Rochfort, on how Doutelle should be ridden. The colt was thus anchored in the rear, in the process compromising Almeria, who was left alone to lead the field when she would have gained much from Doutelle's company. It was no disgrace for Almeria and Doutelle to chase home Ballymoss, the outstanding horse of the season, but the reverse was a portent of things to come. Pall Mall would meet his match, while Miner's Lamp sustained a tendon injury too severe to allow him to race on. And while Agreement's Doncaster Cup triumph in September saw the flame flicker, the Queen was narrowly denied the coveted accolade of leading owner in 1958. Conversely, Boyd-Rochfort topped the trainers' charts after Alcide, whom he trained for Sir Humphrey de Trafford, won the St Leger. It was the fifth and final time Boyd-Rochfort would celebrate the gong.

From left: Princess Margaret, the Queen Mother and the Queen, Royal Ascot 1958.

The following year brought further royal success. There was certainly no sign of an imminent drought. Pall Mall won the Lockinge Stakes for the second consecutive year; likewise Agreement the Doncaster Cup. There was a second Royal Ascot double in three years, courtesy of Above Suspicion and Pindari. And Boyd-Rochfort successfully concluded his own quest to win the Derby when he saddled Parthia, again for de Trafford, to victory at Epsom.

However, 1959 would prove the last of its kind. It marked the final year in which Boyd-Rochfort and the Queen would share in mutual success. Both Boyd-Rochfort and Moore were of advancing years. The former was now into his eighth decade; Moore not far away from his ninetieth year. Their alliance propelled the royal livery to moments of supreme triumph, but the floorboards were now creaking – and they would not so much splinter as collapse completely. Six unbroken seasons of excellence would subside beneath the debris of a shocking campaign in 1960, when neither Boyd-Rochfort nor Murless saddled a single royal winner of any description from nineteen horses in training. It was an all-time low the like of which the Queen had never previously encountered.

Again, however, the assessment that trainer and manager were almost certainly past their best is afforded by hindsight. It could have been an aberration; in 1960 Boyd-Rochfort's stable was blighted by a debilitating virus. Indeed, although his stable's strength gradually diminished, he would saddle other notable royal winners from horses bred under Moore's stewardship. Apprentice's triumphs in the Goodwood and Yorkshire Cups of 1965 were cases in point, as was Canisbay's nail-biting victory in that year's Eclipse Stakes.

Canisbay's triumph thrilled the Queen on two counts. His dam was Stroma, whose charms the Queen fell for when she instructed Moore

Nail-biting: Canisbay (Stan Clayton) just beats Roan Rocket (right) in the 1965 Eclipse Stakes at Sandown Park.

to buy her for 1,150 guineas at Doncaster nine years previously. And Canisbay only contested the Eclipse because the Queen expressed her wish for him to do so. Unconvinced of Canisbay's merit, Boyd-Rochfort was keener to run him in races far below the status of the Sandown Park contest.

For all that, question over the respective abilities of Boyd-Rochfort and Moore remained. They were also complicated in nature. Were the

146

horses Moore was responsible for breeding simply no good? Was Boyd-Rochfort turning Moore's silk purses into sow's ears? Or was each as ripe for retirement as the other? The Queen herself seemed in no hurry for definitive answers. She was fond of Moore, and also young enough for this popular, charming man with a witty turn of phrase to have exerted a paternalistic influence. From abject royal fortune in the 1930s, and with Boyd-Rochfort's invaluable help, Moore had brought about a remarkable transformation. The subsequent golden chapter for the royal silks resulted from his immense command of the subject. It would have been invidious to dispense with the pair of them at the first sign of adversity – although no such latitude was to extend to Dick Hern, who trained royal horses with distinction until he was controversially dismissed in 1988.

What was certain was that the royal broodmare band dripped with stamina-laden blood. Moore was a firm advocate of it; each year he recommended stallions long on stamina as suitable mates for the royal mares. Early results from the racecourse attested to the success of Moore's policy, although when these 'staying' racemares were themselves mated to staying stallions, the emphasis on stamina became overabundant. In these circumstances it can take a succession of matings to faster sires to recalibrate the balance at a time when speed was becoming increasingly requisite for racecourse success.

In Moore's day it was virtually unknown for a staying mare to be bred to a sprinting stallion. The contrast was perceived as too great, yet contemporary thinking is very different. The finish to the 2009 Oaks was fought out between Sariska and Midday, who were daughters of sprinters in Pivotal and Oasis Dream respectively. Dancing Rain, winner of the 2011 Oaks, is by another sprinter in Danehill Dancer. Moore would have recoiled at that, yet looking back, his philosophy did not evolve with the times. He was also an advocate of inbreeding, which occurs when mares are mated to stallions of similar genetic backgrounds. He would breed a granddaughter of Hyperion to a great grandson of the same sire with the purpose of increasing the concentration of Hyperion's blood in the resultant foal. Almeria was the product of such a mating. She was a supreme runner, but the concentration of Hyperion's blood in her came with the less welcome trait of Hyperion's fiery temperament. Inbreeding was a successful strategy deployed by many breeders in Moore's generation. The best of them, Marcel Boussac, dominated racing in France for two decades from the 1930s but his fortunes, rather like those of the Royal Studs, turned for the worse in the 1960s.

Like the Royal Studs under Moore's tenure, Boussac sent mares to his own stallions in an effort to boost the latter's standing. There is much to be gained financially from 'making' a stallion in this way, although most efforts are doomed to fail for the simple fact that most racehorses to take up stallion duties are doomed to failure. To commit your mares to your own unproven stallion is to flirt with failure on both fronts. A stallion's ultimate worth is preordained, no matter the quality of mares bred to him. Equally, to patronise one destined to fail is to bring about a dilution in the quality of blood in your mare. Moore was convinced of the merits of Kingstone and Rising Light, who both resided at the Royal Studs. The two were bred to royal mares each year; each year they failed to sire a horse of particular renown. The consequences were equally dire for Boussac, who advocated inbreeding to an unusually concentrated degree and who made far greater use of his own unproven stallions. On Boussac's death in 1980 his entire band of mares was bought by the Aga Khan, who promptly reversed the policy. He bred Boussac's mares to stallions from different genetic backgrounds. In this way would he revive some classic lines that Boussac had driven into a state of temporary impotence.

Over at Sandringham, a change of tack had to wait until Moore was ultimately cajoled into retirement in 1962. In his twenty-five years as racing manager, the first fifteen of them for George VI, Moore swore by the merits of Hyperion, one of the two outstanding stallions in post-war Newmarket, while steadfastly resisting the lure of the other, Nearco. Time would illustrate that Moore had backed the wrong horse. Hyperion's huge early influence would soon subside while Nearco, owned and bred by Federico Tesio, would effectively become the founder of the modern Thoroughbred.

By the early 1950s the Queen's interest in bloodlines was both strong and well-informed. She gently started to challenge Moore's dismissal of Nearco, who was champion sire three times. At her behest Beginner's Luck was sent to the great stallion in 1956; the consequence, Near Miss, would become granddam of Joking Apart, who carried the Queen's silks into third place in the 1975 One Thousand Guineas. At a time when rival studs were stocking up on Nearco's blood, Near Miss was the only filly by that stallion to graze the royal pastures. It was an omission that flew in the face of Nearco's ongoing success.

Moore's retirement signalled a period of major change in the royal racing arrangements. He was succeeded in 1962 by his deputy Brigadier Tony Wingfield, who gave way to Major Richard Shelley one year later. Yet Wingfield and Shelley served specifically as managers of the Royal Studs, from which the latter would stand down through ill heath. There would be no official racing manager for a seven-year period from 1962, although it was becoming increasingly apparent that the Queen turned for advice to Lord Porchester – or 'Porchey', as he had been known to her for many years.

Lord Porchester, subsequently Lord Carnarvon, soon became centrally involved in royal racing matters. His profile rose significantly on Moore's retirement as the Queen contemplated her blueprint for the future. The man who accompanied her to see Hypericum win the Dewhurst Stakes in 1945, when he was an officer in the Royal Horse Guards, was well qualified to dispense advice, and he had already spent countless hours with the Queen discussing every aspect of a sport to which they were both in thrall.

In a filmed conversation with Sir Peter O'Sullevan four years after Carnarvon's official appointment as her racing manager, the Queen put it thus: 'My racing manager and I have argued how important the breeding and the influence of the past is over many years' acquaintance. We have had a lot of fun out of it. And now, having put him in charge, we have even more arguments and even more fun – and sometimes I practise what he preaches.'

In the years before he was officially anointed in 1969, Carnarvon was the strongest voice behind the Queen's realignment of her racing and breeding interests. There was much for them to consider.

6

THE 1960s:
A BARREN
DECADE

Cecil Boyd-Rochfort's career never really flourished after the debacle of 1960. A trying season all round closed with his invaluable assistant Bruce Hobbs resigning in frustration at Boyd-Rochfort's persistent refusal to entertain retirement. The transition from one assistant to another is always an anxious one for any trainer. Men of Hobbs's standing play an integral part in the smooth running of a stable. To a large extent they are their employer's hidden eyes and ears, cognisant of problems that can be nipped in the bud. Yet from Hobbs's perspective, there was another factor to consider.

Boyd-Rochfort's stepson Henry Cecil was now seventeen years old. Together with his twin brother David, Henry spent much of his school holidays helping out at Freemason Lodge. In time one of them would inevitably succeed their stepfather, who had no children of his own. When the twins left school they were sent to a succession of stud farms to further their equine education. At that stage David looked a more likely successor than Henry, although that would change in 1964, when Boyd-Rochfort appointed Henry, then twenty-three, as his full-time assistant. The desire to give his young protégé the full benefit of his knowledge is almost certainly what kept Boyd-Rochfort from retirement.

By then, however, the royal homebreds were no longer Boyd-Rochfort's exclusive preserve. By 1968, when he finally drew stumps, Boyd-Rochfort had trained 136 royal winners in his seventeen-year association with the

Royal Family. In that year there were just three royal three-year-olds in his string. The Queen had already chosen to look to the future.

The royal migration from Newmarket was thus under way. All the Queen's horses had been trained in the town since Murless moved his string to Warren Place in 1952. Peter Hastings-Bass received his first draft of royal yearlings ten years later. His recruitment signalled a change of thinking by the Queen and her advisors. So much so that on Boyd-Rochfort's retirement the Queen replaced him with Major Dick Hern. Hastings-Bass trained at Park House stables in Berkshire, within the 1,500-acre Kingsclere estate he had bought in 1953, and which shared boundaries with the Carnarvon family seat at Highclere Castle. With Hern based just across the M4 motorway at West Ilsley, Newmarket's place as home to the Queen's racehorses was no more. A new era was in the making.

These unfolding circumstances conspired against Henry Cecil when he embarked on his own training career in 1969. He received no royal patronage, not then nor since. It seems a curious omission for the man who would quickly become the dominant force among British trainers, and who 'did' Castle Yard, the last winner Boyd-Rochfort trained for the Queen. Cecil could not have been better connected to receive royal horses: in 1967 he married Noel Murless's daughter Julie, thus uniting twin training dynasties that gave the Queen so much to celebrate in the 1950s. Cecil's life has been colourful, to say the least. His divorce from Julie in 1990 presaged a period of personal turbulence that was compounded by serious illness. For decades his eccentric, often wayward behaviour was advanced as the likely reason for the absence of royal patronage, yet such speculation appears groundless in the wake of Cecil's knighthood in 2011.

Royal racehorses have since returned to be trained in Newmarket – although not to Cecil's stables at Warren Place, from where Cecil's father-in-law Noel Murless prepared Carrozza to win the 1957 Oaks. Murless himself would lapse from the royal roster through circumstances beyond his control. The horses he trained for the Queen were all leased from the National Stud, whose directors announced in 1964 the sale of its entire band of broodmares. The decision resulted from a review of the stud's purpose, which was to best serve British breeders.

At the time there was a constant drain of the best of Britain's racehorses to America, where wealthy stud owners were enamoured by their stallion potential. It proved a lucrative and highly successful formula for them. The National Stud would try to staunch a flow that left Britain with few stallions of sufficient quality available to breeders. To achieve it, the stud would fortify its coffers by selling its mares.

A valuable source of talented royal runners was thus lost at a time when the Royal Studs were delivering few of their own. There must have been royal lament: it was the Queen's first sighting of two of the National Stud's produce, Big Game and Sun Chariot, which endeared her to racing in the first place. Historically, racehorses were leased by agents of British monarchs when the Royal Studs were unproductive. On behalf of Edward VII, Lord Marcus Beresford made such an arrangement with the future Lord Wavertree in the early 1900s, with the result that Minoru's 1909 Derby victory was gained in the royal silks. A yard was named in acknowledgement of Lord Wavertree's contribution to the royal cause when the National Stud relocated to state-of-the-art premises in Newmarket in 1964.

Murless was disappointed at the change of policy but saw out the arrangement in style – and with a son of Aureole to boot. In the last leased crop of royal three-year-olds in 1967 was the unraced colt Hopeful Venture, who soon made up for lost time, winning his first two starts with ease to enter calculations for the Derby. However, Murless ignored the temptation, for also in his care was Royal Palace, who had long shown Murless he was something out of the ordinary and confirmed it by winning the Two Thousand Guineas. Hopeful Venture thus stayed at home while Royal Palace returned from Epsom with the Derby garlands. He would stand in for Royal Palace when the latter was cruelly injured in his preparation for the St Leger, in which Hopeful Venture beat all bar the enigmatic Ribocco.

Hopeful Venture then crossed the Channel to give the royal silks their first airing on a French racecourse. The experience was bitter-sweet: Hopeful Venture won the Prix Henry Delamarre but was disqualified after he was deemed to have impeded the runner-up. A repeat journey would be made the following season, when Hopeful Venture landed the

Grand Prix de Saint-Cloud from exceptionally strong opposition. The runner-up Minamota had just filled the same berth in the French Derby, while Vaguely Noble, who finished third, would progress to win France's most important race, the Prix de l'Arc de Triomphe. It was the only time Vaguely Noble, himself a grandson of Aureole, would be defeated in 1968, which closed with neither Murless and Boyd-Rochfort any longer on the royal training roster.

Despite Hopeful Venture's sterling deeds over two seasons he raced in the long shadow of Royal Palace. The latter progressed from landing the Two Thousand Guineas and Derby in 1967 to a blitz of the big races the following year. His winning sequence embracing the Coronation Cup, Prince Of Wales's Stakes, Eclipse Stakes and King George VI and Queen Elizabeth Stakes – in which he broke down but still won – is as good as it gets. In any other year Hopeful Venture would have gained the plaudits, yet he earned recognition as the horse to bring the Murless chapter to an apposite conclusion. If the Queen was in the least bit affronted by muted acclaim for Hopeful Venture, she would eventually raise her glass to Royal Palace when he sired her dual Classic heroine of 1977, Dunfermline.

Hopeful Venture's first trip to France in 1967 followed a few months after the Queen had paid a private visit to that country. She was taken to many

Hopeful Venture (Sandy Barclay) holds off Minamota (Freddie Head) to win the 1968 Grand Prix de Saint-Cloud.

of Normandy's renowned stud farms during a four-day tour in which she saw for herself some of the stallions Charles Moore had recommended for use on the royal mares. The trip underlined how seriously she took her breeding. It was a notable success, and she had followed it up by sending Hopeful Venture to run in France – and beyond that, by recognising the opportunities that French racing presented ahead of Highclere's sterling exploits in 1974. On that visit Alec Head extended the Queen an open invitation to his Haras du Quesnay, where she subsequently stayed on two separate occasions. Then, as now, the arrangements were made by Lord Porchester, who travelled with the royal party each time.

Evidence of Porchester's growing influence came simultaneously with Moore's retirement in 1962. He soon made a major adjustment to a policy that saw the Queen's foals grazing the Hampton Court paddocks until they were shipped to Ireland in the autumn. That would cease when Porchester declared that Hampton Court's paddocks were worn out. The foals would instead roam on new pastures Porchester rented on behalf of the Royal Studs at Polhampton Lodge Stud, near Newbury. It was an eminently sensible move, since London's smoggy boundaries had now expanded to the fringes of Hampton Court. It wasn't ideal for young Thoroughbreds to be raised amid such pollution. So while the studs' central office remained at Hampton Court, its foals were relocated to paddocks a proverbial stone's throw from Porchester's Newbury home.

Furthermore, the practice of sending the Queen's foals to Ireland, where they stayed for eighteen months until they went into training, would be reversed in 1970. They would instead stay at Polhampton, which the Queen bought outright in 1971. The Irish venture was a legacy of Moore, who insisted the royal foals should be exposed to the elements so as to toughen them up. Since they were left to their own devices in Ireland, they had much to learn about routine stable life on their arrival in Newmarket. The formative process of riding them away thus came as something of a shock.

Down the years the Queen has embraced variations to tried-and-trusted methods of handling Thoroughbreds. She starts from the premise that a kinder way is a better way. Horses that are barely handled until the eve of their second birthday – which for convenience of racing administration, is New Year's Day for all Thoroughbreds – are by then strong animals capable of making life difficult for those charged with vaulting on their backs them for the first time. This is commonly called the 'breaking process', and until recently, a degree of stress for the horse was seen as inevitable. The idea that people who had only previously walked around it would suddenly jump on its back is not the kind of thing to which a flighty Thoroughbred would readily accede. There was always a degree of struggle between the horse trying to buck off a rider who was hell-bent on staying aboard until the horse was becalmed – hence the phrase 'breaking in'.

All that changed when Monty Roberts pioneered an alternative approach in the late-1980s. A Californian horseman, Roberts took his cue from studying equine behaviour in herds of wild Mustangs as a teenager in Nevada. He learnt of their silent communication with one another and applied it to breaking horses, which he rechristened the 'join-up' process. On hearing of his work the Queen invited Roberts to Windsor to demonstrate his technique to horsemen at the Royal Mews. Roberts gave three separate displays of 'connecting' with horses in this way, the first of which left Terry Pendry, who was then Warrant Officer of the Household Cavalry's riding staff, in a state of disbelief.

'The first time I saw it I thought it was either very clever or very stupid,' Pendry recalled. 'If it was a trick, it was a bad idea to play it on the Queen. I had no idea how he managed to do it. At first glance it seemed as if he just stood there with his hands in his pockets. But after a while, I got it.'

Pendry subsequently introduced elements of Roberts' method in the breaking – or 'starting', as it was now termed – of cavalry horses. The Queen did likewise when she elected to 'start' her Thoroughbreds at Sandringham instead of delegating that responsibility to her trainers. The Monty Roberts way is far kinder than traditional methods. It is entirely non-confrontational. After his inaugural visit to Windsor, Roberts travelled extensively around Europe demonstrating his technique to countless sets of disbelieving eyes. He made an important breakthrough in deciphering the hidden meaning of movement between one horse and another. He then applied it to his own behaviour around horses. He learnt the significance of walking towards a horse, then walking away when the horse retreated so that it would ultimately follow him around as though connected by an invisible piece of string. Roberts's profound appreciation of horse movement is such that he was widely consulted by the crew behind the play *War Horse* as they made the life-size horse puppets they used in their remarkably successful West End stage production. Roberts' advice was also sought by those inside the puppets in their quest to replicate the horse's unique gait as accurately as possible. Their work was silently appreciated by the Queen and Prince Philip, who snuck in to watch the show one evening just as the curtain rose.

Roberts's methods would change the approach to 'starting' horses at many equine establishments, among them some of the finest Thoroughbred studs. Sea The Stars, who retired to stud in 2009 after an exemplary racing season, was 'started' in this way. 'Like all horse people,' said Pendry, 'the Queen will see something that makes her think: "How can we use this to make it better for the horse?" The Monty Roberts method says there should be no violence. He and I have since become great friends: his wife once told me that she married a cowboy and ended up with a disciple, because ever since he came to Windsor he vowed himself to horse duty. Horses are not born bad. The first day you spend with them is often the most critical of their lives.'

The Queen's first encounter with Roberts came long after Polhampton was leased for the royal Thoroughbreds in 1962. It pleased her to be able to spend more time among her young horses than she was afforded under Moore's regime. Further changes were afoot. Peter Hastings-Bass received his first intake of royal yearlings the year after the Polhampton development, to be followed soon after by Hern. By then a pattern had emerged. All the royal horses were converging on one part of the country.

This was certainly more convenient for the Queen. With barely a car-ride in between, she could make the short journey from Windsor to see the youngsters at Polhampton as well as her horses in training at Park House and West Ilsley. She could get a great deal from a rare day spent in their company. Equally, it was also true that all the Queen's horses now dwelt in the same stretch of the country occupied for more than 200 years by the Carnarvon family. Intentionally or otherwise, the royal racing interest was unfolding very much under the watchful eye of the seventh heir to the earldom even though he was still without official portfolio.

From then on, very little to do with the Queen's horses escaped Carnarvon's attention. All the changes implemented on Moore's retirement bore his fingerprints. He was a long-standing friend of the Queen, having accompanied her, as Princess Elizabeth, to London balls in their youth. He'd had a horse, The Solicitor, in training with Fred Darling at Beckhampton, where he spent school holidays at a time when the princess visited Beckhampton with her father in the 1940s. Other royal advisors came and went but Carnarvon was a constant presence throughout the Queen's involvement in the Turf. From 1969 he would serve as racing manager with unswerving loyalty for 32 years.

Carnarvon is easily the most intriguing individual to serve in the role. He brought aptitude to a broad range of interests beyond racing, which captivated him from a young age as he watched his father compete regularly as an amateur rider. He took prominent roles in local government – he chaired Hampshire County Council – and in matters of planning and conservation. He developed an appetite for public service in his teens after he accompanied his mother to the soup kitchens of London's East End. The squalor and deprivation he saw at first hand made him resolve to do more with his life than farm land at Highclere.

He proceeded with relish. He chaired numerous committees in the public cause while simultaneously throwing open the doors of Highclere Castle in a hugely successful drive to raise funds for maintaining the 6,000-acre estate. He was an old-school aristo with a modern mind; he even found time to serve as chairman of Hampshire County Cricket Club from 1966 to 1968. He was also never ashamed to admit that he enjoyed a bet.

Carnarvon was also active on several fronts within the sport. In 1967 he chaired a Jockey Club committee charged with making sense of the uncoordinated racing programme in Britain. From that committee spawned what came to be known as the 'Pattern' system: a series of races offering suitable opportunities to superior horses at regular intervals throughout the season. Each race within the Pattern was graded to denote its level of importance; the Classics and other races of proven significance were designated Group One events. The Pattern also provided a broad platform for recognition of a horse's ability. It was so successful as a concept that it was adopted in various guises around the world.

As with previous royal racing managers, Carnarvon ran a successful stud of his own before pursuing the royal cause. His passion for breeding prompted him to buy the 260-acre Highclere Stud, within the grounds of the family estate, from his father in 1982. 'My father had started to lose interest and the place was deteriorating, so although I would have inherited it eventually, I bought it,' said the man who inherited the earldom in 1987.

He tasted success long before then. Indeed, his first horse, the aforementioned The Solicitor, determined the course he would pursue throughout his Turf life. Then nineteen, Carnarvon came by the horse when his father asked him to choose one from the family homebreds as a gift. The Solicitor greatly endeared himself to his new owner by winning a pair of competitive races for two-year-olds, yet Carnarvon didn't hesitate to act on Fred Darling's advice to sell him there and then. The sum he cashed amplified the virtue of taking a profit, which Carnarvon reinvested in bloodstock. There were obvious benefits in taking profits but the instinct to sell, thus ingrained, would govern the approach Carnarvon adopted in his royal role.

It served him well in the interim. He showed a sharp eye for a young horse when buying Tamerlane as a yearling for 4,500 guineas in 1953. Tamerlane enjoyed a fruitful racing career; he led the field into the final furlong of the Two Thousand Guineas before he was caught by Our Babu. Subsequent victories, among them one at Royal Ascot, preceded Tamerlane's sale to Ireland – and another handsome deposit in the Highclere Stud coffers.

Carnarvon also displayed an uncanny knack of reviving previously successful but now-dormant families abandoned by others. His father's waning interest had left Highclere bereft of some of the female lines it had previously cultivated. In the 1950s Carnarvon made two cheap purchases to redress the loss. He gave £800 for Minstrel Girl and £2,000 for Jojo, whom he bought from a friend in dire financial straits on the eve of his daughter's wedding. These two mares became ancestress respectively of Lemon Souffle and Niche, the pair of fillies Richard Hannon trained to a host of big-race wins in 1992-93.

It was an extraordinary achievement. Carnarvon had taken two unwanted mares and transformed their ailing fortunes. Furthermore,

Niche and Lemon Souffle were by unfashionable sires; Carnarvon had worked his magic on a very limited budget. Time and again he would breed fine racehorses by inexpensive stallions. It characterised his approach. And time and again, he refused to allow emotion to intrude on the business of taking profits. A case in point was Lyric Fantasy, a contemporary of Niche whom he'd bought as a yearling for 12,500 guineas. The pair ran amok as two-year-olds in 1992, after which Carnarvon decided to keep Niche and sell Lyric Fantasy. He did not believe Lyric Fantasy would race as effectively the following season, and he was proved right. Some years later he would say with a cold eye of her sale for 340,000 guineas: 'Lyric Fantasy was just a hyped star who was always going to make a lot of money.'

Much of what Carnarvon touched turned to gold. He would cash in the crown-jewel representative of a Thoroughbred family and work with less illustrious relatives to telling effect. Then he would repeat the process, over and over again. To his immense satisfaction, Highclere Stud became synonymous with high-class horses. Moreover, he achieved it with the primal instinct of a dealer utterly convinced that he would end up on the right side of any trade.

There was no shortage of evidence to back him up. Satinette, a talented filly Carnarvon sold for 600,000 guineas in 1984, would trudge through the same Newmarket auction ring thirteen years later, when her disenchanted owner was glad to sell her on for 32,000 guineas. In 1989 Carnarvon banked 1.1 million guineas from the sale of another homebred filly, Roseate Tern, who would achieve little when she subsequently joined the broodmare band of Sheikh Hamdan Al-Maktoum. But there was a very different legacy when the sheikh, on Carnarvon's prompting, bought the Queen's filly Height Of Fashion in a private deal for £1.2 million in 1982. In time Height Of Fashion's worth would far exceed that sum. Although her sale was not driven by the profit motive, its consequences would irredeemably tarnish Carnarvon's royal tenure. Some maintain it was simply bad luck; others that the flame is one day bound to burn those who play with fire.

Height Of Fashion's example is not without parallel within the Royal Studs. The fate of one of Feola's daughters is documented earlier: ten-year-old Knight's Daughter was culled from the books in 1951. She fetched just

2,500 guineas at auction, after which she produced the great American champion, Round Table, for Claiborne Farm. It was a mistake the Royal Studs could contend with, since other daughters of Feola were making good her loss. Feola herself was still going strong. During her fertile life she would produce an embarrassment of female riches: eight fillies from ten live foals, of which three – Hypericum, Angelola and Above Board – won races of championship calibre. All three were quite properly retained by the Royal Studs.

Given the number of fillies Feola produced it was understandable the studs would sell on the less successful ones. It was impossible to keep them all with a ceiling on numbers, as there was at the Royal Studs. Knight's Daughter was among the first to go, yet even as she would reveal her hidden merits the collective breeding exploits of Hypericum, Angelola and Above Board left little reason to regret her sale. Above Board produced two talented colts in Above Suspicion and Doutelle; Angelola was dam of Aureole, who swept the board in 1954; while Hypericum's son Restoration finished runner-up in the Eclipse Stakes after winning the King Edward VII Stakes on his racecourse debut. This was top-of-the-range stuff, but there was one problem. All these superior runners were colts.

Although Feola was a gem of a broodmare, the realisation of it came too late. Knight's Daughter was among Feola's first three foals; all were fillies, all were sold off. It wasn't long before their collective influence came to bear. One of them, Foretaste, produced a grandson, Lassalle, who won the Ascot Gold Cup in 1973. And the other, Starling, bred three champion runners on her export to Argentina, where her son Sideral became one of that country's most potent stallions.

As for Knight's Daughter, she carried an unborn foal at the time of her sale that would shape the breed in her own right. Named Yarmouth, she became ancestress of the top-class runner Bemissed, herself dam of Jet Ski Lady, winner of the Oaks in 1991. Furthermore, Knight's Daughter left another notable legacy for Claiborne Farm through one more of her daughters, the aptly named Monarchy. She spawned a line responsible for two more recent Group One winners in Johannesburg and Minardi.

Simultaneously, over at the Royal Studs, the more glamorous trio of Feola's daughters were beginning to run aground. Angelola foaled one talented filly in Angel Bright who, despite winning the Oaks Trial at Lingfield, was sold on account of her ongoing unsoundness. Above Board never foaled a filly that would perpetuate her within the Royal Studs. Only Hypericum's line flourished, and then solely via one daughter: Highlight. Indeed, Highlight's daughter Highclere is the last Group One winner from Feola's family to race for the Queen – and that was back in 1974.

Angelola with her foal by Borealis just days before her three-year-old son, Aureole, would finish runner-up in the 1953 Derby.

Remarkably, however, Feola's descendants beyond the Royal Studs continue to thrive. By the close of 2011 the grand old royal matriarch's clan had thrown seventy individual winners of championship calibre in eleven countries around the world. No fewer than thirty-one were gained in South America, where Feola's influence is profound and where Hypericum's culled daughter Prescription made a huge impact in Chile. There have been others closer to home: household names like Pebbles and Nashwan, and in Japan, the phenomenal racehorse Deep Impact. The Queen has also had to digest the salty fact that a pair of recent Group One winners abroad, Right Approach and Kingdom Of Fife, raced initially in the royal livery before their sale to greater glories.

These, then, are the dastardly tricks Mother Nature can inflict on the undeserving. Feola was not far short of top class as a racehorse. In that, she earned the right to be bred to the best stallions. It made perfect sense to keep her talented daughters and discard the others. To do this is to work in harmony with principles that have guided breeders over hundreds of years. For breeders, the racecourse is the ultimate proving ground. It is where offspring born of years of thought and theory are put to the test. Racecourse performance is the tried and trusted platform on which long-standing breeding practice has been established – and with good reason. Yet none of this was any help where Feola was concerned. The mare who was nineteen years old when the Queen inherited her defied all convention. She would produce no more foals.

George VI would reap a small part of Feola's fabulous legacy. The Queen would reap another small part of it through Highclere. As it transpired, Highclere's daughter Height Of Fashion did follow convention. Highclere's best runner was also her best representative at stud, yet she was sold before her breeding merit could be explored. Height Of Fashion's sale was governed by circumstances other than the need to cull, as were so many of Feola's descendants. The proceeds from her sale were used to buy the Queen a racing stable, and towards that end a once-in-a-lifetime mare slipped through the Queen's fingers. Whatever the merits of it, and some of the fallout was incendiary, it is unreasonable to expect the Queen to unearth another mare of Height Of Fashion's calibre in her lifetime. In the years ahead a relative of Height Of Fashion might reignite the family's fortunes from surviving members within the Royal Studs, although it is too much to anticipate a firework party. As for the Queen, the only thing to say about this dispiriting sequence of events is that they were manifestly unwarranted. Justice was hard to divine, especially when Height Of Fashion's sale coincided with the start of another fallow period for the Royal Studs.

But then, the scales of justice have never applied to breeding racehorses. They are impotent in the face of nature's whims. Carnarvon's breeding interests thrived in spite of him selling on seemingly irreplaceable jewels. He somehow managed to make light of it. The Royal Studs, by contrast, sold inferior products which flourished in other hands. They always retained the best. On the one occasion they sold a jewel, as Height Of Fashion was, they would come to rue it.

Carnarvon's successful exploits with Highclere Stud made him the ideal sounding board for ways to improve the royal racing and breeding fortunes on Charles Moore's departure in 1962. He worked tirelessly behind the scenes, and from a low ebb they regained momentum towards the end of the decade. Several important changes were made. Some had an instant effect; others took much longer to percolate. The lease at Polhampton and the Queen's new training arrangements were easy enough to implement. Overhauling the Royal Studs was a more time-consuming process. Care was required to take long-established bloodlines down different paths for fear of losing their essence altogether. Nevertheless, the time for a new approach was nigh, and in 1964 the Queen sent her first mare to America – Near Miss – to be bred to the iconic racehorse Native Dancer. Others would follow on an annual basis as the Queen sought a fusion of blood from two continents that was shaping the contemporary racehorse.

Over the years more and more of the Queen's mares were dispatched to Kentucky. Indeed, by 1989, the royal crop harboured six foals by American-based stallions as opposed to eleven by sires in Europe. Contrarily, however, the move yielded little by way of racecourse success. Early results were sufficiently encouraging for the extension of a policy that was largely dictated by unrest in Ireland, yet despite using some of the best stallions in America over more than two decades, the Queen never bred a headline horse by them. The green shoots of recovery would sprout much closer to home.

The outcome of the American venture remains baffling to this day. Nor could the explanation rest with the quality of mares stationed in Kentucky. Some of the best made the journey, to no avail. 'We would leave the mares out there for three or four years at a time and bring back their weaned foals every year,' recalled Sir Michael Oswald, who managed the Royal Studs at that time. 'Looking back on it now, I think we should have brought the young horses back when they were yearlings, not foals. In Kentucky there is a much bigger contrast between winter and summer. Winters are very cold and dry, and summers very hot. If I could do it all over again I'd have left the foals in Kentucky for another year until they were ready to be broken and put into training. I think it would have suited them better.'

It was on Sir Michael's appointment as manager of the Royal Studs in 1970 that the pace of change accelerated. He joined a triumvirate completed by Carnarvon and the Queen that would decide how the royal mares were mated. In his first year at the helm no fewer than five mares were sent to stallions from the Phalaris line which Moore had been so anxious to avoid. Bred by Lord Derby, Phalaris was for the most part a product of bloodlines developed at Hampton Court in Queen Victoria's time. He was an extremely influential stallion whose descendants were not short of speed. No contemporary stud could afford to ignore his line completely. The Queen herself amplified the change in philosophy during her filmed conversation with Sir Peter O'Sullevan in 1974. 'The emphasis was on staying blood and recently I've been trying to inject a bit more speed,' she said.

Among the mares mated to a faster type of stallion in 1970 was Highlight. She was sent to Carnarvon's resident stallion at Highclere, Queen's Hussar, who forged his racing reputation over a mile. From their tryst came Highclere.

The union of Highlight and Queen's Hussar brought further evidence of a shift in thinking at the Royal Studs. The Queen herself advocated the mating in her desire to bring into play what breeding theorists call 'hybrid vigour'. In simple terms hybrid vigour is diametrically opposed to the concept of inbreeding which Moore strongly advocated. Hybrid vigour is achieved by mating a mare from a virile male line with a stallion from another. It represents the fusion of two dominant lines, rather than the duplication of a single line common to both the mare and the stallion. The Queen plainly wanted to explore the theory, since Highlight was again sent to Queen's Hussar the following year. And when Highclere started catching the eye as a yearling towards the end of 1972, Highlight revisited Queen's Hussar in 1973 and 1974.

Highclere proved much the best of her mother Highlight's four matings to Queen's Hussar. No one can explain why that was. The four were siblings in blood, after all, but then, so are many human brothers of diverse athletic ability. Any dip into the gene pool will always retain the element of chance, no matter how plausible the explanations that may follow. Everything else is no more than theory.

Great racehorses sometimes result from the most implausible thinking. In 1901 Cavaliere Edoardo Ginistrelli, an Italian owner/breeder based in Newmarket, noticed that every time his acclaimed mare Signorina walked past a male horse in a nearby stable the two would exchange equine pleasantries. Inquiries about his mare's potential suitor revealed he went by the name of Chaleureux. He was of such low standing that he was used as a 'teaser' on mares believed to be in season, and therefore ripe for mating. The teaser's lot is a rum one. He risks being kicked if the mare is unreceptive, yet when she 'shows' she is immediately whisked off to a more glamorous mate. Ginistrelli was undeterred by Chaleureux's humble status. In declaring his mare and the humble teaser to be in love, he sanctioned their union, to loud hoots of derision. The outcome was Signorinetta, winner of both the Oaks and the Derby in 1908. A semblance of sanity was restored at Epsom the following year when Minoru, running for Edward VII, returned the Derby to its blue-blooded heritage. All the same, the lesson of Signorinetta speaks for itself.

The Royal Studs' inclination towards sires with more speed continued in 1971, when seven royal mares visited stallions which excelled over distances of one mile or less. Again, the effect was tangible. By 1976 the Queen had a pair of fast two-year-olds in Card Player and Fife And Drum. They came in sharp contrast to the late-maturing Thoroughbreds favoured by Moore. In the broodmare bands of most successful studs are a broad mix of inmates: some of them fast runners, others proven over middle distances. Great store is set by maintaining the balance, especially when stamina starts to gain the upper hand. In part, this is a consequence of the growing prestige of races run over a mile or less, although many breeders aver that the pure middle-distance galloper of the 1970s would struggle to contend in such races today. The thought is eminently plausible, since contemporary Derby winners are rarely devoid of finishing speed.

The use of faster stallions thus provided the platform for the Royal Studs' regeneration. The Queen and her two advisors were a team to rival the expertise of any stud in the country, although their thoughts did not immediately gel. The story goes that in the early 1960s Carnarvon handed the Queen a detailed written assessment of her studs, together with a breeding blueprint for the future. Her Majesty, none too impressed at first, subsequently came to see the merit in some of its suggestions. As she alluded to Sir Peter O'Sullevan in their filmed conversation, there was considerable debate over the best way forward. Sir Michael Oswald engaged in the debate from 1970, bringing to it knowledge gained from his stewardship of Egerton Stud, where Persimmon, Diamond Jubilee and Minoru had been trained by Richard Marsh for Edward VII.

Egerton was a flourishing nursery during Sir Michael's tenure as manager. Bought in 1941 by Lady Macdonald-Buchanan, who inherited a sizeable bloodstock portfolio from her father Lord Woolavington, Egerton was home to some important stallions. Among them were Owen Tudor, winner of the wartime Derby in 1942 and the Gold Cup at Ascot the following year, and his remarkable son Abernant, whom Sir Gordon Richards described as the fastest horse he ever rode. It was Noel Murless who recommended Sir Michael to fill a vacancy at Egerton in 1962. 'He said to me that if I was as mad about the business as I sounded I should join Egerton,' Sir Michael reflected. 'He told me it was run by a dear old general who didn't know what was going on any more, but it had the best stud groom in Europe. He was right on both counts.'

Sir Michael recalls his time at Egerton with affection. Conversely, the year he spent in a merchant bank on leaving the Army was eminently forgettable. 'It was the most boring thing I've ever done,' he lamented. 'The only excitement came when you paid an awful lot of money to the wrong person and then had to unravel it. I kept asking how I could get into racing and was told there was no money in it, and very few gentlemen within it. The first part was right and the second wrong.'

The vacancy at Egerton thus came as a godsend, even though Sir Michael and his wife Lady Angela lived in a bitterly cold house within the grounds. They survived on optimism and a deal of good humour. 'The stud groom once rang at two in the morning so I could go and watch a foal being born,' Sir Michael said. 'The phone was on my wife's side of the bed and when she answered it the stud groom inquired: "Lady Angela?" And she replied: "Well, who else did you expect to find in my husband's bed at this time of the night?" We had some wonderful times there.'

Sir Michael's love of racing led to his first encounter with Lady Angela. It might well have been the last but for his split-second decision to resist an impulse propelling him at high speed towards the Royal Ascot grandstand. Having arrived late, he was running with Thoroughbred zest to catch the opening race when he came to an abrupt halt to avoid cutting across a mother-and-daughter combination at a bottleneck – even though he had first run. Two weeks later the mother, suitably impressed by the man's gallantry, invited him to a dinner party and sat him next to her daughter. Sir Michael and Lady Angela were soon engaged.

On the Thoroughbred front, the wisdom of decisions made by Sir Michael as part of the Royal Studs' triumvirate could not be assessed until the produce of those matings reached racing maturity four years down the line. This wait was rendered all the more anxious for the lack of racecourse success posted by the royal horses in training. From the dismal racing returns of the 1960 season it became clear that the royal broodmares started losing their vibrancy in the late 1950s. Conversely, and in keeping with the contrary nature of the game, Aureole ended 1960 as champion sire.

The stud at Sandringham is divided by a public road. On one side of it the Queen might have cast a frustrated eye at a tribe of mares falling short of expectations; on the other she could gaze in wonder at Aureole, her beloved racehorse who was proving a stallion of considerable repute. In 1960 he was represented by Derby and St Leger winner St Paddy in addition to Vienna, subsequently sire of Vaguely Noble. He would be

Champion Sire again in 1961, when gains posted by St Paddy and Vienna were augmented by Aurelius, who won the St Leger. For all that, none of them carried the royal silks.

The Queen regularly visited Aureole in his paddock, where she enjoyed feeding him mints. Proud as she was of his stallion deeds, she must have quietly implored him to do some good for her personally. This strapping horse, who'd fought tooth and nail to repel Vamos at Ascot in 1954, was withholding his genetic prowess from the royal brood. He would not bestow upon the Queen the Group One winners he bequeathed to others. More than that, Aureole would not sire a talented filly for the Queen to breed from even though he was used on royal mares every year. It must have been exasperating. In the circumstances the Queen was entitled to feel as affronted as was Daniel Wildenstein at the thought of losing Allez France's precious blood from his studs. Except that the Queen is not prone to outbursts. She accepts what comes her way. Even so, there is nothing more tantalising than to be within touching distance of a cherished ambition. Aureole had sired a Derby winner for someone else; why not her? Failing that, why not a single decent filly for the Queen to breed from? Ah, those eternal questions once more. So close, and yet...

As it was, the royal racing drought persisted for much of the 1960s. The decade started well enough in 1961, when Aiming High's Coronation Stakes triumph allowed the royal party to visit Royal Ascot's winner's enclosure for the eighth time in nine years. Aiming High was decidedly talented yet prone to injury, but for which Noel Murless felt she would have achieved as much as Carrozza. But Aiming High, like all the royal horses with Murless, was leased from the National Stud and would return there, rather than to Sandringham, at the end of her racing days.

Seven years would pass before the Queen had her next winner at Royal Ascot. It was gained by Hopeful Venture in the Hardwicke Stakes, although he was another graduate of the National Stud. During this period the Royal Studs' own drought at Royal Ascot would stretch from the double posted by Pindari and Above Suspicion in 1959 to Magna Carta's victory in the 1970 Ascot Stakes. Royal winners at the royal racecourse, once very much on tap, had run dry.

Magna Carta's victory marked a first royal winner at the venue for Ian Balding. He'd succeeded Peter Hastings-Bass at Park House stables on the latter's death in 1964. The news came as a shock: cancer struck Hastings-Bass down at the tender age of 43, when he was poised for a rewarding career from a stable steeped in history. Kingsclere was where John Porter trained for Edward VII, then Prince of Wales, a century earlier. It was subsequently home to a succession of able trainers, although none could match Porter's haul of seven Derby winners. In the royal shift away from Newmarket, Hastings-Bass received his first batch of yearlings in the autumn of 1963. Balding was simultaneously approached to join Hastings-Bass as his assistant.

The offer placed Balding on the horns of a dilemma. Any disinclination was prompted by his amateur riding career, which was then in full cry. It was something he cherished beyond his other sporting pursuits – and there were several, among them rugby, for which he'd earned a blue at Cambridge. There was also the difficult matter of his own family circumstances: his father had recently died and his brother Toby had been thrust into the family training breach in his early twenties. Balding, then twenty-four, accepted the position with reservations, although he had a more daunting decision to make when Hastings-Bass died less than three months later. Taking over at Park House would end Balding's riding career and might easily alienate his mother. He was in a quandary even though the opportunity of a lifetime stared him full in the face.

Over this, Prince Philip rode to the rescue – albeit with no carriage behind his horse. For Goodwood week in 1964, Balding was asked with Hastings-Bass's widow, Priscilla, to stay with the Duke and Duchess of Norfolk at Arundel Castle, where it so happened that the Queen and her husband were also staying. Balding thought it a good opportunity for an introduction to an owner he had yet to meet, and for whom he trained six two-year-olds. But there was an agenda unbeknown to him. After supper one evening Prince Philip took him aside to say he knew of Balding's predicament. 'He then said something that made a difference,' Balding recalled. 'He told me that if all our bright young men were to turn down such a wonderful opportunity our country would be much the worst for it. I probably realised then that riding was not the be-all and end-all.'

The Queen with trainer Dick Hern and jockey Joe Mercer after St Patrick's Blue's victory at Ascot, July 1968.

Quite the opposite, as things turned out. Balding's decision to take over from Hastings-Bass proved the springboard for a life more rewarding then he could have imagined. He became engaged to the late trainer's daughter Emma in 1969. He would have by her two children, Clare and Andrew, both of whom are significant career achievers: the former in broadcasting, the latter as resident trainer at Park House, which houses royal racehorses to this day. He would be able to indulge his twin passions of hunting and polo, the latter at which his father captained England, within the Kingsclere estate that became his family home. He would train some big-race winners for the Queen, who provided his young children with their first riding pony. And he would train one of the finest post-war racehorses in Mill Reef, who would become Europe's pre-eminent stallion after winning the Derby in 1971, when Balding was champion trainer.

The chances are that none of this would have come Balding's way had he forsaken the opportunity to prolong an amateur riding career that would invariably have ended with him being stretchered away from a racecourse with badly broken bones. It makes no sense at all to think about Balding's options in this way, yet for him to have even contemplated it illustrates the addictive lure of race-riding. It may also help to explain why the Queen, for whom breeding horses is the favoured angle, is similarly passionate about her own equine calling. The joy horses bring is indescribable for the inability of words to convey it. Perhaps Lord Mildmay, the Corinthian amateur rider and avid story-teller, came closest to portraying its essence. It was he who charmed the Queen Mother into buying Monaveen, the horse she shared with Princess Elizabeth, by regaling her with tales from the saddle at a dinner thrown by George VI to celebrate Avila's victory at Royal Ascot in 1949.

Balding enjoyed a fruitful first season with the royal horses in 1964. He sent out ten winners, somewhat to the chagrin of Boyd-Rochfort in Newmarket, who wasn't accustomed to sharing the royal string with anyone else. After another moderate season he was doubtless casting beady eyes in Balding's direction. In frustration at his dwindling returns he was beginning to think he was no longer being sent the best of the yearlings. So much so that he asked of the Queen, a little too directly for her liking, how decisions on the yearling allocation were made. Boyd-Rochfort had become a bad workman, blaming his tools for shortcomings resulting from nothing more sinister than his advancing age. And when Dick Hern trained a small complement of royal horses for the first time in 1967, the implications for Boyd-Rochfort were impossible to ignore. He retired the following year.

Between them, Balding and Hern wrote the next instalment in the Queen's racing fortunes. With royal winners scarce as the decade drew to a close, they might have wondered whether the raw material in their hands was sufficiently good for purpose. They need not have worried. After years of frugal pickings, the Royal Studs were about to turn their own page. The new decade opened as it would carry on, with Magna Carta's Ascot Stakes triumph commemorating the Queen's first win at the royal meeting for eleven years. It was a portent of things to come.

7

TWIN PEAKS:
HIGHCLERE AND
DUNFERMLINE

Previous spread: Just after the start of the
1977 St Leger. Dunfermline and Willie
Carson on the right, Alleged and Lester
Piggott to their outside.

Dick Hern was not someone to trifle with. The son of an Army Captain, he was born and bred to serve in the Forces before making a career from horses. He grew up at a time when such things were almost preordained at birth. Commissioned into the North Irish Horse in 1939, he saw active service in north Africa and later Italy, where he whiled away the days before his recall to Britain by organising a series of race meetings at Ravenna, on the north-west coast. The runners were spoils of war, the riders anyone who fancied a spin at high speed. He was abetted in Ravenna by another major, Michael Pope, who would become one of his closest friends. Throughout his second career Hern's militaristic inclinations saw him known to all and sundry as 'the Major' – just as his royal forerunner in the training ranks Cecil Boyd-Rochfort was universally known as 'the Captain'.

There was little to do with horses that Hern hadn't encountered. In his youth he hunted prolifically with most of the Somerset packs. On leaving the Army he became a qualified riding instructor of such repute that he was appointed chief instructor and coach to Britain's three-day event team that returned from the 1952 Olympics in Helsinki with the gold medal. He would certainly have ridden on the team himself had he not been adjudged a professional horseman.

A career in racing came later to Hern than most others with the calling. He was thirty-one when he joined Pope as assistant, and thirty-six when he successfully applied for the vacancy as private trainer to Major Lionel Holliday in 1957. It was a risky move for Hern, since Holliday, an uncompromising Yorkshireman, had worked his way through thirteen trainers in almost as many years. He complained bitterly that many who arrived on bicycles would depart in Rolls-Royces.

Hern was almost certainly the only one to leave Holliday on his own terms. By 1962 he'd trained Hethersett to win the St Leger en route to the first of four trainers' titles. Over five seasons he gave Holliday more success than he had previously known. Many thought Hethersett unfortunate not to win the Derby when he was brought down in a seven-horse pile-up. Holliday was immensely proud of the achievements of his studs at Copgrove Hall and Cleaboy, in Ireland, although he wouldn't live to see Vaguely Noble, the best horse he bred, cut a swathe through the 1968 season.

Hern was on the move soon after Hethersett's St Leger victory. He accepted an offer to train from the Astor family's West Ilsley stables in

From left: Dick Hern, Willie Carson, the Queen Mother, the Queen and Lord Porchester, Sandown Park, 1978.

Berkshire, where his achievements quickly caught the royal eye. He first yearlings from the Royal Studs arrived in 1966, although to his lament, there wasn't a good one among them. His time would come. Together with Ian Balding, he was in the new vanguard of trainers that would overthrow the generation headed by Noel Murless. His prowess was such that the Queen was far from the only prominent owner/breeder to throw her hat in with Hern.

Hern and Balding were thus in competition for the best of the royal horses. It was a good-natured, professional rivalry that extended beyond the Queen's patronage. In the race preceding Magna Carta's Royal Ascot triumph in 1970, Balding saddled a colt he held in the highest regard for the Coventry Stakes. Mill Reef did not disappoint. He moved on from a six-length victory to dominate the two-year-old canvas. He followed a narrow defeat to My Swallow after an arduous journey to France by winning the prestigious Gimcrack Stakes by ten lengths and the Dewhurst Stakes by four. In essence, he was a champion two-year-old with the world at his feet.

Meanwhile, over at West Ilsley, Hern took the low road with Mill Reef's contemporary, Brigadier Gerard. Despite winning each of his four starts as a two-year-old, culminating with the Middle Park Stakes, Brigadier Gerard did not capture public imagination in the same way as Mill Reef. As a result few enthusiasts entertained his chance when he lined up alongside Mill Reef and My Swallow for one of the most keenly anticipated renewals of the Two Thousand Guineas in 1971.

Collectively, the three colts had won eighteen of their nineteen starts, the sole loss arising when My Swallow beat Mill Reef in France the previous year. Something had to give – and it wasn't Brigadier Gerard's unbeaten record. Hern brought him into the Classic directly from the winter recess, without a preparatory race, yet the colt showed a clean pair of heels to Mill Reef and My Swallow, who came home in that order. Even his most devoted admirers could not have envisaged a winning distance of three lengths. It was scarcely credible.

From that point Brigadier Gerard and Mill Reef went their separate ways. Mill Reef stepped up from a mile to compile a fabulous winning sequence in the Derby, Eclipse, King George VI and Queen Elizabeth

Stakes and Prix de l'Arc de Triomphe, while Brigadier Gerard campaigned over a mile to win the St James's Palace Stakes, Sussex Stakes, Goodwood Mile and Queen Elizabeth II Stakes. He won the last three of those races by an aggregate of twenty-three lengths, after which Hern saddled him to one more victory in the Champion Stakes over one and a quarter miles. It is extremely rare for two horses of such merit to be foaled in the same year. By their flawless achievements they conferred great credit on their respective trainers.

Both colts stayed in training the following season, although their paths never crossed. After winning twice from as many starts Mill Reef succumbed to sickness in the summer. He then suffered multiple fractures to a foreleg and was saved only by pioneering surgery. After a long and complicated convalescence he recovered to sire two Derby winners in Reference Point and before him Shirley Heights. Brigadier Gerard, by contrast, pressed on to championship honours. In all he won seventeen of his eighteen starts, his sole reverse coming at Roberto's hands in the 1972 Benson and Hedges Gold Cup at York.

Just as they had with Brigadier Gerard and Mill Reef, Hern and Balding jousted for early supremacy with the royal horses. Balding had the better of it in 1971, when Example's deeds just outweighed those of the Hern-trained Albany. Lester Piggott developed a fine rapport with Example, who flourished in the autumn to win two significant races. One was gained in France, where the royal silks had been increasingly seen since the Queen's private visit four years earlier – and to where Example returned to win again in 1972.

Albany was an altogether different proposition: she won at Newbury on an afternoon in May after the Queen had seen her exercise at West Ilsley in the morning. Albany wasn't quite up to contesting the finish to the Oaks, although after a respectable fifth place she too was sent to France to win a race of merit.

Example and Albany fuelled belief that the Royal Studs were in productive mode once more. Their racecourse achievements made them guaranteed additions to the broodmare band, since each was of a type to throw superior runners. Albany in particular seemed blessed by the right credentials. She was by the Queen's Classic winner Pall Mall out of her Group One winner Almeria. Among her early foals were two talented runners in Card Player and English Harbour, yet just when expectations rose they would taper away.

Two decades later a solitary daughter of Albany roamed the royal paddocks. It would not be long before there were none at all. As for Example, it was indicative of her potential that she was sent to the court of the mighty Nijinsky, in Kentucky, for her maiden covering. She returned to Sandringham safely pregnant, yet in the act of giving birth the foal inside her inadvertently thrust a leg through her colonic wall, rupturing it beyond repair. It was a shocking loss, and one felt more profoundly for the fact that Stroma, bought on the Queen's instructions at Doncaster sales in 1956, had also perished to the same freakish accident.

Two more royal fillies – one trained by Hern, the other by Balding – would come to the fore in 1973. The previous autumn Hern was preoccupied with closing Brigadier Gerard's career on a winning note. The colt's swansong came in the Champion Stakes, a race he'd won twelve months previously and would win for the second time. With that mission accomplished, Hern turned his attention to the annual intake of yearlings. The choice of 'doing' the new recruits is usually determined by stable staff in order of status and seniority. Senior staff always look for yearlings with obvious potential on pedigree and physical appearance – or in some cases, because the yearling belonged to an owner known to tip generously on stable visits, irrespective of the horse's merit. When this process was complete at Hern's stables in the autumn of 1972, a big bay filly was left with no takers.

It was hardly surprising, since she was particularly highly strung. She had no preference for biting or kicking but a predilection for both. No stable-hand would willingly volunteer to be confronted by her at the break of every day. She was named after the place where she was born: Highclere, the stud where her mother Highlight had foaled her ahead of a repeat covering by the resident stallion Queen's Hussar. It must have pleased Lord Carnarvon, although there is no record of his early take on a filly who seemed to want to maim anyone in her vicinity.

Over at Park House, Escorial was being equally antisocial to Balding's staff. She was placid enough in her box but would lash out with her hind legs when she was out at morning exercise. Escorial was from the Avila family of Albany. Given Hern's recent success with the latter it was surprising Escorial had been sent to Balding, since trainers who excel with a horse from one family tend to receive other members of it. Perhaps it was beyond the call of duty for one man to end up with a troublesome brace like Highclere and Escorial, although as it turned out, their early prowess on the gallops was such that both trainers were delighted with what they had.

Hern resolved the question of who should 'do' Highclere when the filly was adopted by the only stable-lass in his yard. She was made over to Betty Brister, whom the Queen would recognise on her first visit to Richard Hannon's stable twenty-five years later. Brister made light of Highclere's foibles but all who worked at the yard readily attested to the groom's patience. Without her guiding hand Highclere might easily have become unmanageable.

Racing wisdom holds that a difficult filly is much harder to handle then a difficult colt. There is no doubting its veracity. An unruly colt is usually just that: no more than a boisterous adolescent with no inherent vices. Conversely, some fillies are plain nasty. Once so disposed, their lighter side is virtually impossible to retrieve within the short time span of their racing careers. Only when they retire to the paddocks will they shed inhibitions often implanted in them by a bad formative experience. It was largely thanks to Brister's patience that Highclere never trawled the depths of her darker side.

Besides, high-mettled aggression, properly channelled, is no bad thing in a racehorse. Better that than one who wilts when battle is joined in earnest. Highclere was certainly no quitter, as she showed on her racecourse debut at Newmarket. She was engaged by Polygamy, who'd had the benefit of a previous run, and fought hard before she was obliged to yield narrowly. Of the hundreds of races for non-winners at starting, it was extraordinary that Highclere should run into Polygamy, who would become a formidable racecourse rival. The pair clashed again the following month, when Highclere had Polygamy behind her but could not get to an inherently faster filly over six furlongs at Ascot. Nevertheless, it was another encouraging run from Highclere, who was on her way to vindicating Hern's high opinion of her.

Hern's confidence then took a knock. After a hard race in strong company, Highclere's sights were lowered in anticipation of a facile victory that would raise her morale. In the event, her victory at Newbury was less than bloodless. More visually impressive was Escorial, who had made a striking debut in a similar race half an hour earlier. On that basis Escorial's future looked gilt-edged. Given the pick of the pair, any impartial observer would have taken Escorial over Highclere. Hern was neither impartial nor impressed; likewise Joe Mercer, who rode Highclere to victory. Only Carnarvon, perhaps emboldened by the inspiration for her name, resolutely kept the faith.

Conversely, Balding would not have swapped Escorial for anything – especially when she followed up in stronger company at Ascot with an ease that made Lester Piggott describe her in glowing terms. Escorial was now a prime Oaks candidate, while Highclere's claims on the One Thousand Guineas were less secure. Carnarvon, however, had plans for Highclere. After her Newbury victory he suggested Highclere should return to his stud for a short break from the stable routine at West Ilsley. He also felt the filly would gain from the fitting of blinkers that had worked wonders for her sire Queen's Hussar – whose traits Carnarvon, as his breeder, knew only too well.

Suitably becalmed after her break, Highclere started to regain Hern's faith in the One Thousand Guineas build-up. He tried her in blinkers at home and was suitably encouraged to fit them for the race itself. She came forward with every piece of work so that, come One Thousand Guineas day, the only one despondent about Highclere's chance was Joe Mercer. Not that anyone would have known it, since Mercer rode Highclere with the utmost conviction. He sent her to the front two furlongs from the finish, just ahead of the steady climb to the winning post at Newmarket. Highclere's raking stride seemed as if it must sweep her to victory, yet Polygamy – who else? – suddenly found her best stride. She gained on Highclere hand over fist: would the winning post come in time for the royal runner?

There was simply no telling when the pair flashed past the post in unison. There followed a long, tense wait while the judge deliberated. There was pessimism in the stewards' room, where the Queen watched

With groom Betty Brister after Highclere's
One Thousand Guineas victory, 1974.

the race in company with Hern, Carnarvon and Sir Michael Oswald. To them it appeared that Polygamy's late thrust had just snatched the spoils. A sense of foreboding was palpable – which meant that joy rose up from the pit of despondency when the judge proclaimed for Highclere. She had it by a short head: the identical margin by which Carrozza had won the Oaks seventeen years before.

It was an epic struggle in which Highclere's fighting spirit made the difference, yet there was more to celebrate than victory alone. The Queen had won two previous Classics but this was the first without an accompanying caveat. Pall Mall's Two Thousand Guineas triumph, which the Queen missed through illness, was tempered by the fact that the colt's entire family had been culled from the Royal Studs. As for Carrozza, she was obliged to return to the National Stud after her triumph at Epsom.

Highclere was different. She would one day return to Sandringham, where the idea of her very existence was originally conceived. In the moment of victory an emotional maelstrom coursed through the Queen, who subsequently expressed it in a letter sent to Mercer. 'For once I don't remember much about the race owing to the excitement,' she wrote, 'but I do know that a homebred Guineas winner has given me more pleasure than anything for a long time.'

Here, finally, was apposite reward for decades of perseverance. It was a rare triumph for hope over despair, enriched all the more by the memory of so many previous failures. And it was all down to Highclere. The yearling filly with no early admirers among the staff at West Ilsley was now the belle of them all.

After the race the Queen was a bastion of reason in the face of an exultant press corps. She suggested that Epsom's gradients would not suit Highclere, who would bypass the Oaks in favour of the French equivalent, the Prix de Diane. Besides, the Queen was hoping to be represented in the Oaks by Escorial, whose seasonal reappearance beckoned. But the long winter wait for Escorial ended in anguish when she flopped under Balding's stable jockey Philip Waldron at Newmarket.

Disappointing though it was for Escorial to finish a well-beaten third, her antics raised further questions. She ran away from Waldron's whip, in the process making plain her intolerance of her jockey's demands for greater effort. She was difficult at home but had never previously transferred her quirks to the racecourse. There were evidently two sides to her: this was a very different Escorial from the one Piggott had extolled on riding her to victory at Ascot seven months earlier. With the Oaks on the horizon, perhaps the solution was to reunite her with Piggott, whose understanding of horses was instinctive. Piggott could never express this talent in words but it always rose up from his silent depths whenever he rode a racehorse.

So he was duly summoned when Balding sent Escorial to York in a bid to redeem her reputation. Balding took no chances: he arranged for Escorial to be ridden over from the racecourse stables, across the open expanse of the Knavesmire, with another man on the ground to lead her. In the blink of an eye, however, Escorial shed the pair of them before she cantered nonchalantly back to the racecourse stables. She was up to mischief once more.

Curiously, Escorial's antics were as unfit for a queen as they would be impossible to fault when she was eventually saddled for the race. In the course of it she advanced from the rear, with Piggott sitting motionless, to win as she pleased from Lauretta – who'd beaten her easily on their Newmarket encounter two weeks earlier. The contrast was extreme, although no sooner had Piggott dismounted than he was booked to ride Escorial in the Oaks.

Having raised expectations once more, Escorial proceeded to dash them by running abjectly at Epsom. She reduced Piggott to the status of a helpless passenger as she singularly failed to improve from her position in the rear. Up ahead of her, Polygamy capitalised on Dibidale's slipping saddle to gain handsome compensation for her narrow One Thousand Guineas defeat by Highclere. Escorial, for her part, was in disgrace.

Escorial never again showed her better side on the racecourse. Unlike Highclere, she channelled her nervous energy in the wrong direction. The Queen's own take on Escorial was perfectly accurate, as she explained to Sir Peter O'Sullevan in their filmed conversation some months later. 'We had very high hopes of Escorial in the spring … but she became wayward, swishing her tail and bucking. She was perfectly genuine when I saw her win at York, but maybe Piggott kidded her into doing it – and kidded us too.'

Temperament is an important element within the breeding calculation. Some breeders heed it less than a horse's conformation, its bloodlines, its soundness, or racing prowess. Each to their own, although racehorses have become highly bred animals in the quest to optimise their speed. They are extraordinarily graceful creatures, yet entirely man-made. It is up to man how far he dares to stretch already-taut boundaries to the very limit. Yet just as unsoundness can compromise a breeder's efforts, so too can issues of temperament. One small infusion of blood with a propensity to transmit temperament can overload the equation. Sometimes it works wonders; at others it is the drop that causes the swollen dam to breach. And of course, the way the equation is resolved is entirely down to Mother Nature. If she cursed Escorial, she chose to smile on Highclere.

Above: The Prix de Diane at Chantilly, 1974: Highclere (Joe Mercer) cruises home from Comtesse de Loir … and (opposite) receives an appreciative pat from her owner.

Part of the Queen's reasoning in sending Highclere to France after the One Thousand Guineas was that the Prix de Diane is run over an extended mile and a quarter. The step up in distance, from one mile at Newmarket, would not be as pronounced as it would be for the Oaks, which is run over one and a half miles. Since Highclere's sire Queen's Hussar had excelled over a mile, it amounted to a happy compromise – although Highclere's victory was so comprehensive she would have gained it over any distance.

Events on Prix de Diane day will never dim in the minds of those centrally involved. Highclere's itinerary went without a hitch, which is rare indeed when a horse travels beyond its country of residence. The only snag came when the taxi taking the Queen's entourage to Chantilly racecourse was caught up in traffic which, the driver informed his cargo, was down to the royal visit. When told that they were, in fact, the Queen's men, the driver charged down the hard shoulder with an abandon familiar to anyone who has ever ridden in the back of a Parisian taxi.

Everything else was just so from the moment Highclere boarded a flight that would whisk her over to France without turning a hair – which was no certainty, given her disposition. And in the race itself a passage opened up for Joe Mercer that was every bit as inviting as the one by which he had just reached the racecourse. Highclere entered the home straight on the tail of the leader, Hippodamia, whose efforts to hold her advantage were laboured. As Hippodamia toiled she veered away from the inside rail, where Highclere was waiting to pounce. One second Highclere was in danger of hitting racing traffic, the next she was into the clear and bounding away to a famous victory.

At two lengths, Highclere's winning margin over Comtesse de Loir brooked no argument. There was no need to call on the judge, as there had been at Newmarket. Indeed, Highclere was so emphatically superior to the opposition that the Queen's entourage spent much of the final furlong dancing a victory jig. 'It was absolutely not the way to behave in Her Majesty's company,' Sir Michael Oswald reflected with a smile many years later. Yet the royal party was not alone. The huge crowd at Chantilly rose as one to acclaim Highclere's victory, in the process triggering scenes of disorganised pandemonium.

If the local gendarmes felt victory for the Queen would afford them a quiet afternoon, they were quite mistaken. The winner's enclosure was quickly swamped by ecstatic turfistes. For a while there was a danger the Queen might be caught in the crush – as was Sir Peter O'Sullevan, at Chantilly on duty of his own. 'Porchey saw me in the crowd and waved me towards him,' Sir Peter recalled, 'but as I stepped forward someone trod on my heel and dislodged my shoe. So there I was, congratulating the Queen in one shoe and one stockinged foot. Happily there was no big toe poking out of it, because she of all people would have noticed it.'

At least Sir Peter hadn't shed a critical part of his attire in the royal presence. That fate so nearly befell Charles Engelhard when the Derby triumph of his Nijinsky in 1970 earned him a post-race audience with the Queen. As Engelhard climbed the steps to the royal box, the braces holding up his trousers suddenly snapped. He thus entered the fray with his arms clamping his top hat and binocular case to either side of his waist. By all accounts the Queen Mother's face was a picture when Engelhard abruptly declined her offer to take the accessories from him in the interests of comfort.

Over at Chantilly, the gendarmes finally prevailed in their efforts to contain the exuberance. It was still a scrum: even Alec Head, who in normal circumstances walks a metaphorical royal carpet on French racecourses, was grid-locked out of the winner's circle. 'I have not seen anything like it; the crowd went berserk,' Head recalled. 'It was one of the very great days, and it showed that racing is an international language, with no barriers.'

It was something the Queen herself will not forget in a hurry – right down to the encroaching, euphoric well-wishers. Later that year, in her filmed conversation with Sir Peter O'Sullevan, she said: 'I had never been racing in France when I had a horse running, and it was a lovely outing for me being there. The President [of France] was of course very kind and made it very easy for me to get to Chantilly. The crowd was tremendously friendly and after the race, when Highclere had won, they seemed even more friendly – luckily.'

There was also a fascinating role reversal between the Queen, who was there in a private capacity, and Marcel Boussac, the doyen of French breeders who hosted the Queen's visit. Although Boussac often wore a stern expression there were moments on that day when his face betrayed the excessive strain as his country's designated representative. The Queen, by contrast, exuded joie de vivre. The boot was on the other foot: it was Boussac who bore the facade of concentration redolent of the Queen at official functions. Photographers keen to capture the full-blooded royal smile had ample opportunity in the long interval between Highclere surging to victory and the trophy presentation in Boussac's box. 'I think it was one of the happiest racing days of the Queen's life because she received such a welcome,' Sir Peter averred. 'Usually, everything seems to get coated in dullness if royalty is involved. The cordon sanitaire goes up.'

Highclere's victory also highlighted a royal penchant for spontaneity. On the plane home, as spirits rose on the depletion of in-flight champagne stocks, the royal horsemen received an invitation via the cockpit radio. A car would be waiting at the airport to sweep them straight to Windsor Castle for an impromptu dinner celebration. With no time to change, Hern and Mercer were in their jeans as they toasted Highclere's victory later that night. It was clear the Queen did not want a magical day to end.

Highclere was now at the peak of her powers. Mercer rated her victory in France superior to her One Thousand Guineas defeat of Polygamy, who'd won the Oaks eight days before Highclere's triumph at Chantilly. Highclere was now among the best fillies of her generation, if not the best, and in these circumstances the adventurous way forward is to confront older horses of both sexes in the King George VI and Queen Elizabeth Stakes at Ascot. It had the makings of a tough assignment for a filly on only the sixth start of her career, and so it proved.

A feature of Highclere's sterling victories at Newmarket and Chantilly was that she raced prominently on both occasions. She seemed happy to stalk the leaders before seizing the baton from them. Perhaps the strength of the opposition at Ascot inhibited her natural style, for she was anchored in midfield when the field rounded the bend ahead of Ascot's relatively short home straight. Perhaps Mercer wanted to conserve Highclere's energy on her first attempt at racing over one and a half miles. Either way, she had ground to make up as she negotiated the turn in the immediate wake of Dahlia, aboard whom Lester Piggott oozed confidence.

Dahlia was at her destructive best, as she had been twelve months earlier in winning the King George by six lengths. She was in imperious form here, too, as she glided into the lead 200 yards from the finish. To her credit, Highclere never gave up the chase. Dahlia was simply too strong, yet Highclere ran past one horse after another to beat all except the illustrious French racemare. It required a huge effort to carry her that close, and the strain took its toll. In two subsequent starts Highclere never showed her previous zest.

It is not uncommon for the spirit of a racehorse to fracture in this way. The sheer intensity of the effort they make sometimes obliges them to run through the pain barrier. As with human athletes, there is no telling how they will respond. Highclere would have reached that threshold in the One Thousand Guineas, when she outfought Polygamy. She almost certainly went beyond it in her vain chase of Dahlia at Ascot. In the aftermath, as she heaved for air, she almost certainly resolved to excuse herself from a similar state of exhaustion in the future heat of any subsequent battle. It is in a horse's nature to do anything once. Once bitten, twice shy; and for that, Highclere could not be blamed in the slightest. She had given her all in the royal cause. She was also by some margin the most exciting addition to Sandringham's paddocks in twenty-one years of the Queen's reign.

For most owners, the retirement of a horse of Highclere's ability is a sad development. For most breeders it represents an exciting transition. At long last the Queen had a splendid product from her beloved Feola family in the Royal Studs. And there was more to anticipate. Highlight's second visit to Queen's Hussar had resulted in a year-younger full-sister to Highclere who was sent to Hern. Named Light Duty, she made a highly encouraging debut to finish runner-up within a cast of previous winners at Newbury. She was only denied in a photo-finish but the experience, rather than bringing her forward, caused her to regress. It wasn't apparent at the time but Light Duty had a harder race than was ideal on her baptism. It seemed she lacked Highclere's mental constitution. She would rebound again the following season when she twice finished second in two important races for fillies, but she did not achieve the level of success her debut suggested she was capable of. Nevertheless, in view of Highclere's achievements, not to mention her own, Light Duty was welcomed with open arms when she, too, joined the cast at the Royal Studs.

With Light Duty failing to excel, the royal racing highlight in 1975 was Joking Apart, who led the One Thousand Guineas field into the final furlong before she was caught and beaten into third place. Her sterling effort lent succour to the Queen's decision to send mares to be bred to North American stallions in 1964. Joking Part's dam, Strip The Willow, was produced by the inaugural visit of her dam, Near Miss, to Kentucky. However, as with the venture as a whole, Joking Apart started out promisingly enough as a broodmare before her influence faded into obscurity. It didn't help her cause that she was intermittently unsound in her racing days.

Joking Apart was one more product from the royal paddocks that were now flourishing. The next was imminent, although from her two-year-old season in 1976 Dunfermline's dazzling exploits as a three-year-old could not have been envisaged. Dunfermline's mother, the ordinary racemare Strathcona, was given her chance at stud almost certainly because she was Stroma's last foal. But for that, Strathcona would have been ripe for culling. Instead she produced Dunfermline, whose brace of Classic victories in 1977 made a perfect accompaniment to the Silver Jubilee celebrations.

Ironically, Dunfermline was a contemporary of Highclere's latest half-sister Circlet, who was seen as much the better prospect when the two were dispatched to Hern's stables towards the end of 1975. The assessment still held firm when the pair started working in earnest the following spring, although Dunfermline, a big, unfurnished filly, was never likely to be precocious. Each was beaten on their respective debuts – however Dunfermline's third place came in pleasing contrast to Circlet's disappointing run at Goodwood, where Hern expected much better of her.

The baton changed hands after that. Circlet won a competitive race at Ascot with ease but Dunfermline was beaten twice, albeit in a higher class, in a manner that raised some doubts about her will to win. However, the assumption that she'd surrendered all too tamely was sternly rebuked the following season, which opened for Dunfermline with a change of jockey.

Genuine surprise greeted the announcement towards the end of 1976 that Joe Mercer had been dismissed as Hern's stable jockey. He was displaced by the increasingly powerful turf alliance of Sir Michael Sobell and his son-in-law Arnold Weinstock (later Lord Weinstock), who had bought West Ilsley stables from the Astor family. Mercer enjoyed considerable success in the role, especially in the royal silks worn before him by his father-in-law Harry Carr as stable jockey to Cecil Boyd-Rochfort. Such sackings are usually prefaced by tell-tale smoke signals but Mercer's came like a bolt of lightning from a clear blue sky. If nothing else it was a sign that the proprietors of Hern's stables paid little heed to public sentiment in pursuing their own agenda. Other patrons within West Ilsley were equally capable of protecting their interests without turning a hair.

Mercer was replaced by Willie Carson, who quickly adopted the prevailing view that Circlet was Dunfermline's superior. That would change only when the pair reached the racecourse as three-year-olds after the winter recess. Circlet succumbed in the Oaks Trial at Lingfield, after which Carson reported problems with her breathing that would soon usher her towards retirement. Conversely, Dunfermline made a winning return on Two Thousand Guineas day at Newmarket, when the Queen was on hand. Carson felt that Dunfermline was long on stamina. He rode her accordingly and the big filly did not disappoint as she galloped to a resounding victory. It was Dunfermline's first rebuttal of the suggestion that she was faint of heart. Her second came on Oaks day at Epsom.

A consequence of Dunfermline's emergence in Silver Jubilee year was that her owner's diary was saturated with public engagements in celebration of it. As ever, the Queen had been at Epsom three days before to see Lester Piggott drive The Minstrel past Hot Grove in the Derby's closing strides. Come the Oaks, however, and she was consigned to watching on television from Windsor Castle as Piggott endeavoured to complete a Classic double aboard the favourite, Durtal. At least the Queen enjoyed a more leisurely big-race build-up than Carson, who pranged his Ferrari on the way to Epsom and was running dangerously late to weigh out.

The drive that delivered Carson to Epsom in the nick of time was as hair-raising a ride as he would have in the Oaks itself. After some early scrimmaging he recovered the lost ground into midfield as the leaders reached halfway. Then a weakening horse, the bane of every jockey's life at Epsom, dragged Carson back through the field so that he had just two horses behind him on the approach to Tattenham Corner. Carson thus decided to throw caution to the wind. Having angled Dunfermline towards the outside, he made headway around the treacherous bend and continued his progress down the home straight – where he identified Freeze The Secret, ridden by Frankie Dettori's father Gianfranco, as the filly to beat.

At that point Carson fully expected Dunfermline's efforts to catch up with her, yet the big, rangy filly maintained her rhythm. On and on she galloped, cutting into Freeze The Secret's advantage until she was suddenly alongside and then past her. Dunfermline reached the end of her tether soon after, yet just when her detractors might have expected her to falter she summoned one last effort to resist Freeze The Secret by three quarters of a length.

The 1977 Oaks: Dunfermline and Willie Carson go to post under the expert eye of the Queen Mother.

It felt to Carson that he had just taken a spin on the nearby fairground carousel that is an annual fixture in Derby week. Dunfermline had proved a perfect match for the jockey's bustling riding style. She responded to his urgings with an urgency of her own, in the process hoisting a first victory by a royal homebred in the Oaks at Epsom since La Fleche's triumph in 1892 – although that one, bred as she was in Queen Victoria's time, did not carry the royal silks. Well beaten back in fourth place was Triple First, a fancied runner who had beaten Dunfermline the previous season and whose great-grandson, Carlton House, came so close to winning the Derby for the Queen in 2011.

Durtal's anticipated challenge had never materialised. Her saddle started slipping from her sweat-laden back on the way to the start, setting off a chain of events that saw Piggott jettisoned and Durtal injure herself while running loose. Nevertheless, Carson was adamant Dunfermline would take taken the measure of an opponent who lived on her nerves. The

royal combination had not won by default. Victory was gained entirely on
merit, as Dunfermline would prove when she next resurfaced in Classic
competition for the St Leger. She did so in company with Gregarious,
another in the Queen's ownership who would set a level gallop all the way
round Town Moor at Doncaster.

Hern's decision to deploy Gregarious in that role was born of Dunfermline's defeat in the Yorkshire Oaks, when a sedate pace reduced the race to more of a sprint than the test of stamina Dunfermline so plainly relished. These tactics were nothing new; Hern had adopted them for Bustino's King George assault on Grundy two years earlier. Any horse with strong reserves of stamina, as Bustino and Dunfermline had in abundance, is instantly compromised in a race where the early gallop is little faster than a leisurely hack. To guard against the eventuality in the St Leger, Gregarious would set off at an honest gallop and try to win the race for himself. Failing that, he would ensure the race unfolded at a tempo to Dunfermline's liking.

There was certainly no shortage of confidence behind Dunfermline even though she was lined up against a talented cluster of colts – among them Alleged, unbeaten in five previous starts and a red-hot favourite. For the first time in her life Dunfermline had excelled in her homework at West Ilsley, where the staff had long noted her inclination to idleness. Sir Michael Oswald, then manager of the Royal Studs, was on hand to see Dunfermline complete the gallop that would conclude her preparation. 'It was staggering to watch her on that morning,' he recalled. 'Dunfermline galloped with a good horse that had just won well at the big York meeting and she pulled away from him by seven or eight lengths without making an effort.'

The St Leger postscript is that Carson and Hern felt Lester Piggott rode an injudicious race aboard Alleged. With Piggott tracking Gregarious into the long Doncaster straight, Carson was able to track the favourite's every move. He positioned Dunfermline on Alleged's tail and waited. It looked ominous when Alleged duly answered Piggott's prompt to open up in the straight. For a few strides Dunfermline could not match the unbeaten colt, but she reached inside herself, as she had at Epsom, to narrow the gap once more. The duel was back on.

It didn't last much longer. Carson knew that he would take Piggott's measure two furlongs from the finish, when Piggott crouched into the drive position to no discernible response from Alleged. And sure enough, Carson moved up to Piggott to engage in a brief tussle before biding Piggott farewell to win by one and a half lengths. There was clear daylight

More Classic success for Dunfermline as she and Willie Carson floor Alleged and Lester Piggott in the 1977 St Leger.

Opposite: Horse and jockey return in triumph, with trainer Dick Hern on the extreme right.

between the two at the end of a searching examination in which the third horse home, Classic Example, finished ten lengths further adrift.

As at Epsom, however, the Queen was unable to witness Dunfermline's triumph in person. Plans for her to travel to Doncaster were abandoned at the last minute; she would instead stay at Balmoral to welcome the Prime Minister Jim Callaghan. So she watched on television, doubtless enchanted by the outcome – and doubtless as unaware as everyone else watching from their sofas that a late twist to the tale was unfolding at Doncaster. Before the intrusion of a commercial break, television presenters somehow failed to mention that the Doncaster stewards had opened an official inquest into interference between Dunfermline and Alleged. Like the Queen, viewers only became aware of an inquiry now ominous by its duration on resumption of coverage from Doncaster. Most inquiries conclude within minutes if racecourse stewards are satisfied that any interference is accidental and academic to the outcome. The longer

these inquiries last, however, the greater the prospect of a disqualification – and this one went on for twenty minutes before the result was allowed to stand. It turned out Dunfermline had indeed collided with Alleged in the closing stages – but inconsequentially, ruled the stewards after no little deliberation.

The least perturbed by events at Doncaster was Carson. Piggott had told him there would be no problem; Alleged had been beaten by the better horse on the day. It was a magnanimous gesture from Piggott, who perhaps remembered the spontaneous outpouring of public joy when he rode Carrozza to win the Oaks. To play a part in the demotion of Dunfermline would have ensured a dramatic reversal of public sentiment in a year when the Queen's reign was celebrated the length and breadth of the country – although Piggott was so ruthless a competitor he might well have objected with stronger evidence to support him.

As it transpired, Alleged carried Piggott to handsome compensation soon afterwards. He responded to defeat by turning the tables on Dunfermline in the Prix de l'Arc de Triomphe where, in the absence of a pacemaker like Gregarious, Piggott made all the running at a tempo to suit Alleged for a famous victory. Carson shouldered some of the blame for Dunfermline's eclipse in Paris. It didn't help that Dunfermline shed a shoe in running, as Carlton House would do in the 2011 Derby. Given his chance again, however, Carson would have ridden more aggressively in an effort to bring Dunfermline's stamina into play. The filly ran on gamely throughout the closing stages to take fourth place, yet with her rests the honour of being the only horse to better Alleged in the latter's illustrious career, which he closed with a repeat victory in the Arc twelve months later. This was high praise indeed. The yearling prematurely dismissed as inferior to Circlet, with which she once shared a royal paddock, now had no peer among fillies in the whole of Europe.

There was a pleasing postscript to Dunfermline's St Leger triumph. Carson was still breathing the intoxicating fumes of victory half an hour later when he went out to ride Dunfermline's half-sister Tartan Pimpernel in an important race for two-year-olds. Perhaps those fumes propelled Tartan Pimpernel to victory in the May Hill Stakes, a race Dunfermline had proved unable to win twelve months previously. Tartan Pimpernel's

victory set the seal on a memorable season, which closed with the Queen faring best among breeders in Britain. It paid handsome tribute to the Royal Studs and to those who engineered its revival. What's more, the future looked bright after a campaign when seven individual royal two-year-olds reached the winner's circle. This promising state of affairs augured well for the policy of using stallions from speedy origins.

From a state of recent impotence, the Royal Studs were now churning out one beguiling prospect after another. Having produced two Classic winners in three years they would slake a nine-year drought at Royal Ascot in 1979, when Hern dispatched Expansive and Buttress at the double. Hern also struck again later that year when he saddled Milford to win the Princess of Wales's Stakes at Newmarket. Milford was Highclere's first foal. Following on from her naming of Highclere, the Queen named Milford after Lord Carnarvon's home, Milford Lake House. Unlike Highclere, however, Milford was born with little mental resilience. Whereas Highclere was a fighter, her son was less inclined to bloody himself in defence of family honour. For all that, Milford was as good a racehorse as the owner of any mare of Highclere's lustre could expect from her first foal.

Tartan Pimpernel and Willie Carson win the 1977 May Hill Stakes – the race after Dunfermline's St Leger – from Fiordiligi (Lester Pigggott).

The Royal Studs now possessed several broodmares that were throwing high-class stock. And the trainer entrusted with converting that promise into high achievement was at the top of his game. To his successes with the Queen's homebreds in 1979, Hern added Troy's scintillating victory in the Derby for his landlords, the Sobell/Weinstock alliance. It set the seal on an unforgettable year. The momentum was firmly with a trainer who would return to Epsom twelve months later to win a second Derby with Henbit, whose victory preceded that of Bireme, also trained by Hern, in the Oaks. The man was in command of a powerful equine battalion. His list of patrons was as formidable as any in the land. Several others were lined up outside the gates of West Ilsley, where the sign read 'No Vacancies'.

Hern's remarkable exploits had ramifications for Ian Balding, who had matched him in the early years of royal patronage but could no longer sustain that pace. There would be consequences: towards the end of the 1970s Balding received notice to the effect that the best of the royal yearlings would be sent Hern's way. Although Balding sensed the policy had been in place for the past few seasons, the effect was to confirm Hern's status as the Queen's principal trainer. It was also clear that Balding's brother-in-law William Hastings-Bass – who had been too young to take over the family string on the death of his father Peter in 1964 – had been earmarked for a future role. Hastings-Bass, subsequently Lord Huntingdon, was sent a pair of royal horses to train for the first time in 1977. It was a frustrating moment for Balding, but then no trainer in Britain – with the possible exception of Henry Cecil – could match the Hern express.

At that stage every link in the royal racing chain was secure, from the Royal Studs' output to the quality of mares returning from the racecourse to continue the cycle. With several prize fillies joining their mothers at Sandringham, the next generation of royal runners would descend from proven stock. Dunfermline and Highclere were the most prized new members of the fold – but that's where the comparison ended. One would greatly enhance the Royal Studs; the other would disappear in a cloud of worthless dust.

To Dunfermline befell the ignominy of underachievement that was sadly abetted by her poor fertility. Her dam Strathcona was no longer in the clan: she was culled at the end of Dunfermline's two-year-old career on the grounds that Dunfermline was a younger and infinitely more high-achieving representative of Stroma's family. At that time Dunfermline's year-younger half-sister Tartan Pimpernel was also on tap, although she could not advance on her promising two-year-old campaign. Like Dunfermline, Tartan Pimpernel would depart the royal broodmare band with far less fanfare than had accompanied her joining it. The consequence was that Stroma's line, much treasured by the Queen, would lapse entirely from royal bloodlines.

Highclere, by contrast, entered the Royal Studs with her spirit severed but her matriarchal instincts intact. The careers of many top racehorses conclude in this way. They suffer no physical damage; it is their minds that call a halt. Indeed, only truly great racehorses are immune to the threat of burning themselves out. They are so superior to the opposition that they are never really asked to enter the lexicon of pain. By winning with something in hand they also save themselves for their next assignment. This is what makes them stand out from more ordinary mortals. They can win the biggest races with a good deal to spare.

Genuinely outstanding racehorses enter into our midst at the rate of one a decade. Indeed, twelve months after Dahlia defeated Highclere in the race from which Highclere failed to rebound, two colts fought out a lung-bursting finish that did for them both. In the 1975 King George VI and Queen Elizabeth Stakes Grundy repelled Bustino, who was trained by Hern, in what is often described as the 'Race of the Century'. As the pair locked horns in the closing stages they drew well clear from a cast of other champions, Dahlia among them. Grundy's winning time lowered the Ascot track record by two and a half seconds. Both horses contrived monstrous efforts for which they would pay the price.

Grundy ran once more in the Benson and Hedges Gold Cup, as Highclere had twelve months earlier, and finished a weary fourth. As for Bustino, he never again pointed his toe with purpose at West Ilsley and moved on to life as the new resident inmate at Wolferton in the wake of Aureole's retirement from stallion duties. As chance would have it, Bustino's union with Highclere three years later would result in Height Of Fashion.

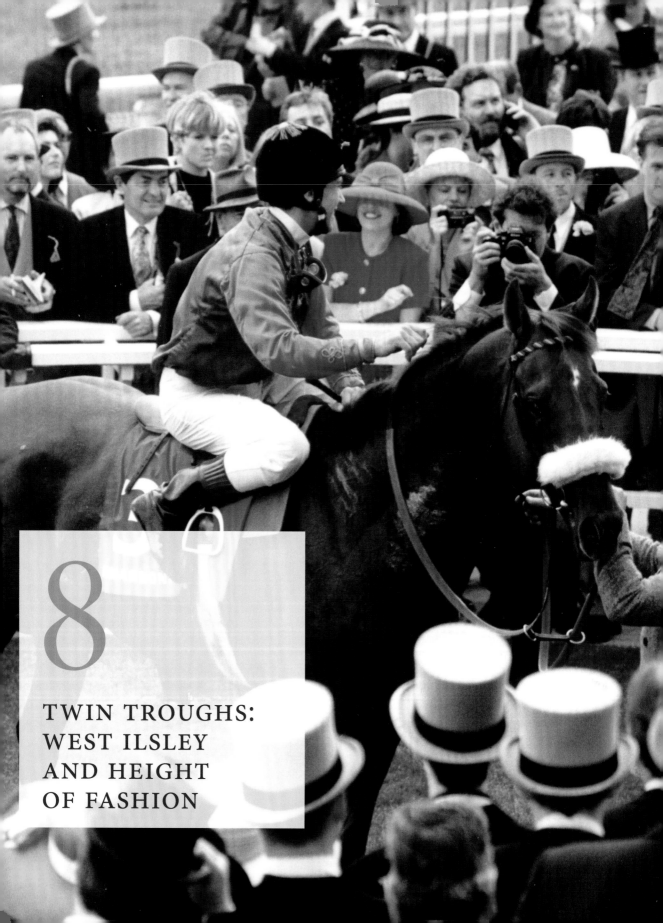

8

TWIN TROUGHS:
WEST ILSLEY
AND HEIGHT
OF FASHION

Ian Balding has no hesitation in describing the Queen as the unluckiest racehorse owner he has ever encountered. He emphasises his words with a rueful shake of the head, as if he is reliving the succession of freak accidents to befall royal horses in his care. As Edward VII declared, racing is the 'glorious uncertainty'. It has spawned a saying that any triumph must be savoured, since disaster would be hot on its heels. How true that is. Just as the Queen's racing and breeding structure looked ready to flourish, it would start to crumble.

The 1980s unfolded to the theme of a Greek tragedy in which Zeus himself could not have unleashed a wrath more profound than was discharged on the royal racing interests. His retribution knew no bounds. It was as if he made it his personal responsibility to ensure that a once-thriving fiefdom was reduced to rubble.

It was impossible to envisage the ruins at the start of a decade that promised so much. Highclere's fourth foal, Height Of Fashion, closed 1981 with a verve unmatched by any royal two-year-old filly during the Queen's reign. Her victories in a pair of prestigious two-year-old races earned her official recognition as the joint top-rated filly of her generation in Europe. She was unbeaten in three starts and a leading contender for Classic honours the following season. Here was one more gem that Hern was cutting for her proud owner/breeder – except that events didn't follow the preordained script.

After the winter recess, Height Of Fashion missed the more prestigious Oaks trials before taking her chance in the last of them at Goodwood. She duly won, but not in the manner anticipated of a Classic winner in waiting. Sure enough, her connections elected to bypass the Oaks. Epsom's undulations were deemed unsuitable for a powerful, long-striding filly of immense physical range, and the decision to forsake the Classic road gave Height Of Fashion further time to flourish before she was properly tested.

Seven weeks later she was pronounced ready for the Princess of Wales's Stakes at Newmarket's July meeting, where the mighty stayer Ardross was also engaged. It was nevertheless an attractive opportunity. Of her three opponents, Ardross was manifestly better over distances beyond one and a half miles, Amyndas was eminently beatable, and Ashenden out of his depth. There was also the significant, first-time deployment of blinkers on Height Of Fashion. The same piece of headgear had worked wonders on her mother Highclere ahead of her One Thousand Guineas victory.

The royal party's mood in advance of the race was buoyant after Hern had opened proceedings by saddling Joking Apart's son St Boniface to victory in a competitive race for two-year-olds. And Height Of Fashion embellished it when she made all the running to win decisively from Amyndas, with Ardross unable to land a blow in third place. The filly raced with great zest in her blinkers, and Willie Carson took the measure of his opponents by allowing Height Of Fashion to use her giant stride to telling effect. On this evidence Height Of Fashion deserved a shot against the best. The imminent King George VI and Queen Elizabeth Stakes was an obvious target for a monarch with fond memories of Aureole's triumph in 1954.

Height Of Fashion duly contested the King George, but not in the royal silks. Soon after her Newmarket victory she was sold to Sheikh Hamdan Al-Maktoum, Dubai's Minister of Finance, for £1.2 million. It was a huge sum, although far from unprecedented at a time when the Maktoums were voraciously building their bloodstock empires. Similar deals were being reported with remarkable frequency. Money was no object to near-Bedouin brothers from Middle Eastern deserts with a rich equine heritage of their own.

Height Of Fashion thus sported Sheikh Hamdan's silks at Ascot, where she ran below expectations in finishing well adrift of the winner Kalaglow.

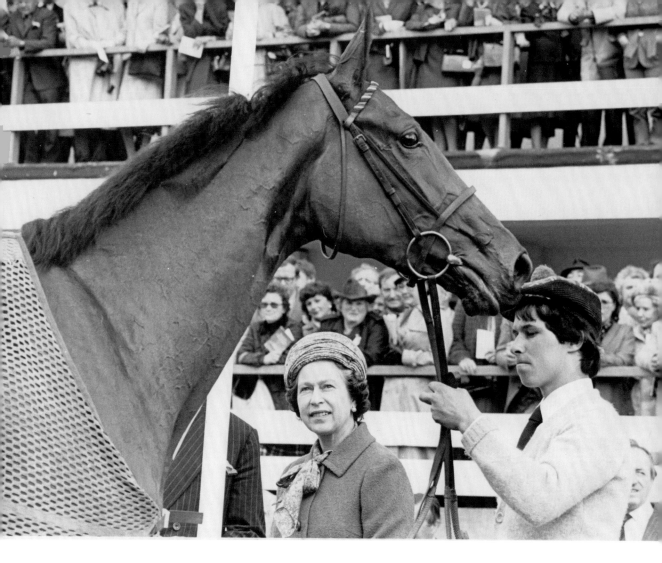

And when she was equally disappointing in the Yorkshire Oaks on her next start, the royal perspective must have been that Height Of Fashion had been sold at precisely the right time. All the more so when it emerged that the Queen put the proceeds from her sale towards the purchase of Hodcott House, which included West Ilsley stables, from the Sobell/Weinstock alliance. Weinstock, though surprised by the offer, was happy to sell if the Queen so wished.

It was very much her wish. The cost of keeping horses in training was rising fast; significant sums from the Queen's private purse were required to meet them. Her capital injection into West Ilsley stables thus allowed her to rationalise the cost of keeping her horses in training. In simple terms her purchase of the stables saw her replace the Sobell/Weinstock alliance as the landlord who dictated the terms of the lease. Everything else would

The Queen gives Height Of Fashion an appreciative look in the Ascot winner's enclosure after the 1981 Fillies' Mile.

Sheikh Hamdan al-Maktoum with the Queen after Malhub's victory in the Golden Jubilee Stakes at Royal Ascot, 2002.

proceed as normal, with Hern renting the stables and collecting training fees from affluent owners.

Carnarvon, who acted for the Queen in selling Height Of Fashion, played a central part in securing the purchase of West Ilsley. It was financed in large part by the sale of a horse that would fail to build on her achievements. Height Of Fashion won five races from as many starts for the Queen; in two starts for Sheikh Hamdan she was beaten all ends up. Through regrettable, it wasn't a huge concern that Height Of Fashion would not be joining the Royal Studs. There was no public outcry over her sale. On the contrary, it was seen as one more bit of excellent business orchestrated by Carnarvon, the man with an uncanny knack of selling equine assets at the right time.

Moreover, Height Of Fashion's loss from the paddocks was more than offset by the preponderance of her relatives at the Royal Studs. Her full-sister Beacon Hill was already on the pastures. Her dam Highclere had several productive years ahead of her and had foaled a filly by Mill Reef earlier that spring. As if to round things off Special Leave, a son of Highclere's full-sister Light Duty, had just raced to an impressive debut victory in demanding company at Ascot. As things stood it was hard to see how Carnarvon and the monarch he served could be anything but pleased with the sequence of events.

It is a measure of Sheikh Hamdan that Hern was not held to account for Height Of Fashion's racing failures. In fact they had the opposite effect, since the sheikh was able to add Hern to his roster of trainers. This might not have been possible but for Height Of Fashion's purchase. Hern never trained a large string. There were more owners keen to patronise him than he could accommodate at West Ilsley, but that tide was turning.

Hern's owner base was largely comprised of aristocratic owner/breeders who were becoming increasingly scarce. Death duties mounted and large estates were being divided up. Very few of them could afford to breed horses on the scale of their forefathers, and those who could were increasingly frustrated in their efforts to win races by the torrent of expensive horses of Middle-Eastern owners. By the mid 1980s it was becoming clear that trainers bereft of Arab patrons would struggle to play at the top table. With weight of money beginning to talk, Hern would have been delighted to welcome Sheikh Hamdan to West Ilsley. In the years ahead the pair would combine to make a potent alliance.

That was some way distant as Hern braced himself for the 1983 season. The previous year's highlight had seen Swiftfoot win the Irish Oaks for Lord Rotherwick. This time Hern would take aim at the Oaks itself with Sun Princess, who was still without a win in two starts when she converged on Epsom. If it seemed most unlike Hern to run a maiden in a Classic, the reason was soon forthcoming. Sun Princess led her opponents into the straight before galloping further and further away from them. Her record winning distance of twelve lengths still stood at the onset of Diamond Jubilee year. Hern then saddled Sun Princess to win the St Leger on her next start – doubtless emboldened by Dunfermline's exploits in completing an unusual double five years earlier.

Hern achieved another notable success in 1983 with Little Wolf in the Gold Cup at Ascot. Little Wolf carried the Eton Blue silks of Lord Porchester, as he was then. Victory emphasised the enduring relationship between Hern and the Queen's racing manager, who had had horses at West Ilsley long before the Queen started patronising the stable in 1966. Hern trained Little Wolf's half-brother Smuggler to a spate of big-race wins in Porchester's colours in the mid-1970s. The two men were firm friends who took their respective families on holiday together.

Carnarvon recognised Hern's talent from an early stage in the latter's career. With Hern in his corner he had built up his successful breeding operation at Highclere, just as Hern was now vindicating the overhaul of the Royal Studs undertaken by the Queen with Carnarvon at her side. As Carnarvon came to appreciate Hern's often blunt assessment of his horses, so, too, did the Queen of her own. There is no sense in pursuing a lost cause – especially one as expensive as a Thoroughbred racehorse. All in all, relations between West Ilsley's main protagonists could not have been better. The point was emphasised at the end of 1979, when the Sobell/Weinstock alliance decided to place Troy, whom Hern trained to win that year's Derby, at Carnarvon's Highclere Stud for stallion duties. Carnarvon rewarded them by completing a then record £7.2 million syndication of the horse. Everyone was happy.

Then, out of the blue, an accident in December 1984 radically changed Hern's life. A love of hunting that never waned saw him out with the

Quorn when his horse jumped what appeared to be a routine obstacle on that fabled strip of Leicestershire. Only when airborne did horse and rider spot the stone water trough on the landing side. Hern took a heavy fall from which he was lucky to escape with his life. A broken neck kept him in traction for six weeks; he was paralysed from the neck down. He would spend the rest of his days in a wheelchair.

Training horses in these circumstances might seem impractical, yet in truth, it is no serious impediment. A trainer sits atop the chain of command; his instructions are implemented by trusty employees around him. It is the stable's head lad, for example, who does the early morning rounds of feeding and checking fragile limbs for signs of wear and tear. The trainer is summoned only if his attention is required. Even then, he will often heed his head lad's advice on a leg problem. These are no more than the minutiae of stable life. The real skill in training racehorses is in the interpretation of their work: whether it should be stepped up or pared down in accordance with how the horse responds. The one indispensable requirement is a keen eye, and there was nothing wrong with Hern's eyesight. Being wheelchair-bound was more or less academic, albeit immensely frustrating for a man of his active hue.

Nevertheless, Hern's achievements in the years immediately after his accident did not match the level he established before it. The two may not have been directly related: Hern often complained of campaigns blighted by 'the dreaded virus'. Ian Balding was another whose string would succumb to it. In its early stages 'the virus' would lie dormant in horses, invisible to the naked eye. Only when a horse made maximum effort in a race would the tell-tale mucus discharge from its nostrils. Veterinarians grappled unsuccessfully with 'the virus' for many years before they came up with an effective vaccine that is now a routine part of stable management. All viruses mutate; this one in its varying forms played havoc with strings up and down the country. It blighted several promising careers. Trainers previously rampant were stopped dead in their tracks. To this day 'the virus' remains a source of paranoia among trainers who experienced the worst of it in the 1980s. And with good reason.

Equally, however, 'the virus' quickly became a convenient excuse for a poor campaign. For those like Carnarvon, whose business it was to keep a firm handle on the progress of royal racehorses, it was hard to know how much credence to lend such excuses. It is often folly to look beyond the numbers, and by the end of 1985, the first in his unfortunate predicament, Hern's numbers were not encouraging. He had not trained a royal horse of note for three years. A poor season by his standards was rescued by Petoski's surprise victory, at odds of 16/1, in the King George VI and Queen Elizabeth Stakes. In 1986, another year of royal disappointment, Hern's only triumph in a championship race came via Dick Hollingsworth's Longboat in the Gold Cup. In 1987 there was nothing at all to speak of. For Hern, it was the first such omission for twelve seasons and a far cry from 1983, when he was champion trainer for the fourth time.

The loyalty of owners is sorely tested in a succession of lean years. Hern's career was hardly in free fall but it had known better days. There was no question of anyone jumping ship, least of all the Queen, yet many owners in the stable must have wondered whether they were presiding over the start of an irreversible decline. It had happened to Cecil Boyd-Rochfort, whose ebbing fortunes in the 1960s were witnessed – and perhaps supported for too long – by a royal entourage now obliged to ponder the same of Hern.

Of course, some trainers rebound from a series of poor seasons to reclaim their hegemony. There is no finer example than Boyd-Rochfort's stepson Henry Cecil, whose career appeared beyond redemption until he consigned a spell in the wilderness to history. For Cecil, the new millennium was a new dawn. He was 64 when his renaissance gained momentum with Light Shift's Oaks triumph in 2007. Shortly afterwards he would unearth Frankel, the best of several great racehorses he has trained.

As for Hern's expectant patrons, they must have wondered what lay in store at the start of 1988, even though none would have dreamt of saying so in public. One with rare cause for optimism at West Ilsley was Sheikh Hamdan. The pick of his horses in residence was Unfuwain, a strong-galloping colt by the world's pre-eminent sire Northern Dancer. He was also Height Of Fashion's second foal. The first, also by Northern Dancer, was Alwasmi, who had proved himself well above average, if short of the highest class. Height Of Fashion may have disappointed the sheikh in two

Three generations of royal racing enthusiasts at Epsom on Derby day, 1988.

racecourse visits but he was plainly determined to give her every chance at stud. At the time of her visits to Northern Dancer, the fee for using that great stallion's services stood at $1 million. With no guarantees. In other words, if your mare returned from her tryst without producing a live foal, the $1 million fee was payable none the less.

For those two visits to Northern Dancer the sheikh paid an identical sum to what Height Of Fashion had cost him in the first place. The steep price was governed by the prevailing boom in bloodstock values around the world. It was driven by men of the private means of Sheikh Hamdan, for whom $1 million was a drop in the ocean. It was also a reflection of Northern Dancer's dominance among stallions, both in Europe and north America. He excelled in every respect, particularly in Federico Tesio's diktat on the Derby's overriding importance in Thoroughbred evolution. He had already sired two celebrated Derby winners, Nijinsky and The Minstrel, before his unions with Height Of Fashion. One month after the second of them, which would result in Unfuwain, Northern Dancer raised his status still further when two of his sons, Secreto and El Gran Senor, fought out a pulsating finish to the 1984 Derby. He was simply without peer.

Unfuwain wasted little time in advertising his own Derby prospects in the spring of 1988. He opened with a crushing victory in Epsom's Derby trial before making equally short work of three opponents in the Chester Vase. Come the Derby and sentiment alone persuaded Willie Carson to forsake Unfuwain for the ride on his stablemate, Minster Son. Carson had bred Minster Son, who'd stated his own Derby case with a pair of less flamboyant trial victories. In Carson's absence Steve Cauthen was drafted for the ride aboard Unfuwain, whose free-running style seemed perfectly suited to the crack American's acute tactical prowess.

In the end Carson's ruminations proved academic. Neither Unfuwain nor Minster Son made an impact in finishing seventh and eighth respectively. There was disappointment with the outcome at West Ilsley, in particular with Unfuwain's tame effort. The colt took the lead early in the home straight but his effort petered out just when he was expected to impose himself. Indeed, the mood at West Ilsley was still sombre when the curtain rose on Royal Ascot two weeks later.

Hern was not there to see it; he had been taken ill at the start of the week. By Thursday he was in Cromwell Hospital, west London, where he underwent surgery to arrest a leaking valve in his heart. He returned home six weeks later but was back in the same hospital within a fortnight for emergency surgery to drain a build-up of fluid in his heart. He was still there nine days later when he was informed, on 14 August, that his West Ilsley lease would not be renewed on its expiry the following year.

Those close to Hern were taken aback. The man who had trained for the Queen with conspicuous success for more than twenty years was being turned away when he needed royal support. The news was delivered to Hern's wife by Carnarvon, who had already sanctioned Neil Graham's recruitment from California to help at West Ilsley in Hern's hospitalised absence.

Soon after that bombshell Hern's condition was discussed by a panel of five medics. Three of them, all of whom had been treating Hern, opined he would be able to continue training. The other two – the Queen's physician, Sir John Batten, and Jockey Club Medical Officer, Dr Michael Allen – were less than convinced. The royal advisors chose to heed the latter opinion.

With minds made up, Hern's removal from West Ilsley could not now wait until his lease expired towards the end of the following year. It became a more pressing concern – and a delicate one, given the confidentiality of medical advice that could not be relayed to Hern. Nevertheless, events continued to unfold at bewildering speed. On 25 August, Hern was persuaded to sign a letter written on his behalf stating that he would relinquish his trainer's licence with immediate effect, and that Graham, recently arrived, would take over temporarily until Carnarvon appointed Hern's successor at West Ilsley for the 1989 season.

The letter nearly sealed Hern's fate. In his authorised biography, written by Peter Willett and published in 2000, Hern claimed he was unaware of an important clause in the terms of his West Ilsley lease. The act of relinquishing his licence would render the lease null and void. When informed of it, he resolved instead to retain the licence in suspended form until he was ready to reactivate it. There was provision for this within Jockey Club licensing rules. Had he relinquished his licence altogether Hern would have simultaneously signed away his entitlement to train from West Ilsley. He would have no legal basis to return from hospital to the place where he had lived and trained for the previous 26 years.

Hern's account is stark about the way in which the Queen's advisors sought to bring about an enforced conclusion to his lease. Yet no sooner had the episode run its course than the royal mood changed. Someone high up the chain was concerned by Hern's plight. Within days of signing the letter that so nearly undermined him, Hern received one from the

Queen that stated he and his wife could continue to live at The Old Rectory for as long as they wanted.

It was an olive branch of sorts. The sense of urgency that punctuated Hern's removal from West Ilsley was no longer paramount. The matter was plainly exercising minds beyond the Queen's racing coterie – and all of this before any public announcement had been made. When it came, in March 1989, it provoked such a hostile reaction that royal advisors senior to Carnarvon felt compelled to intervene.

All the manoeuvring of the previous seven months was distilled down to a simple declaration from the Palace. 'The Queen has appointed Mr William Hastings-Bass to take over the West Ilsley stables when Major Hern's lease runs out in November this year [1989],' the statement said. 'Major and Mrs Hern will continue to live at The Old Rectory and Mr Hastings-Bass will train from Hodcott House, previously the home of the late Mr Jack Colling, Major Hern's predecessor at West Ilsley.'

The official statement was pre-empted by a young journalist, Alan Byrne. A subsequent editor of the sport's dedicated newspaper, the *Racing Post*, Byrne was then news editor on the weekly trade publication, *Racing and Breeding Update*. Like many other journalists, he had heard the rumours and decided to act. Byrne telephoned Carvarvon and put to him what he had heard, to which Carnarvon replied: 'There will be an official announcement next week.' There could be no doubting the story's veracity after that.

Byrne thus delivered a notable scoop, although the circumstances opened a revealing window into the workings of Carnarvon's mind. It was hardly the way to suppress a thorny story. It betrayed a lack of mental agility that was surprising in a man of Carnarvon's profile, never mind one with decades of public service behind him. Against that, it told of his basic honesty. Many of Carnarvon's ilk who are obliged to confront a similar dilemma would have brought the full force of their status to bear – or at least, brazenly failed to answer the question. In the event, however, there was no way of knowing whether Carnarvon felt he had successfully quashed the inquiry or whether he realised that he had, in fact, served up the answer Byrne sought on a silver platter.

On that basis, Carnarvon may have been surprised by the extent of the furore generated by the Palace's announcement. There was evidently some concern about its impact since the statement was released on 13 March, one day before the start of the Cheltenham Festival, when journalists would be besieged by editors calling for more and more words to fill their Cheltenham supplements. Then again, the hope that Hern's imminent eviction from West Ilsley might be confined to the racing pages was severely misplaced.

It wasn't long before the Palace reacted to the clamour from a hostile media. Within a month of the announcement, and on the private prompting of the Queen's Deputy Private Secretary, Sir Robert Fellowes, Hern welcomed senior racing journalists to The Old Rectory to request they cease writing articles in support of him. He described having trained for the Queen for the last twenty-three years as an honour, and that he was sure the Queen and her advisors wanted to terminate the West Ilsley lease solely on the grounds of his health. He also affirmed his plan to continue training beyond the end of the year.

Hern's bidding may well have had the desired effect but for a turn of events that returned the sorry episode to the spotlight three weeks later. Coming nicely to the boil on the West Ilsley training grounds was a chestnut colt who'd won both his two-year-old starts with something to spare. Although neither had come in demanding company, there was something about Nashwan that tantalised Hern and his senior staff. Inexperienced colts are rarely asked to gallop flat out at home, yet even at half-speed the seasoned eye will detect the presence of something out of the ordinary. Such hopes were entertained for Nashwan, who duly confirmed them with a blistering gallop at West Ilsley in April. With word of his prowess spreading like wildfire, Nashwan's odds for the imminent Classics entered free fall.

So much so that Nashwan approached the stalls for the Two Thousand Guineas as favourite at 3/1 even though he had never run against the best. It was enough for punters that he came with the blessing of a stable that knew a thing or two about top-class horses. There was abundant confidence behind him and it was not misplaced. Willie Carson rode the colt with rare conviction and Nashwan responded by winning with something to spare.

For Hern, the moment of vindication had arrived. He was in the Classic winner's enclosure nine months after his ability to train had been questioned by a pair of doctors. He would later describe it as the sweetest moment of his life, rendered all the more so by the rousing reception he received when Nashwan returned to unsaddle. The Newmarket galleries are the most informed in racing. They stood united in their support for a man they perceived had been wrongly cast aside by his royal landlord. 'Everyone was right behind me,' Hern would say years later. 'I could feel the pleasure they were expressing in their cheers and applause.' Up in the saddle, Carson beamed from ear to ear in the soft light of a sun-kissed spring afternoon.

Such joyous scenes were the last thing the royal advisors needed. There was no longer room for doubt that the public stood squarely behind Hern. Taking their cue from it, journalists embarked on another round of uproar over the way he was being treated. Two weeks later the Palace responded with another statement, this time announcing that agreement between all parties had been reached for Hern to stay at West Ilsley for twelve months beyond the end of his lease, until November 1990. In that season he would share the facility with Hastings-Bass.

The announcement brought some respite, although Nashwan's vice-like grip on the lengthy Derby preamble never allowed the clouds to disperse. If Nashwan proved the conduit for Palace embarrassment over the public show of support for Hern, his heritage was another source of profound royal lament. Nashwan was Height Of Fashion's third foal. The horse who stoked anti-royal fires at Newmarket was entirely of the Queen's breeding until his mother had been sold to finance the purchase of stables that were now blighting the public's perception of their monarch. The tall, supple colt with a stride of grace and power was homing in as the overwhelming favourite on the race in which the Queen cherishes victory above all others. He would not disappoint. After a brief tussle with Cacoethes he forged clear halfway down the home straight to win by five lengths. The consummate ease of his victory suggested Nashwan was a model Thoroughbred. It was an impression he confirmed with supplementary triumphs in the Eclipse Stakes and the King George VI and Queen Elizabeth Stakes.

Carnarvon must have watched this improbable sequence of events unfold with a sense of foreboding. He was portrayed as the villain of the piece and subsequently cast as the man who did untold damage to the Queen's reputation on the Turf. They were grave accusations, although judgement was passed as much by inference and supposition as by the flurry of rumours doing the rounds. For the rest of his life Carnarvon maintained that he could not elaborate on circumstances he insisted were more than met the eye. It was convenient for him to say so, just as it was convenient for detractors to goad him for keeping silent. Those of royal affiliation take their cue from the Queen, who maintains a public silence at all times.

It was noticeable that the strongest attacks on Carnarvon were penned by journalists within Hern's narrow circle of friends. Hern was notoriously and habitually short-tempered with journalists he did not know in person. Those he did know were influential, of contemporary age, and from similar public school backgrounds. To them he was a man of great charm and no little humour behind closed doors at The Old Rectory. Yet many friendly with Hern were on the same terms with Carnarvon; suffice to say that any journalist obliged to express an opinion that divides two friends is in an invidious position.

The media's role in commenting on Hern's plight must also be seen in tandem with the prevailing public mood. In the late 1980s newspapers were becoming increasingly frustrated with the royal family's puerile treatment by television, which became the family's favoured media platform. Television continued to portray the House of Windsor as a modern-day Camelot despite suggestions of a rift in the marriage between the Prince and Princess of Wales. Inevitably, newspapers excluded from the inner royal loop sought their own retribution. Stories undermining the closely guarded image of the so-called 'fairy-tale marriage' were appearing with growing frequency.

They marked the beginning of an end to the understanding that royal private lives were out of bounds to reporters. The Windsors were thus becoming fair game at a time when a heavy royal hand seemed intent on sweeping Hern away. Criticism of the family became rife and Hern's treatment offered further ammunition. It was another small step on the road that would culminate in the Queen's 'Annus Horribilis' speech in November 1992.

From Carnarvon's perspective, his advice was governed by what he felt was in the best interests of the royal racehorses that it was his responsibility to manage. Publish and be damned: in many ways he was caught between one close friend and another. Just as Carnarvon took family holidays with Hern, he was a childhood friend of the Queen. There is no disputing the weight that the Queen always attached to his advice. He was a man of great influence, yet one prone to overreact in the heat of the moment.

This inclination surfaced in 2001, when Flight Of Fancy returned to unsaddle after her luckless second place in the Oaks at Epsom. At first glance it seemed as though Kieren Fallon, who would close the season with a fourth jockey's title in five years, had ridden an injudicious race aboard the royal filly. Carnarvon said as much, describing Fallon's ride as 'awful'. It was an impetuous observation rendered obsolete almost as soon as it was made. A post-race veterinary inspection revealed Flight Of Fancy had fractured her pelvis in running. Her wayward passage through the closing stages was almost certainly down to an injury so severe that she would never race again.

The 2001 Oaks at Epsom: Flight Of Fancy (white face) falters when holding every chance as Imagine (blue cap) goes on to win.

As for West Ilsley, Willie Carson felt the response to Hern's health problems was too abrupt. 'Carnarvon wanted to get out of the situation quickly,' he ventured some years later. Carnarvon was technically correct in his assertion that the doctor whose opinion mattered most in the racing context belonged to the Jockey Club's Medical Officer. 'I had to take the view of the doctor with the authority, the Jockey Club doctor,' Carnarvon said in 2000. 'How could I do anything else? As far as I was concerned I was responsible entirely for one thing, and that was the management of the stable by someone who was fit and capable of running the stable properly.'

It was also plain that Carnarvon wanted to be seen to act decisively. He was not alone: other significant owners with horses at West Ilsley expressed the same wish to Carnarvon in private. The stable was a going concern, owned by the Queen. Owners who were anxious about a possible waning of Hern's talent before his heart problems in 1988 now felt a quick resolution to the impasse was warranted.

It was a difficult dilemma, and if Carnarvon was guilty of misjudgement it was by acting with undue haste. The sheer speed of decisions relating to Hern's future was unwarranted by the circumstances. In the limited time Hern remained at West Ilsley he proved more than equal to the demands of training. He would continue in that vein when Sheikh Hamdan installed him at purpose-built premises at Farncombe Down, on the fringe of Lambourn, in 1991. Other owners who questioned Hern's prowess were also wide of the mark, yet they remained anonymous – and thus beyond reproach. Carnarvon, by contrast, was in a no-win position. On the one hand, he would have derived no pleasure at all from a slump in Hern's career. On the other, Hern's ongoing success at Farncombe Down brought him further opprobrium.

The fallout from this chapter of royal involvement in racing was considerable. Lifelong friendships were said to have been damaged beyond reconciliation. The Queen herself came in for criticism; some even ventured that her reputation within the sport would never recover. It became an extremely sensitive issue for the Palace. The Queen was more exposed than in most matters, where layer upon layer of courtiers, officials and advisors serve to distance her from involvement. Those within the royal racing circle, Ian Balding and Willie Carson included, were openly critical. So was Lord Oaksey, an amateur rider of Corinthian ideals and a younger contemporary of Carnarvon at Eton. The breach seemed beyond repair.

Nevertheless, time's passage allowed most of the wounds to heal. Entrenched positions taken in the heat of the affair have since subsided at all levels. Distinguished guests at Balmoral who were no longer invited have since returned with the regularity of old. The Queen converses frequently with Willie Carson at Royal Ascot. Hern himself was made a Commander of the British Empire (CBE) in 1998, the year after his retirement. Balding felt that he paid for his perceived lack of loyalty when he was told in 1999 he would be receiving no more royal yearlings – although he conceded that his results, even with the 'second pick' of yearlings from the Royal Studs, had been disappointing. However, Balding remained on the Queen Mother's training roster, and the royal silks returned to Park House stables when the Queen took over the royal jumping string on her mother's death in 2002. And the wheel of redemption turned full circle in 2011, when the Queen sent three yearlings to Balding's son Andrew, who had succeeded him at Park House.

As for West Ilsley, it became something of a royal millstone. The argument for buying it made sense only until the onset of the unforeseen. Finding a replacement of similar calibre to Hern was always going to be a thankless task, since moving there held no appeal for established trainers of the day. They owned thriving set-ups of their own, capable of housing twice as many horses as West Ilsley, where capacity never much exceeded 100 boxes.

Indeed, had the Queen not owned West Ilsley she could simply have moved her horses to another trainer. That was no longer an option. In the absence of any like-for-like replacement for Hern the summons went to William Hastings-Bass, who'd trained a string of royal horses since 1977. In different circumstances Hastings-Bass would almost certainly have trained from Park House Stables at Kingsclere. He was just sixteen when his father Peter died of cancer in 1964, thus leaving a training vacuum filled by Ian Balding, his assistant at the time. Hastings-Bass was an appropriate appointment at West Ilsley in the sense that he would have

Phantom Gold and Frankie Dettori win the
Ribblesdale Stakes at Royal Ascot, 1995.

taken over his father's string, and the royal horses within it, but for the
impediment of his young age.

For the first five years Hastings-Bass made West Ilsley work in a financial
context. He won the Ascot Gold Cup three years running from 1990, albeit
not with royal horses. But the burden of making it pay rested squarely with
him. Not salaried by the Queen, he was responsible for meeting other estate
costs in addition to the annual lease. To the Queen's annual string of twenty-
five horses Hastings-Bass added a further sixty belonging to other clients,
yet he still needed to win championship races to show a profit. It proved an
unequal struggle to which Hastings-Bass, by now Lord Huntingdon, called
a halt with his decision to vacate West Ilsley in 1998. It was to royal relief all
round when the property was sold the following year.

Although not in the highest echelon, Lord Huntingdon's training career
was far from pedestrian. In 1989 he sent Unknown Quantity across the

Atlantic for the Arlington Handicap – and victory marked the first race of championship class won by the Queen in North America. He arrested the Queen's twelve-year absence from the Royal Ascot's winner's enclosure in 1992, when Colour Sergeant won the Royal Hunt Cup. And there were big-race wins for the likes of Enharmonic and Phantom Gold, the latter at Royal Ascot under Frankie Dettori in 1995.

By the time of his retirement, Lord Huntingdon had been joined on the royal training roster by Roger Charlton at Beckhampton. Other royal appointments were imminent: horses previously sent to West Ilsley were divided between Richard Hannon, Sir Michael Stoute and Michael Bell, the latter two in Newmarket. Collectively, these trainers discovered what Huntingdon had learnt for himself. Slouches they were not, but the royal horses were not up to winning the quality of race they had annexed so regularly in the 1970s.

By general consent the Arab influx made racing in Britain the most competitive in the world. Winning a Flat race of any denomination became an achievement in itself; hence the transfer of several wealthy owners to the National Hunt code. Equally, Height Of Fashion's sale coincided with an overall lapse into unproductivity at the Royal Studs. Height Of Fashion was the last good horse Hern trained for the Queen. She would breed a Derby winner for her new owner at a time when the royal racing fortunes reached a low ebb.

It was not the first time a mare of Height Of Fashion's influence had been denied to the Royal Studs. The culling of Feola's daughters in the 1950s had serious long-term ramifications. However, unlike that episode, Height Of Fashion's sale was governed by more than routine culling, since the Queen was keen to buy West Ilsley. But the extent of her desire becomes evident on closer inspection of the prevailing circumstances. On the face of it the sale of one filly – out of a mare, Highclere, still young enough to breed many subsequent foals – did not seem like an overt risk. But there were other portentous elements into the bargain.

Highclere's first foal was the talented colt Milford. Her second was Burghclere, a superior royal runner who reached a place in two important races: Royal Ascot's Ribblesdale Stakes and the Pretty Polly Stakes at Newmarket. Burghclere might have been as good a filly as Highclere would ever produce, yet she was sold at public auction straight off the racecourse for 460,000 guineas. That alone underlined her gilt-edged breeding credentials. Highclere's third foal was another filly, Beacon Hill, who failed to win but was retained by the Royal Studs. Her residual value was nothing like Burghclere's. In that respect her retention mirrored the policy Carnarvon had so successfully pursued in his own breeding venture. Carnarvon was more than willing to cash in racecourse stars while breeding successfully from their less-illustrious relatives.

Beacon Hill's retention also signalled a departure from the prior case of Feola. In that instance Feola's best racing daughters were retained by the Royal Studs while those of no account were sold off. It was happening the other way round with Highclere's daughters – especially when her fourth foal, Height Of Fashion, was sold to Sheikh Hamdan in 1982. Her sale was insulated by the fact that Highclere had just foaled a filly by Mill Reef, but from that moment the barometer swung violently to settle on stormy weather. Highclere spent two unproductive years in Kentucky before she produced her foal by Mill Reef. That foal was culled after she proved unable to make the racecourse, while Highclere's next two foals both met with early deaths. There was now an urgent need for Highclere to bequeath daughters for the Royal Studs to breed from, yet few were forthcoming. She was now fourteen and her only daughter on the pasture was Beacon Hill. A position of strength was now deteriorating quickly.

Highclere's next foal was a blessing: Highbrow was both healthy and talented enough to finish runner-up in the Ribblesdale Stakes at Royal Ascot. Highbrow was duly retained, yet any sense of relief proved fleeting after Highclere spent the last six years of her breeding life in Kentucky without the desired effect. The decision to send her there was straightforward, given that Height Of Fashion was achieving outstanding results in her trysts with Kentucky-based sires.

An eagerly anticipated mating in Kentucky was Highclere's union with Blushing Groom, who sired Nashwan when Height Of Fashion was bred to him. The Royal Studs would have dearly loved a filly to breed from; she would have been a three-quarters sister in blood to Height Of Fashion. The consequence, of course, was a colt. Highclere would breed another colt to Nureyev and one more to Diesis. Of the two fillies she produced in

Kentucky, Wily Trick never won, and bred two runners of no account for the Queen before she was culled in 1995 – after which she promptly bred the Hong Kong Derby winner, Elegant Fashion. The other was Highclere's last foal Clear Attraction, who did not win and died, aged ten, after breeding little of note.

In the course of her breeding life Highclere produced seven fillies but only one, Highbrow, did well for the Royal Studs. Highbrow's son Blueprint won twice at Royal Ascot, while her daughter Fairy Godmother showed a high level of ability before she retired to Sandringham. Yet while Fairy Godmother has been among the Queen's more successful broodmares of late, her record pales in comparison with those established by other descendants of Highclere that were sold out of the Royal Studs. Request, a daughter of Highbrow who was culled in 2000, bred the 2009 Coronation Cup winner Ask for her new owners.

Of the others, Burghclere's daughter Wind In Her Hair finished runner-up in the 2005 Oaks before she produced Deep Impact, one of the best horses ever to race in Japan. But the one that really got away, of course, was Height Of Fashion. Her son, the outstanding Nashwan, was among ten foals she produced. Seven of them had sufficient talent to compete in Pattern races. More importantly, Height Of Fashion bequeathed five daughters to Sheikh Hamdan. It was just as well he was in a position to keep them all, since four of them bred winners of Pattern races. Their influence has since extended to the next generation: recent champions Ghanaati and Lahudood are granddaughters of Height Of Fashion, who has been largely responsible for the excellent reputation forged by Sheikh Hamdan's Shadwell Stud.

When events conspire against them, some owner/breeders respond by extravagant means. They are driven entirely by passion. Just as Daniel Wildenstein was mortified to contemplate anyone else breeding from Allez France's only daughter, Sheikh Mohammed could not countenance the thought that others would be racing the sons and daughters of his beloved racehorse Dubai Millennium. When that great horse died midway through his first season at stud in 2001, the sheikh was so distraught that he resolved to buy every one of Dubai Millennium's sons and daughters. He started by making offers to breeders with mares carrying unborn

Opposite: An Epsom Derby winner for the
Queen – the 'Amateurs' Derby', that is, as
Senor Urbano-Grajales drives Arabian Story
well clear of his rivals in the 1996 Moët et
Chandon Silver Magnum.

foals to the horse. Though many obliged him, others preferred to wait.
The sheikh then redoubled his efforts to buy those foals when they were
born. Those he could not buy as foals he pursued a year later, when they
were yearlings. On he pressed, until he managed to secure 51 of Dubai
Millennium's 54 live offspring.

The sheikh spent untold millions in his quest to redress Mother Nature's
cruel act. To him, the horse's offspring were like family. No price was too
great – except in a small handful of instances when breeders seemed
intent on exploiting the situation excessively to their financial advantage.
Of course, nothing could fully compensate him for Dubai Millennium's
tragic loss, yet the sheikh cherished a moment of exceptional resonance
when Dubawi, a son of Dubai Millennium, won the Irish Two Thousand
Guineas in 2005. It is also refreshing to record that Dubawi himself is now
flourishing as a stallion. In every one of Dubawi's foals Sheikh Mohammed
will look for physical traits handed down by Dubai Millennium, in the
process rekindling memories of his exceptional racehorse. They will never
disperse.

In Height Of Fashion's case, the Queen could do nothing to retrieve
any of her daughters, since Sheikh Hamdan kept them all. And the
parallel between Height Of Fashion and Dubai Millennium underlines
an important distinction. Whereas such a stallion as Dubai Millennium
can sire more than a hundred foals every year, broodmares like Height Of
Fashion can deliver only one, since they are eleven months in gestation.
On average, a broodmare is expected to produce ten foals in her lifetime.
Probability decrees that half will be colts, leaving five fillies for their
breeder to develop the bloodline into the future. Female lines govern the
thinking of all breeders. In essence, they are the vehicles of success. Sheikh
Mohammed has plenty of mares by Dubai Millennium on his studs. He
will cherish them all, yet none so much as other mares descending in their
female line from Dubai Millennium's mother and her immediate relatives.
On them does the sheikh pin his hopes for the future.

Height Of Fashion's sale raised a question that preoccupied the
bloodstock community for many years. Would she have enjoyed such
outstanding results had she stayed within the Royal Studs? One thing is
certain: she would not have been sent to the dazzling array of stallions

Sheikh Hamdan chose for her. Height Of Fashion's two visits to Northern Dancer cost the sheikh an estimated $2 million alone. Three separate trysts with Mr Prospector cost between $250,000 and $325,000 each, while others with Blushing Groom, Danzig and Lyphard would collectively have left little change from $1 million.

These were not sums of money the Royal Studs would routinely spend. Like her father before her, the Queen keeps a firm handle on running costs. It later transpired that an influence within the decision to sell Height Of Fashion was the question of which stallions she could be bred to on her retirement from racing. With stallions in Ireland out of bounds, only a small handful in Britain had the requisite quality. There might have been little option but to send Height Of Fashion to Kentucky, if not to the court of stallions aligned for her by Sheikh Hamdan. It would not have pleased the Queen, who missed seeing her Kentucky-born foals until they arrived in Britain many months later. Her particular pleasure in breeding horses is to watch youngsters develop. She likes to see them at regular intervals, camera in hand, to record the considerable physical evolution made by horses of that age. Equally, the lack of previous racecourse achievement by her Kentucky-bred horses might well have persuaded the Queen to keep Height Of Fashion at home. That is not to say she would have failed to flourish; rather, that the likes of Nashwan and Unfuwain would never have been born. In all likelihood Height Of Fashion's legacy would have been quite different.

Nor did the Royal Studs enjoy any luck by their efforts to redeem Height Of Fashion's sale. Highclere's latter years in Kentucky proved unproductive even though her retracing of Height Of Fashion's footsteps to the court of sires based in America was the obvious way to approach it – and that despite the Queen's reluctance to spend excessively on stallion fees. It is often said that the cost of patronising expensive stallions did not arise, since the Queen was gifted breeding rights to them by their owners. This argument holds little water on close inspection. Had the syndicates owning stallions of the status of Danzig, Lyphard, Mr Prospector and Northern Dancer been willing donors, then Highclere would surely have visited them. In any case, the royal racing and breeding interests are not disposed to accept gifts. Any reciprocal arrangements, as in the case of Carlton House, involve an exchange of horses between the parties concerned. There are times when gifts are bestowed on birthdays and state visits: the Queen was given a filly on her visit to Australia in 1980, which she named Australia Fair. But this is common to all and sundry. We commemorate birthdays and Christmas – and in the Queen's case, state visits – by exchanging gifts.

The footnote to the second half of Highclere's life is simply that Mother Nature would not cooperate. Nor was she kindly disposed to the breeding career of her full-sister Light Duty who bred nothing of note and whose line would lapse entirely from the Royal Studs. In Feola's time the sale of daughters that would excel in other hands was offset by the deeds of those retained by the Royal Studs. No such redemption was afforded Highclere's daughters.

Nor was there any logic to the twist that Height Of Fashion's sale coincided with the start of a decline in the influence of the royal broodmare band that would affect the Queen's fortunes on the racetrack. No reason was apparent: female lines that flourished right up to Height Of Fashion's birth were now withering. Success in the highest class would prove elusive; so much so that the last Group One victory savoured by the Queen in Europe came during Dunfermline's heyday in the Silver Jubilee year of 1977.

In his role as the BBC's television commentator and racing correspondent at the *Daily Express*, Sir Peter O'Sullevan watched the related consequences of the West Ilsley episode and Height Of Fashion's sale unfold with a heavy heart. His perspective lends a different slant to events as most saw them at the time. 'I remember Her Majesty saying to me on one occasion: "It's all very well, but I couldn't have bought West Ilsley without selling Height Of Fashion." She said it quite querulously, really, as if to say: "People ought to think further ahead." But with hindsight, it was an ambitious thing to do. And of course, some ill-feeling was naturally engendered over Dick Hern. Height Of Fashion could not go to Irish stallions. That was hugely constricting to the Queen, although it was perfectly understandable.'

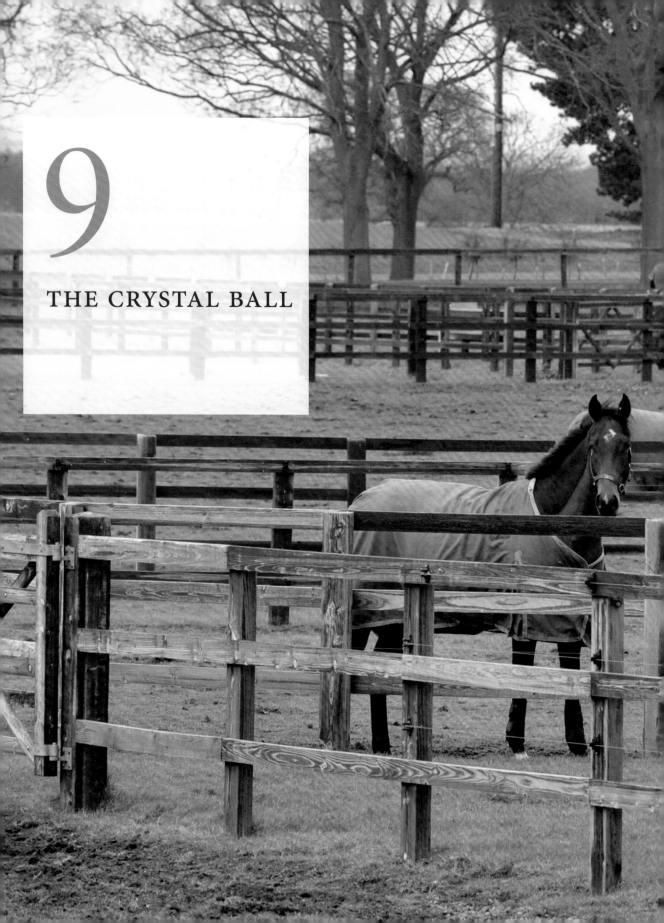

9

THE CRYSTAL BALL

The last thing you'd expect to see when you walk past Buckingham Palace is a gang of cowboy builders swinging from makeshift scaffolding with music blaring loudly from a radio. If you did, the chances are they would have to return time and again to patch up a job badly done.

The same is true of a valuable painting. The owner of a masterpiece in need of restoration will not send it to an artist who peddles his wares on the railings at Hyde Park. To place such assets in unprofessional hands is instantly to devalue them.

A band of broodmares is no different. Mares are assets that require investment if they are to maintain or advance their value. A high-class racemare retiring to stud has earned the right to be bred to high-class stallions. To deny her the opportunity is to diminish her prospects. There are exceptions, of course, but they serve only to make the rule. In rare instances a mare will throw a succession of talented runners by a series of undistinguished stallions. It is every breeder's dream to stumble upon such a mare. They are like gold dust, and every bit as hard to find.

The Royal Studs have not had one of these since Edward VII's time. Perdita was a distinctly average runner but she proved a revelation at stud, where she bred three outstanding runners in Florizel, Persimmon and Diamond Jubilee – all of them by the notable sire St Simon. All three retired to stallion duties at Sandringham, where Edward VII, as Prince of Wales, set up the stud in 1886. Florizel did well enough while Diamond

Jubilee was exported to Argentina, where he also flourished. But the best of them was undoubtedly Persimmon, who was champion sire four times. Conversely, Perdita's daughters wielded no influence at all. Her line would soon dissolve from the royal broodmare band.

Then, as now, successful stallions earn their owners a fortune in stud fees, and Persimmon's innings ensured the Royal Studs more than paid their way. Much of the infrastructure at Sandringham was built from income generated by Persimmon, who is commemorated by an arresting bronze statue at the entrance.

The closest the Queen has come to having a standout mare in her reign is Highlight, whose story underlines just how much the breeding business owes to chance. Although Highlight deserved her place at stud through her racecourse achievements, the first half of her breeding life was distinctly unproductive. He first foal failed to win, she failed to get in foal in year two, her third foal died young, her fourth failed to win, her fifth also died young, she again failed to get in foal in year six and in year seven she 'slipped' her pregnancy. Here, surely, was a mare unworthy of perseverance, yet the Queen felt otherwise. By now the equine dynasty founded by Highlight's grandmother, Feola, was taking shape, and the Queen's persistence paid off when for her ninth foal, Highlight produced Highclere.

It was as if Highlight suddenly found Mother Nature's favour. In quick succession she produced three more daughters of laudable racing merit in Light Duty, Circlet and Blaze Of Glory. Each of them showed promise as broodmares without managing to come up trumps. The one to do so, of course, was Highclere via her daughter Height Of Fashion. Despite a healthy scattering of Highclere's relatives on the Royal Studs, none came close to matching Height Of Fashion breeding exploits. So much so that the studs housed just five broodmares descending from Highlight among twenty-seven mares in residence at the start of Diamond Jubilee year. In contrast, there were twelve tracing to Amicable who, largely through her daughter Expansive, has wielded a more purposeful influence over the past thirty years. The other ten mares are from lines new to the Royal Studs, that have undergone considerable change since John Warren succeeded his father-in-law Lord Carnarvon as Bloodstock and Racing Advisor to the Queen in 2001.

Carnarvon's legacy over three decades of tenure divides sharply into two. His advice was fundamental to the Royal Studs' revival in the 1970s. It was he who advocated the mating of Highlight with Queen's Hussar, which produced Highclere. Against that, the studs have regressed since Height Of Fashion's sale in 1982. The royal silks achieved only sporadic success throughout the 1990s, but then, very few breeding ventures of similar size managed to remain competitive. The last decade of the twentieth century saw British racing became the most competitive in the world. Arab concerns were harvesting the fruits of their massive investment, while the Coolmore outfit fronted by John Magnier was beginning to hit its straps.

Never before have the Royal Studs been aligned against such daunting competition. A heavy financial outlay on the Queen's part would be required to match strides with them, and that is not her way. Indeed, today's royal racing and breeding preserve is a very different institution from that of its forbears. Earlier monarchs spent more lavishly on their Thoroughbreds. There is also no alternative source of horses available to the Queen – as there was for Edward VII, who won the 1909 Derby with the lessee Minoru; or even George VI, who won four of the five Classics in 1942 with the National Stud lessees Big Game and Sun Chariot. And while this lends context to the Royal Studs' fortunes, it fails to acknowledge that racing and breeding are the Queen's hobby. Racecourse results are paramount to those who breed racehorses as a profession, but the Queen is not among them.

Indeed, the Queen as custodian of the Royal Studs has been a model of financial restraint. It is plain that proprietors of some competing entities have more money than sense. There is no method in their madness. They breed distinctly ordinary mares to the best stallions on the lucky-dip principle. Money is spent in unprecedented amounts with no prospect of a financial return on the road to self-sufficiency. Such people should not breed their own. They would be better served by replenishing their racing strings from the yearling sales, since their enjoyment is governed entirely by racecourse success and the attendant kudos. By contrast, the enjoyment of breeders with a successful racehorse emanates from the years of heartbreak and application required to produce it.

The Queen is firmly in the latter camp. Warren attests that she is less preoccupied by competing with rival studs than by the knowledge that

The statue of Persimmon at Sandringham.

the horses she breeds have been given every chance to attain their full potential. It is folly to countenance a champion racehorse from the mating of a relatively ordinary mare to a stallion of commensurate ability. But there is much satisfaction to be had if that horse achieves more than might reasonably have been expected of it.

In the twenty years following Height Of Fashion, the Queen's passion never waned in proportion with the level of success she once enjoyed. She was happy to immerse herself in the aesthetics of breeding. It was a calling she shared with Carnarvon, whose ethos for using stallions was rooted in the quality of their blood. He always preferred the lure of a less expensive stallion of immaculate lineage to a more acclaimed one of equally regal blood – and with a stud fee to match. It worked a treat for him, although the magic did not rub off on the Queen's mares.

Before he took over from Carnarvon in 2001, Warren spent six years as a consultant to the royal breeding interests. This allowed him to acquire an understanding of the way the Queen and his father-in-law wanted to develop the Royal Studs. 'The perception I had was that they chose stallions [to use on the royal mares] in the purest sense,' Warren related. 'It was down to whether they liked a particular nick, or a cross [of blood]. That's probably why the likes of Highclere came about: they liked the nick between Highlight [her dam] and Queen's Hussar, who was an inexpensive stallion. My father-in-law studied pedigrees closely and taught me a tremendous amount. I always think he treated the Queen's broodmare band as he did his own, which was basically on a shoestring. He knew the Queen was conscientious and in no way self-indulgent.'

Warren's assessment emphasises the frame within which the Queen's racecourse achievements should be viewed. They stem from a limited budget. In that respect the Royal Studs have not been performing too far below expectations. Some seasons have been punctuated by a healthy number of winners, although in critical analysis it is fair to say the studs might have done better. In this, they are probably paying a price for using stallions that, although pure of blood, did not leave an influential genetic imprint on subsequent generations. This is akin to a garment whose colour loses a bit of vibrancy each time it is washed. 'Like any other breeder,' Warren averred, 'you start with a good mare and breed from a lesser daughter, then a lesser daughter of hers, and so on. It is inevitable you will thin the blood.'

In these circumstances breeders who spend fortunes mating their mares are at a distinct advantage. Even if the resultant foal is of little account the influence of these stallions prevents the blood from thinning. The colour retains its vibrancy; the masterpiece retains its value. It is also why a good broodmare band requires investment if its influence is to persist. That Carnarvon was able to make his stud retain vigour through several decades of selling prize fillies and using inexpensive stallions is a tribute to him. That the Queen was unable to achieve similar success, even with Carnarvon's assistance over more than thirty years, demonstrates the fickle nature of the game.

For all that, there has been one impediment on the Royal Studs greater than the collective influence of all the above. It concerned the studs' inability to use stallions based in Ireland, which came to dominate the racing landscape in Europe. It arose in the first instance when Robert Sangster, heir to the Vernons pools business, chose to make racing and breeding his preferred vehicle of investment. He aligned himself with Vincent O'Brien and John Magnier to establish Coolmore Stud and its racing subsidiary, Ballydoyle Stables, from where O'Brien trained a string of champions destined for stud duties at Coolmore.

To initiate the turning of that circle, the three men went on annual sales trips to the premier yearling sales at Keeneland in Kentucky. They spent small fortunes on the best of them, in the process raising the value of Thoroughbreds. Given their collective expertise, the odds on them striking equine gold were short, and the hit duly arrived in the late 1980s. His name was Sadler's Wells. A son of Northern Dancer, Sadler's Wells would become a genuine stallion phenomenon. In his prime he generated an annual income of eight-figure proportions for Coolmore and its partners. They would reinvest the proceeds wisely. They spent heavily to buy Danehill, who repaid their faith in spades when in 2005 he was the stallion to finally end Sadler's Wells' thirteen-year stranglehold as champion sire. It was the first of three sire's titles for Danehill. Together with Sadler's Wells, he has proved an immensely successful sire of sires. Coolmore thus had the seed corn of an influence that will extend well into the twenty-first century. The best of Sadler's Wells' and Danehill's sons stand today at Coolmore and its annexes in Kentucky and Australia.

Ireland is portrayed as home to some of the world's best stallions but its reputation owes much to Coolmore. To be denied access to its stallions is to be condemned to near-certain failure. In 2005 the Maktoum family stopped using Coolmore's stallions after the two behemoths fell out. Their racing fortunes ebbed in tandem. Even their huge investment could not uncover stallions of sufficient quality for a collective broodmare band in excess of 1,000 head. Four years later Sheikh Mohammed moved to address the problem: he spent a sum approaching £200 million on a dozen proven racehorses in an effort to bolster his stallion ranks. At the start of the Diamond Jubilee there were signs that one or two of them might reach the highest grade, although none can hope to match the deeds of Sadler's Wells or Danehill. If a man of Sheikh Mohammed's vast resources struggles to swim against the Irish tide, what chance the Queen?

The Irish stallion impasse would endure for thirty years. There was no royal winner in Ireland after the Queen Mother's Mascara won at the now-defunct Baldoyle racetrack, north of Dublin, in 1971. Mascara was trained at The Curragh by John Oxx senior, whose son, also John, gained recognition of his own training talent through the stellar exploits of Sea The Stars. John Oxx junior worked in his father's stables at the time and remembers how events in Northern Ireland were shaping a deteriorating political landscape.

'Mascara ran at Leopardstown one day and I remember there was a lot of security around the parade ring,' Oxx told the *Irish Times* ahead of the Queen's visit to Ireland in 2011. 'The security situation was changing and there was no question of [the Queen Mother] ever having another horse in training here.'

No one would have lamented that necessary absence more than the Queen Mother. Her love of jump racing was shared by a nation whose population has an affinity with the horse unmatched anywhere else. Furthermore, the Queen Mother was seen over several decades as the most visible royal connection with Ireland. She had been to Down Royal racecourse in 1962 to watch her horse Laffy win the Ulster National. In the circumstances it was appropriate that when the Troubles quelled sufficiently for royal silks to return to Ireland in 1996, the Queen Mother led the way.

In addition to his groom and trainer, Norman Conqueror was accompanied to Fairyhouse for the Irish Grand National by the Queen Mother's racing manager, Sir Michael Oswald. After Norman Conqueror made little impact Sir Michael was befriended by a local man with whom he shared a glass. He had no compunction in telling the truth when the man asked him the purpose of his visit. To which his new-found acquaintance replied: 'Yes, and I'm the Duke of Alburquerque.'

The Queen Mother's affection for Ireland manifested itself every year when she attended the Cheltenham Festival in March. 'The meeting usually coincides with St Patrick's Day,' said Terry Pendry, manager and head groom of the Royal Mews at Windsor Castle. 'Every year she would stop off at a little shop on the way and pick up some shamrock, which she handed out at Cheltenham. The Irish loved her; there is no other word to describe it. As for jumps racing in general, I think a little bit of it died with Queen Elizabeth.'

Racing and the myriad characters within it held the Queen Mother in thrall. A vivid example of it surfaced when Sir Michael was handed a most unusual letter that arrived from Australia. 'Somewhere out in the backwoods of Queensland is a drinking establishment called The Liar's Lounge,' Sir Michael related. 'There were eighty-five members and when they won a yearling filly in a raffle they wrote to offer Queen Elizabeth a 1/86th share in her. I don't think they expected to hear back from her but she was so thrilled she asked me to write on her behalf to tell them so. Then we received another letter saying: "Tell Her Maj, the next time she comes out here she must come to the Lounge, where the shout's on us." She desperately wanted to go, too, but unfortunately, it couldn't be done. She was ninety-seven at the time.'

For the Queen at home, a more pressing matter was the question of how she should mate her broodmares without recourse to Ireland. In the face of Britain's diminished stallion ranks the only other option was Kentucky, and that did not work for the Royal Studs. In keeping with the Queen's desire to keep a lid on costs, only the best of royal mares based in Kentucky were bred to high-ranking stallions. Even then, the margins are small: a top-class stallion is one whose progeny compete in the premier league at a rate of one foal out of every ten born to him. The other nine are underachievers.

'I have always been sceptical about the American angle,' John Warren said. 'It is a bit like planting a cactus in the middle of The Curragh. You can't expect an American-bred horse to operate as well in Europe because the entire US bloodline has been developed from racing on dirt. It has become a very different animal to one descending from European bloodlines.' The fundamental difference is that European bloodlines have been developed on the back of racing on turf.

When the Kentucky venture was scaled down, the royal mares were effectively consigned to visiting stallions based in Britain. A cursory look at the leading sires in Britain and Ireland in 1990 serves to illustrate the extent of that handicap. Of the top twenty stallions on the list, only four were based in Britain. The other sixteen were off limits to the royal mares. And 1990 was no rogue year; it was an accurate snapshot of the day. This obliged the Queen to patronise many of the young and unproven stallions assembled by the Maktoum brothers at their Newmarket studs. The Maktoums have always been strong supporters of the royal cause but their stallions failed to buck established trends. As with everything else in breeding, most were destined to fail.

'I think the Queen and my father-in-law felt very frustrated at the time,' Warren recalled. 'Every year they would scratch their heads over which stallions they should use. When Height Of Fashion was racing I know they spent quite some time talking about how they might mate her, and there weren't many options. I think the Royal Studs did suffer for the lack of opportunities. To my mind that is why they experienced a dip.'

This also played its part in the absence of new additions to the Royal Studs throughout the 1990s. There was little sense in amalgamating mares of different blood when they could not be mated to best effect. Introducing fresh blood is important to any breeding venture. In addition to broadening the bottom of the pyramid it offers the opportunity to experiment with successful contemporary strains. Again, the Queen will have recognised the imperative for it, yet what was the point? Instead she reacted with prudence. She effectively placed the studs' development on hold until such time as she was in a position to revive it. That time has now arrived.

The Queen's state visit to Ireland in 2011, the first of its kind by a British monarch for 100 years, was successful beyond expectations. She was

The Queen and the Duke of Edinburgh admiring the stallion Invincible Spirit at the Irish National Stud, 2011.

warmly welcomed wherever she went over three days, which included visits to four of Ireland's prominent stud farms. It was no indulgence on her part, since breeding racehorses is a rich part of Ireland's heritage. It is something at which the country is a world leader. The business is a huge employer and a significant generator of national income. As much was acknowledged by an Irish government that accorded tax-free status to income accrued from stallion fees until such time as Ireland's hegemony within Europe was firmly established. In essence, breeding horses is part of Ireland's soul.

Accordingly, the Queen was received at the National Stud of Ireland, whose links with Britain are long-standing and pronounced. Minoru was foaled and reared at the Kildare nursery before his transfer to the royal livery, which he carried to victory in the 1909 Derby and Two Thousand Guineas for Edward VII. At that time the stud belonged to Colonel William Hall Walker, subsequently Lord Wavertree, who left the property and its bloodstock to the British government for the creation of a National Stud. His bloodstock was transferred to Britain and the Irish government bought the Kildare property to establish its own National Stud in 1943, the year after another of its protégés, Sun Chariot, had won three Classics for George VI.

During her visit to the Irish National Stud the Queen was able to see Invincible Spirit for the first time in the flesh. She had previously used the stallion on royal mares more than once. The Queen also visited Gilltown Stud, where she set eyes on Sea The Stars. She had seen this supreme racehorse two years earlier, when Sea The Stars won the 2009 Derby at Epsom. But the visit she would have anticipated most of all was the trip to Coolmore Stud, with its glittering array of stallions, in County Tipperary. Like every visitor, she would have felt like a child allowed to run amok in a sweet shop. To see so many iconic Thoroughbreds at first hand is as good as it gets.

The Queen's visit gave rise to speculation that she might be about to send mares to the stallions at Coolmore. Ladbrokes, the bookmakers, even offered odds on the likelihood of imminent matings with Galileo and Montjeu. In reality, this had been happening in a discreet way for upwards of fifteen years. In an annexe to the Coolmore boardroom hangs a letter on official paper from Sir Michael Oswald. In it Sir Michael offers appreciation for the fact that Coolmore had returned all four of the royal broodmares to Sandringham safely in foal. He also enclosed a cheque for £100 as a gift to be distributed among the staff. The letter is dated 4 December 1997. It sits proudly inside a frame with the original royal cheque, presumably uncashed, attached to it. That it hangs in the Sadler's Wells suite, which is named after the stud's totemic stallion, underlines Coolmore's pride in playing host to those royal mares. It serves to underpin the bond that unites horse people around the world. As Alec Head, the French breeder of repute, observed in an earlier chapter, racing and breeding are international languages that know no boundaries. As if to underline the point, the British monarchy has retained an unbroken association with a race in Ireland for nearly two centuries. The Royal Whip Stakes has been renewed at The Curragh ever since a perpetual trophy was presented to the Turf Club of Ireland by William IV in the 1830s.

According to Joe Grimwade, manager of the Royal Studs, the Coolmore stallion that really filled the Queen's eye was Galileo. She had seen Galileo twice previously but not since 2001, when he raced to victories in the Derby and King George VI and Queen Elizabeth Stakes at Ascot. Galileo has since become a Coolmore mainstay; he was champion sire in three of the four years up to 2011. Had her mother been alive to accompany the Queen her gaze would doubtless have settled on Montjeu, who sired three

Derby winners in seven years to 2011. That is because Montjeu, with his size and scope, is more of a jumping model than Galileo, whose physical qualities are perfectly aligned for Flat racing, which the Queen prefers. Staff at the Royal Mews in Windsor cannot help but feel resonance in the Queen's words when she comes across First Love, who is now a riding horse but was one of the Queen Mother's last homebred jumpers. She will look at this equine giant in stature and declare: 'Now that's a proper horse.' They are the very same words her mother would use on seeing a horse in First Love's mould.

The Queen has already savoured success from the progeny of the small number of royal mares bred to Coolmore stallions. In 2000 Interlude, by Sadler's Wells, won a Group Two race in France, while the following year Flight Of Fancy, another filly by Sadler's Wells, might have won the Oaks – in which she finished runner-up – but for sustaining an injury in the closing stages. Stallions based in Ireland are now available to the royal mares. This had been foreshadowed in the previous decade, and with it came the opportunity for the Queen to breed Thoroughbreds without impediment. She has duly taken it.

This welcome development started to unfold when John Warren took office in 2001, when opportunity beckoned. 'When I was an advisor I used to speak to the Queen on occasions,' Warren related, 'but when I took over the position I was able to have long discussions with her about different sire lines. Because Ireland was opening up we could explore what the stallions based there had to offer, and also which of her mares might no longer be suited to the opportunity these stallions presented. We went into this in great detail. At the end of it, the Queen decided to restructure her broodmare band over a period of time.'

Indeed, the royal broodmare band at the start of Diamond Jubilee year differs significantly from the one in place when Warren took office in 2001. Only two among the twenty-seven Flat mares were by American-based sires and both of those sires – Fasliyev and Rahy – did their racing on European grass. The American 'dirt' influence is so negligible as to be virtually non-existent. As a collective tribe the mares are relatively young, and thus retain plenty of opportunity. Of the nine female families the Queen inherited with the Royal Studs in 1952, only two survive: the aforementioned lines of Highlight and Amicable. More importantly, there have been ten new additions, each of them from lines never previously harboured by the studs. All in all it was quite an overhaul, although Warren was anxious to emphasise the context.

'It is important to remember that the Queen and my father-in-law both loved what they had,' Warren said. 'Whatever they bred, they were always thoroughly content. Both of them spent decades getting into the families they wanted. People of their generation, of their age, tend to be happy with their lot, whereas I was looking at it with a fresh eye. And even then, at no point did the Queen say: "Right, let's go out and buy X, Y and Z to put the restructuring into place." It has been a methodical, calculated, gradual process. We have introduced the odd bit of new blood each year. It is successful blood that has added another dimension to the mating plans.'

Warren feels the Royal Studs have much to anticipate. 'The Queen hasn't hit the jackpot yet but there are some very well-bred mares that I feel sure will make their mark,' he said. 'They are, I hope, part of the foundation the Queen has put down. The proof of the pudding is in the eating, but I feel the Royal Studs are very close to achieving something significant.'

It remains to be seen where any success might originate from. In terms of their immediate ancestry the new mares are a cut above most long-standing members of the band. Perhaps they will spearhead a return to greater prominence for the royal silks. Against that, both Alec Head and Sir Michael Oswald believe the Highlight/Highclere clan is far from a spent force. 'It is a wonderful family,' Head averred. 'One of these days I am sure it is going to hit again.'

Part of Warren's remit is constantly to reassess the broodmare band's overall composition, since the Queen is inclined to view each mare as an individual project. She immerses herself in the specific characteristics of each family. She will know the inherent quirks within each family: previous foals from a mare may have a natural aversion to starting stalls, for instance. Others, like Aureole, may be free of spirit. She remembers all the minutiae that have accumulated over her six decades of breeding Thoroughbreds. 'The more time I spent discussing bloodstock with the Queen the more I realised the depth of her knowledge,' Warren said. 'It is second to none among the many people I have dealt with in this industry. She has a natural interest but also a wealth of experience. There is no one in the country, perhaps in the industry worldwide, who has bred more crops of foals.'

Highly bred animals tend to come with particular traits, especially when they are subjected to inbreeding on the lines favoured by the Queen's former racing manager Charles Moore. Even when this is outcrossed, as it was in the case of the full-sisters Highclere and Light Duty, those traits can endure. They can also promote an unwarranted reputation among those obliged to handle such horses. A personal recollection concerns Light Duty's arrival on the National Stud in Newmarket in 1987, when she was bred to Final Straw. Seasoned stud hands were cautioned to handle her with care; on no account should she be patted down the neck. Word spread that the Royal Studs permitted so much blood to be drawn in the interests of research that its broodmares were hostile to any hand placed on their necks lest it should belong to a vet brandishing a needle. It seemed an utterly implausible story. Sure enough, a gentle pat drew nothing more sinister from Light Duty than a look of contentment as she ambled back from the paddocks to her stable.

The episode serves to underline the impression that royal horses of that era tended to be high on mettle. But that, too, seems consigned to the past. Traits of temperament are often at their most pronounced when young horses are put through the process of 'starting' them and riding them away. This process unfolds each year from the Friar Marcus Yard at Sandringham in the lead-up to Christmas, yet to wander among the yearlings then is to see a herd of happy, content young horses. Any sense of unease in one horse in an open barn is inclined to rub off on others stabled alongside it. There was no hint of it on this December day. Elements of the Monty Roberts technique adopted by the Royal Studs may have much do with it, although a glance through the royal collection confirms that very few broodmares carry duplications of sires within five generations other than to Northern Dancer, whose influence in contemporary pedigrees is so ubiquitous it has become the norm.

Breeding Thoroughbreds is a vastly different enterprise from breeding horses for other purposes – and quite a contrast from the Fells and Highlanders from which the Queen draws equal pleasure. Yet one aspect gives rise to a royal lament. It is the sheer speed with which young

The stallion Motivator at Sandringham.

Thoroughbreds are taken to the racecourse. Some are up and racing before they reach their second birthday, when their ongoing skeletal development is under considerable strain. Natural wastage is high; much of it is dictated by commercial concerns driven by the prohibitive cost of keeping a horse in training, which roughly equates to the annual cost of a private education.

Further to that is another inescapable fact: ninety per cent of all Thoroughbreds are destined to disappoint. Animals that commonly live until their mid-twenties are tried and discarded by the time they are three years old. What then? The question has vexed the sport since time immemorial.

Some people take their responsibilities to the post-racing conundrum as seriously as if their horses were extended family. Leading Irish owner J.P. McManus retires every one of the hundreds of jumps horses he owns to his stud in County Limerick, where they graze for the rest of their days.

The Queen's retired Flat horses are of a younger age and therefore ripe for retraining into other equine disciplines. Not all are amenable to it, given their Thoroughbred heritage, but suitable places are found for them once the retraining process is complete.

There have been many successful transfers. The aforementioned First Love, now in the Royal Mews at Windsor, has taken part in two renewals of Trooping the Colour and is earmarked for veterans' class for former racehorses at the Royal Windsor Horse Show. Mister Glum, another former racehorse trained by Ian Balding, has developed into a top-class dressage horse.

'The most important thing to the Queen is that these horses find a good home,' Terry Pendry related. 'She never forgets them, even when we pass them on. Periodically I will drive around to where they have been sent, just to make sure they are happy.'

Next in line to join the Royal Mews is Quadrille, who was narrowly beaten in a photo-finish at Royal Ascot in 2011, and whose racing career ended in premature retirement. His suitability for alternative roles will be explored, although the suspicion is that Pendry won't be too disappointed if Quadrille ends up permanently under his care. Pendry once harboured the ambition to be a jockey; he finished third in a race at Ayr in 1966, when his horse bolted at the start and was only caught in the closing stages. Once a jockey, always a jockey – or so the saying goes. In January 2011, on a snow-covered canter in Windsor Great Park, Pendry lowered his hands onto First Love's withers and the old steeplechaser cut loose. 'He virtually dropped his nose on the dirt,' Pendry recalled. 'I swear he was counting his feet going round, and every other stride he was squeaking like a little girl. It was absolutely wonderful.'

Conversely, Warren is charged with keeping as many of the Queen's Thoroughbreds out of Pendry's willing clutches as possible. It is a challenging role, yet one where a single superior runner atones for the inevitable string of disappointments. Warren takes his cue from the Queen as they exchange ideas and monitor bloodlines that come to the fore on the racetrack. An example of the relationship between proprietor and advisor concerned the Queen's purchase of the mare Daralbayda, then eighteen, back in 2005. It arose from a conversation she had with Warren that amplified her admiration for a particular female family successfully cultivated by the Aga Khan. Daralbayda was from that family. Her advancing age made her an affordable proposition with the aim of trying to breed a filly for the Royal Studs. The plan came to fruition when Sally Forth was foaled in 2006.

John Warren at Highclere Stud.

On the back of that, Warren learned that the Queen was enamoured by much of the blood coursing through the Aga Khan's studs that had been developed initially by Marcel Boussac, whose stock the Aga Khan had purchased in 1980. Warren was also aware that the Aga Khan, a friend of the Queen's for many years, wanted to commemorate her eightieth birthday in 2006. The consequence, after much discussion with all interested parties, was that the Aga Khan made over six broodmares for the Queen's temporary use. A mating was devised for each of them. The Royal Studs would secure a breeding right to each of the chosen stallions and keep the resultant foal if it were a filly. In the event of a colt, the Aga Khan would keep it and reimburse the cost of the mating.

This is potentially the most exciting development at the Royal Studs for many years. The Aga Khan's broodmare band is among the most prized in the game. It has delivered consistent success from a myriad different bloodlines. Indeed, a portent of what may lie ahead came in 2011 when Set To Music, from the distinguished female line of French classic winners Zarkava and Zainta, won four races in the royal silks in addition to running second in the Group Two Park Hill Stakes. Not all the fillies have been as successful but their true worth is in their blood. Star Value never ran but claims as her mother another Classic winner in Shemaka. A third filly, Key Point, is half-sister to a champion racehorse Kalanisi. A fourth, Estimate, is half-sister to yet another classic winner in Ebadiyla, while a fifth, Sequence, is half-sister to the 2000 Derby and Prix de l'Arc de Triomphe winner, Sinndar.

Any stud would welcome such an intake, but there is more besides. The Royal Studs have also reached agreement with Prince Khalid Abdullah's Juddmonte Farms, another paragon of breeding excellence, over an exchange involving two broodmares from each side. 'The Queen had three young mares by Sadler's Wells, all of them full-sisters to Flight Of Fancy,' Warren explained. 'Rather than selling them on, we decided to look into a way of swapping two of them with two of Prince Khalid's mares.'

The prince will thus breed from Well Hidden and Hypoteneuse for two years while the Queen has similar access to Far Shores and Five Fields. Again, this reciprocal arrangement gives the Royal Studs access to some regal blood. Far Shores is a half-sister to no less an equine luminary than Coolmore's champion sire Danehill, whereas Five Fields is half-sister to the dual Grade One winner Senure. In 2011 Five Fields foaled a filly by Galileo that will run for the Queen in due course. Beyond that, she represents a gilt-edged breeding prospect for the Royal Studs.

These arrangements with pre-eminent breeders reflect a heartfelt desire on their part to see a revival in the Queen's fortunes. This has been a constant theme throughout the monarch's long involvement on the Flat, which started when the Aga Khan's grandfather gave the Queen a filly, Astrakhan, as a wedding present in 1947. It has progressed from there: towards the end of 2011 Sheikh Mohammed supplemented his reciprocal gift of four horses to the royal racing cause by making over two more. They are both by his successful stallion Street Cry, whose son Carlton House was among the original quartet and who came so close to winning the Derby for the Queen in 2011. It must be hoped that something tangible arises from the collective yearning on behalf of the royal silks, yet nothing in racing is preordained.

In the 1970s every American owner to win the Derby, and thus gain a post-race introduction to the Queen, embraced this collective desire by making their horse available to a royal mare at the onset of its stallion career. Paul Mellon, the philanthropist who owned Mill Reef, made over an annual breeding right in the horse to the Royal Studs. Despite Mill Reef's immense stallion prowess he did not sire a Group One winner for the royal livery. There have been other instances where favourable odds have yielded far less than the sum of their parts. No hint of an impact was made by Monochrome, a yearling filly given to the Queen as a Silver Wedding present by John Galbreath one year after he had won the 1972 Derby with Roberto. Monochrome was a daughter of Idun, a champion runner in north America for three successive years. A filly of the type to spawn a dynasty instead passed quickly from the Royal Studs. It has been this way with so much of the Queen's racing and breeding experience. Perhaps the new era ushered in on Warren's promptings will herald a change of fortune.

The restructuring of the Royal Studs has also given the Queen a fresh interest. In the daily results section she looks out for winners related to mares new to her fold. She is now exploring lines she had only fleetingly countenanced in passing. There is much for her to contemplate as she strives to maximise the intake's potential. In time she will build mental pictures of successive foals from these new mares. She will cast her eye over individuals with different physical traits to the ones she has become accustomed to seeing over the past three decades, when operational constraints prevented her from experimenting as she would have wanted.

The raw material may be changing but the Queen's habits will endure. At the start of each new year she keenly anticipates the birth of foals at Sandringham, where she resides until the second week of February. She will return to Sandringham in April to run her eye over any new arrivals, or perhaps foals that were born elsewhere to mothers now returning after they have been safely tested in foal. Photographs of her young stock are taken in her absence and sent to her every three weeks. She will visit Polhampton to see her yearlings in May. In that month she will also do the rounds of her Flat trainers, taking in Andrew Balding, Richard Hannon and Roger Charlton to the west of Windsor Castle, and Sir Michael Stoute and Michael Bell to the north east in Newmarket. She will enjoy the banter of stable life but she will be a study in concentration as she banks mental images of her horses in training. She will return to Sandringham once more in July, when all her foals will be on site. Duty permitting, she will see them all again in November.

As yet, none of the Queen's children or grandchildren accompanies her on these visits. This raises an important question in the minds of the racing fraternity in Britain and beyond. Who, if anyone, will pick up the baton in the future? There is no obvious answer. The Queen may have attempted to give her eldest son and his wife, the Duchess of Cornwall, a gentle nudge by her choice of wedding present in 2005. She gifted them Supereva, a young broodmare by Sadler's Wells who resides at the Royal Studs. Supereva bred two winners from her first two foals of racing age but has not, as yet, introduced her owners to the big-race frisson the Queen knows so well. There is still time for that, since Supereva, granted good health, should have plenty more racing offspring. The Duchess, an accomplished rider herself, has always enjoyed racing, but the Prince Of Wales has never been smitten by the sport. He rode in six jumps races as an amateur rider in the early 1980s but his involvement, other than regularly attending Royal Ascot, lapsed with his standing down from the saddle.

Although the Prince and Duchess remain the most likely to carry the Royal Studs forward, that may yet change. 'As of now the younger members of the Royal Family are not as interested in racing as the Queen,' Sir Michael Oswald said. 'But then, they have a lot of other things to do. There may come a point when they can't play polo any longer, for example. But even if there is no obvious candidate there is no reason why the Royal Studs, provided they are financially viable, shouldn't carry on in the same way as the Royal Stamp Collection, for example.'

Sir Michael observed that previous monarchs maintained the Royal Studs even though their own interest was minimal. Indeed, but for that, the Queen is unlikely to have bred and raced horses on the scale she does today. It was as well for her, and to a lesser extent for predecessors like Edward VII, that the Royal Studs survived the ambivalence of monarchs like Queen Victoria and George I. The studs have become an important part of British heritage, just as the Queen is an important fixture on British racecourses. To see the dispersal of the oldest Thoroughbred stud in the world would promote heavy hearts in Turf aficionados.

Perhaps Prince William and his wife were sufficiently enthused by their inaugural visit to the Derby in 2011 to take up the cause. Prince Harry is sometimes seen on the Newmarket gallops at an ungodly hour with his friend, John Warren's son Jake. He also has a minor interest in racehorse ownership; perhaps he will develop a passion for racing and breeding redolent of his grandmother. There is simply no telling which way the pendulum might swing.

Whatever comes to pass, the prospect of any imminent future monarch sharing the Queen's calling was always a 100/1 chance. Historians maintain that the extent of the Queen's knowledge surpasses that of any of her forebears. Her recent overhaul of the royal broodmare band seems to bear this out, especially on the delicate grounds of her age. She has celebrated her 86th birthday in Diamond Jubilee year. Alec Head is of a similar vintage. His passion for breeding has not subsided, yet he observed with a glint in his eye: 'You know, when you are young you work hard to be successful. And when you are old and have been successful, you live on your memories.'

The Queen has known success. She has fond memories of it, yet she has just laid new foundations at the Royal Studs. Her enthusiasm knows no bounds. By any reckoning she has embarked on a long-term project. It may take upwards of twenty years to reach fruition, but then, satisfaction is not drawn from the end-product alone. It will be a voyage of discovery, an odyssey punctuated throughout by emotional extremes. Above all, it will be undertaken with the same sense of energy so evident in the Queen at the 1953 Derby, where her journey started. The intervening six decades have served only to heighten Her Majesty's pleasure.

Looking to the future …

INDEX

Page numbers in *italics* refer to illustration captions.

Abergeldie 99, 109
Abernant 168
Above Board 113-114, *114*, 137, 162, 163
Above Suspicion 115, 121, 144, 145, 162, 170
Aga Khan 20, 35, 67, 122, 139, 148, 249-250
Agreement 22-24, 113, 144, 145
Aiming High 170
Aintree, Grand National 98
al-Maktoum, Sheikh Hamdan bin Rashid 21, 76, 161, 208, 210-211, *210*, 213-214, 215, 222, 226, 227, 228, 242
al-Maktoum, HH Sheikh Mohammed bin Rashid 69, 70, 71, 83, 99, 121, 227-228, 240, 242, 250-251
Albany 60, 181, 182
Alcide 144
Alexander 136
Alleged *178*, 197, 198, *198*, 200
Allen, Dr Michael 216, 221
Allez France 68, 111-112, *112*, 170, 227
Almeria 31, 33, 75, 137-138, 140, 141, 144, 147, 181
Ambush II 98
Amicable 235, 246
Angel Bright 162-163
Angelola 103, 132-133, 162, *163*
Anmer 85
Anne, HRH Princess 117, *214*
Arabian Story *228*
Ardross 208
Arlington Handicap 224
Ascot 25, 29, *48*, *50*, 99, 135, 141, *152*, *173*; British Champions Day 25, 27; Fillies' Mile *209*; HM's Representative at 58-59; Hyperion Stakes 34; King George VI & Queen Elizabeth Stakes 6, 34, 74-75, 108, *108*, 114, 134-135, 136, 155, 191, 203, 208-209, 213, 219; Queen Elizabeth II Stakes 25, 27; races named after royalty 25
Ascot, Royal 25, *30*, 40, 42, 43, 59, 126, 134, 136, 140, 145, *145*, 169, 201, 225; Ascot Stakes 170, 172, 175; Chesham Stakes 53, *56*; Coronation Stakes 170; Gold Cup 49, 98, 162, 211, 213, 223-224; Hardwicke Stakes *23*, *134*, 170, *170*; HM the Queen at *23*, *34*, 38, 42, 43-45, *43*, *44*, 46, 47, 49, 53, 56, *56*, 58, *128*, *131*, *145*, *210*; King Edward VII Stakes 144, 162; Prince of Wales's Stakes 155; Ribblesdale Stakes 140, *224*, 225, 226; Royal Enclosure 53; Royal Hunt Cup 224-225; Royal Procession 43, *43*, 44, 47-48, 52-53; St James's Palace Stakes 27

Ask 227
Astrakhan *30*, 35, 250
Atlas 30-31, 111, 121, 136
Aurelius 170
Aureole 6, *23*, 42, 70-71, 85, 99, 102, 103-106, *105*, *106*, 107, 108, *108*, 110, 111, 121, 133-136, *133*, *134*, 143, 162, 169-170, 203, 208, 247
Australia Fair 230
Ave France 68

Balanchine 69
Bald Eagle 142, 143
Balding, Andrew 35, 45, 173, 174, 223, 252
Balding, Clare 27, 29, 44-46, 53, 56, 58, 84, 90, 93, 173, 174
Balding, Ian *25*, 31, 32-34, 35, 40, 44, 45, 59, 102, 115, 172-175, 180, 181, 182-183, 184, 186, 202, 206, 212, 222, 223, 248
Balding, Toby 172
Ballymoss 75, 144
Balmoral 63, 65, 69, 198, 223
Banknote 40
Barclay, Sandy *155*, *170*
Barrett, George 95
Batten, Sir John 216
BBC 27, 44, 45, 46, 47, 48, 53, 58, 84, 85, 103
Be Friendly 24
Be Tuneful 24-25
Beacon Hill 210, 225-226
Beatrice, HRH Princess *83*, 84
Beckhampton 127, 159, 225
Bell, Michael 225, 252
Beresford, Lord Marcus 154
Big Game 60, 62-63, 127, 128, 154, 237
Bireme 202
Blenheim 75, 132, 149
Blueprint 227
Blushing Groom 226, 228
Bois de Citron 20
Boussac, Marcel 147, 148, 190, 249
Boyd-Rochfort, Capt. Sir Cecil 22, *23*, 24, 31, 35, 59, 61, 75, 78-79, 102, 103, 104, 114, 115, 128, 134, 136, 137, 138, 140, 141, 142-143, 144-145, 146, 152-153, 155, 174, 178, 213
Brand 40
breeding 19-20, 65, 67-68, 92-93, 109, 122-123, 127, 128, 130-131, 147-148, 164, 165-167, 168, 170, 228, 234, 235, 238-239, 241-242, 243, 245, 246-248, 249-251; mares, selecting for 128, 130, 131, 132
Brigadier Gerard 180-181, 182
Brister, Betty 14-15, 183, *185*
Brook, Dr Charles 111, 112
Bunbury, Lord 94
Burghclere 225, 227
Burn, Tommy *30*
Bustino 197, 203

Buttress 201
Byrne, Alan 217

Caergwrle 144
Cambridge, HRH Duke and Duchess of 83, 84, 253
Canisbay 145, *146*
Caramba 19
Card Player 167-168, 181
Carlton House 70, *74*, 77, 78, 79, 80, 81, *81*, 83, 84, 85, 86-87, 90-92, *90*, 93, 99, 121, 195, 200, 230, 251; earlier horse 99
Carnarvon, sixth Earl of 75, 132, 160
Carnarvon, seventh Earl of (formerly Lord Porchester) 13-14, 18, 19, 21, 22, *34*, 59, 69, 75-76, 115, 132, 136, 149, 156, 158-161, 165, 166, 168, *179*, 182, 184, 189, 210, 211, 212-213, 221, 226, 235, 237, 238, 239, 242, 245; and Dick Hern's lease 216, 217, 219-223
Carr, Harry 31, 107, 111, 113, 134, 142, 193
Carrozza 126, 137, 138, *138*, 139, 140, 141, 143, 153, 170, 185, 200
Carson, Willie 44, *56*, 116, 118, 119, 120, *178*, *179*, 193-195, *195*, *196*, 197, *198*, 200, *201*, 208, 215, 218, 219, 221-222, 223
Cartier, Award of Merit 19
Castle Yard 153
Casual Look 45
Cauthen, Steve 215
Cazalet, Peter 31-32
Cecil, David 152
Cecil, Sir Henry 152, 153, 213
Cecil, Julie 153
Chaleureux 167
Channel 4: 48-49
Chariots Of Fire 40
Charles, HRH Prince of Wales 220, 252
Charles II, HM King 84
Charlton, Roger 225, 252
Cheetah 142, 143, 144
Cheltenham Festival *21*, 241
Chêne, Paul 67
Chester 75, 138, 144; Chester Vase 215; Dee Stakes 111
Church Parade 77-78, 120
Circlet 193-194, 200, 235
Claiborne Farm 131, 132, 161-162
Clare Island *206*
Clark, Sterling 136
Clear Attraction 226-227
Colour Sergeant 224-225
Comtesse de Loir *188*
Cook, Robin 24
Coolmore Stud 19, 77, 80, 130, 131, 237, 239-240, 244, 245
Cornwall, HRH Duchess of 252
Crepello 113, 140
Cummings, Bart 42
Curragh, The: Royal Whip Stakes 244-245

Dahlia 135, 136, 191, 203
Dancing Brave 92
Dancing Rain 147
Danehill 239-240, 250
Danzig 228, 230
Daralbayda 249
Darius 134, 135
Darling, Fred 60, 63, 127-128, 159, 160
Davison, Emily 85-86
Deep Impact 164, 227
Derby, Lord 94, 166
Derby, the 34, 58, 60-61, 70-71, 74, 76, 77-78, 85-86, 93, 94-95, 96, 97-98, 99, *102*, *106*, 107-108, 109-110, 111, 113, *113*, 115, 119-120, 121, 140, 167, 194, 201, 202, 215, 219, 237, 244, 253; 2011 race 70, *74*, 77, 83, 85, 86-87, 90-92, *90*, 93, 195, 200, 251
Detroit 121
Dettori, Frankie 71, *206*, *224*, 225
Dettori, Gianfranco 194, *196*
Diamond Jubilee 85, 98, 168, 234, 235
Diana, Princess of Wales 38, 46, 220
Diomed 94
Doncaster: Doncaster Cup 136, 144, 145; May Hill Stakes 200, *201*, *206*; Park Hill Stakes 140; *see also* St Leger
Double Brandy 40
Doutelle 22-24, 74-75, 112-113, *113*, 114-115, 121, 140, 141, 144, 162
Dubai 69, 70, 71
Dubai Millennium 227-228
Dubawi 228
Dunfirmline *10*, 44, 155, *178*, 192, 193, 194-197, *195*, *196*, 198, *198*, 200, 202, 211, 231
Durtal 194, 195

Edinburgh, HRH the Duke of *see* Philip, HRH Prince
Edward, HRH Prince *74*, 84; children 80
Edward VII, HM King (formerly Prince of Wales) 63, 85, 94, *94*, 95-96, 97, 98-99, 127, 154, 167, 168, 172, 206, 234-235, 237, 244, 252-253
Edward VIII, HM King 63
Egerton Stud 97, 168, 169
Elegant Fashion 226
Elizabeth, HM Queen, the Queen Mother 15, *21*, *23*, 27, 32, 38, 39, 40, 113, *145*, 174, *179*, 190, *195*, *214*, 240-241, 245
Elizabeth II, HM Queen: and Aureole 6, *23*, 102, 105, 107-108, 135-136, 169, 170, 208; and breeding 65, 67, 68, 69, 74, 75, 83, 122, 148, 165-167, 168, 170, 235, 238, 239, 241-242, 245, 246-247, 249, 251; and Carlton House's Derby bid *74*, 83, 84, 86, 91-92, 93; concern for people within equine fraternity 25,

29, 30; controversy after Height Of Fashion sale 21, 161, 164, 165, 219-220, 221, 230, 231; controversy over Dick Hern's lease 220, 222-223; Coronation 71, 102, 103; and Derby day 6, 18, 39, 58, 60-61, 70-71, 74, 77, 78, 83-84, 83, 85, 86, 91-92, 102, 107-108, 109, 111, 121, 123, 194, 206, 214; and Dunfermline's classic win 197-198; early interest in racing 40, 60-62, 61, 63, 65, 65, 123, 126, 127; and Escorial 187; financial restraint 237-238, 241-242, 243; first winners 32, 35, 47; and foals at Royal Studs 68-69, 230, 251; forsaking traditional ways with horses 35, 156, 157; and Frankel 27; and future of the Royal Studs 253, 253; and Highclere's wins 184-186, 185, 188, 189, 190, 191; hopes to win the Derby 75, 78, 84, 93, 103, 106, 121, 122; and Hyperion 67; investment in horses 49-50, 237-238; Kentucky visit 132; as leading owner 133, 140, 141; letters to trainers 18-19; love of horses 65, 70, 74, 122, 174; memory for faces 14-15, 183; memory for horses 24-25, 253; misfortune in racing 21-22, 31, 32-33, 34, 115, 182, 206; passion for racing 11, 13, 53, 58, 84, 85, 121-122; patron to equine organisations 65; penchant for company of racing folk 13, 29-30, 45-46, 56, 179; and Prince Philip 59-60; and punctuality 52; racing diary 40, 42; reaction to win at Royal Ascot broadcast 53, 56; recognition of horses 13, 22-24, 112-113; recreational riding 20, 48, 50, 65, 80, 152; and retirement of horses 248; and Richard Hannon 10, 11, 13-15, 18, 19; and royal protocol 53, 56; royal silks 30, 35, 98-99; and Sheikh Mohammed 70; state visit to Ireland 83, 243, 243, 244; taught to ride 63, 65; visits to Normandy 28, 28, 67, 155-156; visits to racecourses 13, 21, 27, 28, 42, 66, 138, 152, 173, 179, 185, 188, 209; visits to stables 18, 25, 78, 251-252; visits to the Royal Studs 10, 51-52, 251; and welfare of her horses 102; Wimbledon visit 46-47; see also Ascot, Royal; HM the Queen at
Emma (Fell pony) 65
Engelhard, Charles 189-190
English Harbour 115-117, 118, 181
Enharmonic 39, 206, 225
Epsom 97, 138, 208; Coronation Cup 133-134, 155; Derby day 6, 18, 39, 40, 42, 48-49, 83-84, 83, 105-107, 214; Diomed Stakes 206; Moet et Chandon Silver Magnum 228; see also Derby, the and Oaks, the
Escorial 60, 75, 182-184, 186-187
Eugenie, HRH Princess 83, 84
Example 35, 181, 182
Exeter, sixth Marquess of 40
Expansive 201, 235

Fahd Salman, Prince 77
Fallon, Kieren 221
Far Shores 250
Farish III, Will 45
Federer, Roger 47
Fell Pony Society 65
Fellowes, Sir Robert 218
Feola 132, 136, 162, 163-164, 192, 225, 226, 235
Fife And Drum 167-168
Fiordiligi 201

Firework Party 75
First Love 245, 248, 249
FitzGerald, Peter 104
Five Fields 250
Flight Of Fancy 79, 221, 221, 245, 250
Florizel 234, 235
Fontwell Park 32, 40, 47
Frankel 27, 213
Free Agent 53, 56
Freeze The Secret 194, 196

Galbraith, John 251
Galileo 77, 120, 244, 245; colt 15; filly 250
Generous 77, 85
George I, HM King 253
George III, HM King 80
George IV, HM King 94
George V, HM King 63, 83, 85-86, 132, 141
George VI, HM King 35, 38, 60, 62, 63, 102, 103, 113-114, 114, 127, 131, 164, 174, 237, 244
Ghanaati 227
Gilles de Retz 111
Gilltown Stud 244
Ginistrelli, Cavaliere Edoardo 167
Godolphin 69-70, 76
Goodwood 116, 118, 140, 208; Goodwood Cup 145; Lillie Langtry Stakes 85; Sussex Stakes 29, 110, 136
Graham, Neil 216
Gran Alba 15
Grand National 98
Grantham, Tony 40
Gregarious 196, 197
Greylights (pony) 65
Grimwade, Joe 51, 245
Grundy 203
Gwyn, Nell 84-85

Hall Walker, Colonel William (later Lord Wavertree) 127, 154, 244
Hallum, John 33
Hampton Court Stud 56, 60, 61, 69, 95, 123, 156, 166
Hancock, Arthur 'Bull' 132
Hannon, Richard 10-11, 13-14, 13, 15, 18-19, 53, 160, 225, 252
Haras du Quesnay 28, 28, 67, 156
Harry, HRH Prince 84, 91, 253
Harvest Song 121
Haslam, Buster 29
Hastings-Bass, Peter 31, 153, 158, 172, 173, 223
Hastings-Bass, William (later Lord Huntingdon) 202, 206, 217, 219, 223-224
Haya of Jordan, Princess 83
Head, Alec 28, 28, 67, 156, 190, 244, 246, 253
Height Of Fashion 21, 60, 76-77, 132, 161, 164-165, 203, 206, 208-209, 209, 210, 213-214, 215, 219, 225, 226, 227, 228, 230, 231, 235, 237, 242
Henbit 202
Henry VIII, HM King 56
Hern, Maj. Dick 14, 29, 147, 153, 173, 174-175, 178-180, 179, 181, 182, 183, 184, 190-191, 192, 193, 196, 197, 198, 201-202, 203, 206, 210-211, 213, 220, 225, 231; hunting accident 211-212; loss of West Ilsley lease 215-220, 221-223; wife 216, 217
Herridge Stables 10-11, 13, 15, 21-22
Hethersett 179

High Veldt 111, 136
Highbrow 226, 227
Highclere 14, 29, 34, 40, 60, 74, 75, 119, 120, 135, 136, 163, 164, 166, 167, 182, 183, 184-186, 185, 187-188, 188, 189, 190, 191-192, 201, 202, 203, 208, 210, 225, 226-227, 230, 231, 235, 237, 247
Highclere Castle 159
Highclere Stud 75-76, 149, 159-160, 161, 165, 182, 211, 249
Highland Glen 70, 71
Highland Pony Society 65
Highlight 163, 166, 167, 182, 192, 235, 237, 238, 246
Hirsch, Baron de 95
Hobbs, Bruce 139, 152
Hodcott House 209, 217
Holliday, Maj. Lionel 179
Hooper, 'Dodger' 30-31
Hopeful Venture 154, 155, 155, 156, 170, 170
Horse Racing Heroes 28
horses: 'breaking in' 156-158; difficult 111-112, 183; legs, broken 34; securing 114-115; in training 50-51; see also breeding
Hughes, Richard 38, 59
Huntingdon, Lord (formerly William Hastings-Bass) 202, 206, 217, 219, 223-224
Hurst Park 32, 35, 61-62
Hypericum 60, 61-62, 61, 63, 69, 103, 104, 132, 142, 149, 162, 163
Hyperion 67, 103, 104, 147, 148
Hypotenuse 250

Idun 251
Imagine 221
Insular 117
Interlude 245
Invincible Spirit 243, 244
Ireland 43, 120-121, 156, 240-241, 243-245; HM the Queen's state visit to 83, 243, 244
Irish Times, The 240

Janitor 134
Jardiniere 136
Jarvis, Willie 128
Jet Ski Lady 162
Jockey Club 65, 216, 221; 'Pattern' system 170
Johannesburg 162
Jojo 162
Joking Apart 75, 148, 192
Juddmonte Farms 250

Kalaglow 208-209
Kemp, Malcolm 46
Kempton Park 138, 140; Christmas Hurdle 15; Victor Wild Stakes 133
Kentucky 132, 165, 166, 192, 226, 230, 241-242; Keeneland sales 239; Lane's End Farm 45
Key Point 250
Khalid Abdullah, Prince 77, 250
Kingdom Of Fife 164
Kingsclere 25, 153, 173-174; Park House stables 31, 32, 33, 45, 153, 172, 173, 182, 223
Kingstone 148
Knight's Daughter 131, 132, 161-162

La Fleche 95, 195
Ladbrokes 244
Lady Arnica 39-40
Laffy 241
Lahudood 227

Lammtarra 83
Landau 29, 109-110, 121, 136
Langtry, Lillie 85
Lassalle 162
Lavandin 111
Lemon Souffle 19-20, 21, 160
Light Duty 34, 192, 210, 231, 235, 247
Light Shift 213
Lilibet 63
Lingfield 105, 118, 118, 162-163
Linklater, Barry 60
Little Wolf 211
London: Carlton House 94; Savoy Hotel 86, 97; Westminster Abbey 103
Longboat 213
Longchamp: Prix de l'Arc de Triomphe 34, 155, 200; Prix Henry Delamarre 154
Lyphard 228, 230
Lyric Fantasy 19-20, 21, 161

Macdonald-Buchanan, Lady 97, 168
Magna Carta 33, 34, 115, 170, 172, 175
Magnier, John 19, 21, 77, 237, 239, 244
Major Portion 126, 142, 143
Maktoum family 76, 208, 240 see also al-Maktoum entries
Malapert 142, 143, 144
Malhub 210
Malta 46
Manitoba 48
Margaret, HRH Princess 49, 60, 128, 145
Marsh, Richard 95, 96, 97, 168
Mascara 240
McManus, J.P. 248
Melbourne Cup 42
Mellon, Paul 33, 251
Melody (Highland pony) 65
Memoir 95
Mercer, Joe 74-75, 114, 116, 118, 173, 184, 185-186, 188, 189, 190-191, 193, 206
Mildmay, Lord 40, 174
Milford 117-118, 118, 119, 120, 121, 201, 225
Mill Reef 33, 34, 109, 119, 174, 180, 181, 210, 226, 251
Millar, Lt Col Sir John 48
Minamota 154-155, 155
Minardi 162
Miner's Lamp 111, 112, 115, 121, 144
Minoru 94, 94, 97, 98, 119, 127, 139, 154, 167, 168, 237, 243-244
Minster Son 215
Mister Glum 248
Monarchy 162
Monaveen 32, 38, 47, 174
Mondellihy Stud 104
Monochrome 251
Montjeu 244, 245
Moonlight Cloud 130, 131
Moore, Capt. Charles 59, 61, 74-75, 109, 110, 114, 126-128, 131, 132, 134, 135, 136, 142, 143, 144, 145-147, 148, 149, 156, 165, 167, 168, 247
Moore, Ryan 80, 81, 81, 87, 90, 91
Moses 95
Motivator 51, 51, 247
Mr Prospector 228, 230
Mulberry Harbour 137, 138-139, 140, 141, 143
Murless, Sir Noel 29, 63, 110, 115, 128, 128, 137, 140, 141, 143-144, 145, 153, 154, 155, 168, 170, 180
Musical Drive 32-33, 115
Nashwan 76, 77, 164, 218-219, 226, 227, 230

National Stud 62, 127, 153, 154, 170, 185, 244, 247
National Stud for Ireland 243-244, *243*
National Velvet 49
Near Miss 148, 165, 192
Nearco 93, 148
Nearula 105
Never Say Die 110, 134, 136
New Approach 83
Newbury *13*, 27, 40, 42, 66, 79, 144, 183; Lockinge Stakes 144, 145; Schweppes Gold Trophy 15
Newmarket 29, 75, *78*, 79, 80, 84, *105*, 144, 153, 253; Beech Hurst stables 79; Cesarewitch 113-114, *114*; Dewhurst Stakes 61, 69, 149; Egerton Stud 97; Falmouth Stakes 19, 21; Freemason Lodge stables 22, 23-24, 78-79, 141, 152; Middle Park Stakes 104, 105; Nell Gwyn Stakes 84-85; Princess of Wales's Stakes 201, 208; Warren Place stables 137, 153; *see also* One Thousand Guineas *and* Two Thousand Guineas
Niche 19, 21-22, 160, 161
Nijinsky 109, 182, 189, 215
Normandy, Haras du Quesnay 28, *28*, 67, 156
North Light 120
Northern Dancer 213, 214-215, 228, 230, 239, 247-248

Oaks, the 45, 62, 69, 79, 83, 138-140, *138*, 143, 147, 188, 194-195, *195*, *196*, 200, 202, 211, 213, *221*
Oaksey, Lord 48-49, 222-223
Obama, President Barack 42
O'Brien, Vincent 130, 239
One Thousand Guineas 60, *61*, 62, 63, 138, 141, 142, 148, 184-186, *185*, 191, 192
O'Sullevan, Lady Patricia 25, 48
O'Sullevan, Sir Peter 24-25, 28, 29, 30, 47-49, 58, 60, 62, 74, 106-108, 126, 135-136, 141, 149, 166, 168, 187, 189, 190, 231
Oswald, Lady Angela 38, 39, 40, 169
Oswald, Sir Michael 10, 38-39, 40, 42, *74*, 97, 123, 166, 168-169, 184, 189, 197, 241, 244, 246, 252
Our Babu 160
Owen Tudor 168
Oxx Snr and Jnr, John 240

Pall Mall 126, *126*, 141-143, *143*, 144, 145, 181, 185
Parthia 145
Pebbles 164
Pendry, Terry 65, 157, 158, 241, 248, 249
Perdita 234, 235
Persimmon 96-98, 119, 168, 234, 235
Petoski 213
Phalaris 166
Phantom Gold *224*, 225
Philip, HRH Prince *44*, 59-60, 83-84, *83*, *102*, 109, *131*, 172-173, *243*
Phillips, Zara 78
Piggott, Lester 87, 110, 119, 120, *138*, 139, 140, 143, *178*, 181, 184, 186, 187, 191, 194, 195, 197, *198*, 200, *201*, *206*
Pindari 145, 170
Pinza 71, 99, *106*, 107
Poincelet, Roger *108*
Polhampton Lodge 69, 156, 158, 165, 251-252
Polygamy 183, 184, 187, 191
Pope, Maj. Michael 178
Porchester, Lord *see* Carnarvon, seventh Earl of

Porter, John 31, 172
Pour Moi 84, *90*, 91, 92
Prescription 164
Price, Ryan 15
Prince Leopold 94-95
Pritchard-Gordon, Coral *78*
Prix de Diane 60, 187-189, *188*, 190, 191
Prix de l'Arc de Triomphe 34, 155, 200

Quadrille 249
Queen's Hussar 75-76, 166, 167, 182, 188, 192, 237, 238
Queensland, The Liar's Lounge 241
Quest For Fame 77
Quorn hunt 211-212

races embracing Queen Elizabeth II in their titles 25, 27
racing: and British royalty, links between 25; growth of interest in Middle East 76, 77; popularity of 42-43; stables, atmosphere of 50-51
Racing Post, The 24
Ravenna 178
Reference Point 181
Request 227
Restoration 144, 162
Ribocco 154
Ribot 93, 136
Richards, Sir Gordon 99, *102*, 106, *106*, 107, 108, 109, 140, 168
Right Approach 164
Rising Light 60, 123, 148
Roan Rocket *146*
Roberto 109, 181, 251
Roberts, Monty 157-158, 247
Roseate Tern 161
Rothschild, Leopold de 119
Round Table 131-132, 161-162
Royal Applause 51
Royal Family: and the Press 220; and racing, links between 25
Royal Palace 154, 155
Royal Studs, the *10*, 11, 14, 24, 35, 38, 39, 40, 51-52, *51*, 56, 63, 65, 68-69, 70, 74, 75, 76, 77, 85, 94, 95-96, 97, 107, 109, 115, 120-121, 123, 126-127, 128, 132-133, 136, 137, 143, 161-162, 166, 167-168, 169-170, 172, 175, 181-182, 192, 200-201, 202-203, 210, 211, 225, 226, 230, 231, 234-235, *234*, 237, *237*, 238-239, 242-243, 246, 247-248, *247*, 249-250, 251, 252-253; Persimmon statue 235, *237*
Royal Windsor Horse Show 80, 248

Sadler's Wells 239-240, 244, 245, 250
Sainfoin 95
Saint-Cloud, Grand Prix de 154-155, *155*
Sally Forth 249
Sandown Park *27*, 99, *179*; Eclipse Stakes 145, *146*, 155, 219
Sandringham 63, 247, 251, 252; Women's Institute 45-46; *see also* Royal Studs, the
Sangster, Robert 239
Sariska 147
Satinette 161
Sceptre 98
Scuttle 63, 141
Sea Shanty 123
Sea The Stars 158, 240, 244
Secreto 215
Sequence 250
Set To Music 250
Shadwell Stud 227

Shahrastani 92
Shelley, Maj. Sir Richard 59, 75, 148-149
Shergar 120
Shirley Heights 39, 115, 181
Sideral 162
Sign Manual 123
Signorina 167
Signorinetta 167
Silken Glider 139, 140
Simmonds, 'Simmy' 97
Sir Thomas 94
Smith, Clive 56
Smith, Doug 62, 74-75, 142, *143*
Smith, Eph *108*, *133*, 134, *134*, 142, *143*
Smuggler 211
Smyth, Willie 35
Snaith, Silvia 29-30, 110-111
Snaith, Willie 29-30, 109-111
Sobell, Sir Michael 118, 193, 201, 209, 211
Special Leave 33-34, 115, 210
St Boniface 208
St Frusquin 96, 97-98, 119
St James 83
St Leger *178*, 195-196, 197, *198*, 200, 211
St Paddy 170
St Patrick's Blue *173*
Star Value 250
Starkey, Greville 92
Starling 162
Stoute, Sir Michael 78-79, *78*, 80, 83, 86, 91, 92, 121-122, 225, 252
Strathcona 192-193, 202
Strawbridge, George 130, 131
Strip The Willow 192
Stroma 136-137, 145, 182, 193, 203
Sun Chariot 60, 62-63, 127, 128, 139-140, 154, 237, 244
Sun Princess 211
Supereva 252
Surprise 48
Swiftfoot 211

Tamerlane 160
Tammuz 15
Tartan Pimpernel 200, *201*, 202-203
Tempest 113
Tesio, Federico 93, 109, 136, 148, 215
Thatcher, Margaret 35, 115
The Minstrel 194, 215
The Solicitor 159, 160
Thoroughbred Breeders' Association 65
Three No Trumps 32
Time Charter *10*
Tindall, Mike and Zara 78
Treasure Beach *90*
Triple First 195
Trooping the Colour ceremonies 65, 248
Troy 118, 119, 120, 201, 211
Tully Stud 127
Two Thousand Guineas 60, 62, 105, 111, *126*, 142-143, *143*, 154, 180, 194, 218-219, 244

Ulster National 240-241
Unfuwain 213, 215, 230
Unknown Quantity 224
Urbano-Grajales, Senor *228*

Vaguely Noble 155, 179
Vamos 168, 170
Ventura 130, 131
Vestey, Lord *74*
Victoria, HM Queen 80, 85, 95, 98, 253
Vienna 170

Waldron, Philip 186
Walsh, Ruby 29
War Horse 157-158
Warren, Jake 253
Warren, John 11, *13*, 19, 24, 53, 59, *78*, 80-81, 84, 86, 87, 91-92, 93, 102, 122, 235, 237, 238-239, 242, 245, 246, 247, 249, *249*, 250, 251
Washington International 110
Wavertree, Lord (formerly Col William Hall Walker) 127, 154, 244
Weatherby, Johnny 58-59
Weinstock, Arnold (later Lord) 118, 119, 120, 193, 201, 209, 211
Well Hidden 250
Wessex, HRH the Countess of 84; children 80
Wessex, HRH the Earl *74*, 84; children 80
West Coast Times (NZ) 98
West Ilsley stables 179, 180, 186, 193, 197, 202, 209-211, 215-218, 219, 221-224, 225
Wildenstein, Daniel 68, 170, 227
William, HRH Prince 83, 84, 253
Williams, Peter 'Caz' 31-32, 33, 34, 35, 115-117
Williams, Rachel 117
Wily Trick 226
Wimbledon Championships 46-47
Wind In Her Hair 227
Windsor *20*, 42
Windsor Castle 24, 25, 29, 63, 65, 190-191, 194; Royal Ascot lunches 15, 25, 47, 48, 52; Royal Mews 65, 241, 248, 249
Wingfield, Brig. Tony 59, 148-149
Wolferton Stud 135, 203

Yarmouth 162
Yeats 45
York 42, 49, 75, 104, 186-187; Dante Stakes 80-81, *81*, 83, 87; Queen Mother's Cup for Lady Amateur Riders 117; Yorkshire Cup 145; Yorkshire Oaks 140, 196-197
York, HRH Frederick, Duke of 94, 95